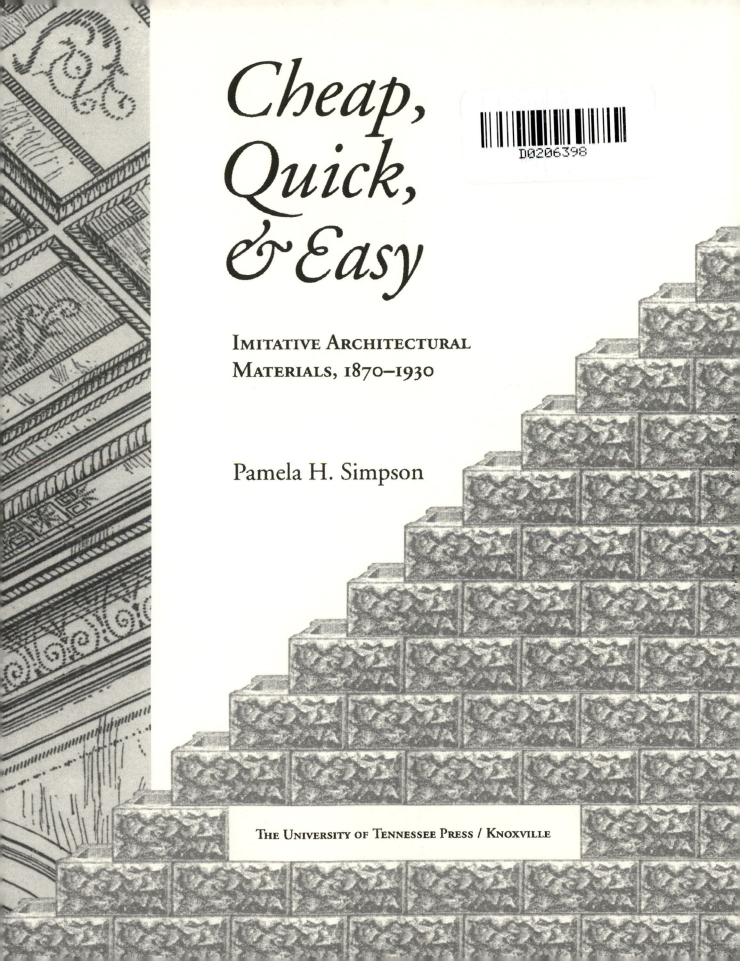

Cheap, Quick, & Easy

Imitative Architectural Materials, 1870–1930

Pamela H. Simpson

The University of Tennessee Press / Knoxville

Cheap, Quick, and Easy

Unless otherwise noted, the photographs were taken by the author.

The author and publisher gratefully acknowledge Furthermore, the publication program of the J. M. Kaplan Fund, for underwriting the production of this book.

LIBRARY OF CONGRESS CATALOGING-IN-PUBLICATION DATA

Simpson, Pamela H. (Pamela Hemenway), 1946–2011
Cheap, quick, and easy : imitative architectural materials,
1870–1930 / Pamela H. Simpson. — 1st ed.
p. cm.
Includes bibliographical references (p.   ) and index.
ISBN 978-1-62190-157-0
1. Building materials—History. 2. Substitute products.
3. Synthetic products. I. Title.
TA403.6 .S55 1999
691'.09—ddc21
98-25486

To Henry and Peter

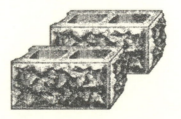

Contents

Illustrations

Acknowledgments

As Tennessee Williams and others have noted, one does rely on the kindnesses of strangers. And if one adds friends to the list, then quite a group has lent me aid and support over the ten years spent researching and writing this book. I thank them all, and I would like to acknowledge a few specifically.

Of the many institutions that provided funding for this project, my own comes first: Washington and Lee University's Glenn Grant Program enabled me to undertake summer travel to various collections in 1991, 1993, 1995, and 1997. Washington and Lee also gave me sabbatical leaves in 1986, 1991, and 1996–97 as well as a Hewlett-Mellon Grant. I am especially grateful to my colleagues John Wilson, John Elrod, Larry Boetsch, Lad Sessions, Cecile West-Settle, and Pat Fallon for their help.

The Mednick Fellowship Program of the Virginia Foundation for Independent Colleges offered support in the summer of 1996. I was fortunate enough to receive two Hagley-Winterthur Research Residency Fellowships, one in 1991, the other in 1996. Working at these two institutions was like being in researchers' heaven. Ministering angels included Roger Horowitz, Philip Scranton, Carol Lockman, Marsha McHugh, Marian Matyn, Jon Williams, Barbara Hall and Susan Hengel at Hagley, and Pat Elliott and Neville Thompson at Winterthur.

A National Endowment for the Humanities Summer Institute at Tufts University in 1989 under the leadership of Sy Bellin provided stimulation in thinking about the relationship of new technology and societal values. But by far the most important institutional support I received was the fellowship year at the National Humanities Center in Research Triangle Park, North Carolina, in 1996–97, where I wrote the manuscript. The fellowship was funded by the Jessie Ball duPont Religious, Educational and Charitable Fund. At the center, the staff, including Bob Connor, Kent Mullikin, Mary Donna Pond, Alan Tuttle, Eliza Robertson, Jean Houston, Karen Carroll, and Linda Morgan, provided the kind of support every researcher needs and several "pig pickin's" as well. The best part of being at the NHC, however, was the company of the other Fellows. I know this book is better for their ideas and encouragement. I would especially like to thank Joy and John Kasson, Fitzhugh Brundage, Peter Coclanis, Susan Cole, Nancy Langston, and Trudier Harris. Our many hours of conversation have richly amplified this study.

There are so many librarians to thank. At Washington and Lee colleagues Betsy Brittigan, Yolanda Warren, Hugh Blackmer, and Barbara Brown deserve special mention. Curator Carolyn Goldstein and the library staff at the National Building Museum, as well as librarians at the Library of Congress, the Avery Library at Columbia University, and the Metropolitan Museum in New York, also gave access to key material. Staff at the Staten Island Historical Society, the Cooper-Hewett Museum and Library, Duke University, the Canadian Centre for Architecture in Montreal, the National Science and Technology Museum Library in Ottawa, the National Archives in Ottawa, the National Art Library at the Victoria and Albert Museum and the British Library in London, and the Bodleian Library in Oxford were all wonderfully helpful. In addition, I would like to give special thanks to Gavin Grant from the Kirkcaldy Museum and Library, Kirkcaldy, Scotland; Joy McKenzie and Terry Griffiths of Akzo-Nobel Decorative Products, Darwen, Lancashire; Larry McNally at the National Archives in Canada; and Charlie Sachs of the Staten Island Historical Society for their assistance.

I am especially indebted to my good friends Catherine Bishir, Delos Hughes, Dan McGilvray, and Michael Ann Williams for reading the manuscript at various stages. Sally McMurry, Jan Jennings, Dennis Domer, Winifred Hadsel, Mark Reinberger, and Jonathan Thornton also read sections and offered helpful advice. Their ideas and critiques and the wealth of their experience were essential to this study.

Many colleagues, including those named above, offered examples, references, and review as well as good company and a bed when I needed it. I would like to thank Annmarie Adams, Joanna Banham, Richard Candee, Marilyn Casto, Jeremy Cragg, Betsy Cromley, Alex and Doreen Cross, David Dickey, Mark Edwards, Ellen Eslinger, Betsy Fahlman, Bryan Green, Herb Gottfried, Peter Goss, Marta Gutman, Joyce Harrison, Bernie Herman, Kim Hoagland, Donna Hole, Kate Hutchinson, Tom Jester, Lawrence Kavanagh, Bill Littmann, Royster Lyle, Richard Longstreth, Carl Lounsbury, Travis MacDonald, Joan and Wes Mattie, Joan and Walter Marter, Ann McCleary, Meredith Morris-Babb, Ozzie Overby, John Pensec, Dan Pezzoni, Fred Peterson, Boyd Pratt, Orlando Rideout V, W. A. Slagle, Bonnie Parks Snyder, Paul Touart, Dell Upton, Abby Van Slyck, David Vaisey, and Camille Wells.

I would also like to thank my colleagues in the Art Department at Washington and Lee for their support and good humor. Betty Hickox, Joan O'Mara, George Bent, Larry Stene, and Kathleen Olson are the best friends anyone could have.

Parts of this study have appeared in another form in articles in *Building Renovation,* in 1992 and 1995; in the *Journal of Architectural and Planning Research,* 1994; in the *Wallpaper History Review,* 1997; and in the Vernacular Architecture Forum's *Perspectives in Vernacular Architecture* series, including volumes 3, 5, and 7. Volume 3 was published by the University of Missouri Press, while the University of Tennessee Press published volumes 5 and 7 (see the bibliography for full citations).

Finally I would like to thank my family for their constant help and support, especially my husband, Henry, who was willing to keep the home fires burning and endure the snows alone while I was enjoying Chapel Hill's rich resources.

Cheap, Quick, and Easy

The development of concrete construction in the United States was fueled by the primary American desire to find ways of doing things that were "cheap, quick, and easy." Its story is a characteristic mixture of the immediate imaginative American recognition of unprecedented technological possibilities and the willingness to do what had never been done before with the tastelessness of a new middle class society that accepted substitute gimcrackery for traditional materials and ideas.

—ADA LOUISE HUXTABLE, 1960

These comments from one of the most prominent architectural critics of our time not only helped to inspire my study of imitative architectural ornament but also provided the title for this book.[1] "Cheap, quick, and easy" is an apt phrase for the qualities of the various new architectural materials that emerged in the late nineteenth and early twentieth centuries. Economical, practical, and durable, products such as hollow concrete block, pressed metal, linoleum, and embossed wall coverings were, indeed, the result of what Huxtable called "unprecedented technological possibilities," as well as a "willingness to do what had never been done before." And both the technological possibilities and the willingness to explore them were present not only in America but also in Great Britain and other industrialized nations.

But wherever one encountered the new materials, an architectural elite stood ready to attack them. Critics, architects, and tastemakers called the imitative architectural ornament "shams," "makeshifts," and, as Huxtable noted, reflections of the "tastelessness of a new middle class society that accepted substitute gimcrackery." There were, however, people ready to defend the new products and champion their qualities. Cheaper, longer lasting, easier to keep clean, and safer than the older handmade forms they replaced, the new mass-produced ornaments were the result of modern industrialization, which had democratically extended the possibilities of ornament to the masses. To the new middle class that embraced them, the new forms represented "progress."

This study began ten years ago with rockface concrete block, that rusticated stonelike material so ubiquitous in early-twentieth-century building. The fact that there was little modern scholarship on concrete block inspired me to look at other, equally understudied late-nineteenth- and early-twentieth-century ornamental forms.

The history of sheet metal and its popular expression as the so-called tin ceiling came next. Having gone from the exterior to the interior, I then turned from ceilings to floors with the history of linoleum, one of the most popular and widely used floor coverings ever produced. Lincrusta-Walton, a wall-covering offshoot of linoleum, invited an investigation of embossed wall coverings. All of these materials had been widely used between 1870 and 1930, but they had been ignored for so long that their histories were largely lost. Even historic preservationists often thought them unimportant. This book is an attempt to recover the histories of the new, "cheap, quick, and easy" ornamental materials and to explain their cultural significance.

In the following five chapters I explore what concrete block, pressed sheet metal, pressed-metal ceilings, linoleum, and embossed wall and ceiling coverings are. I examine their histories, their manufacture, distribution, advertising, and use, and discuss the criticisms leveled against them as well as the arguments of their defenders. Rather than using a strictly chronological organization, I move from exterior to interior in order to logically group the elements together. While I focus on the 1870–1930 period, I consider precedents and subsequent developments where important. In chapter 6 I examine more briefly several other types of imitative materials also popular between 1870 and 1930, though some of these are much older in origin. The arguments attacking and defending all these materials serve as background for the final chapter, which examines the aesthetic debate over the appropriateness of imitation and analyzes social themes revealed in the study.

Huxtable named two relevant themes in her analysis: (1) the impact of technology on new building materials and (2) the aesthetic debate over the propriety of imitation. But she did not address one obvious question. Given the fact that professional architectural writers (like herself) so uniformly condemned the imitative nature of the new ornament as vulgar, cheap, and tasteless, why were the materials so abundant in the built environment? Was it simply bad taste? Concrete block, pressed metal, and linoleum were everywhere. They obviously had broad popular appeal. How could one discern what that appeal was? The people who were happily building with rockface concrete block were not writing about it in architectural journals. Where could one find their point of view?

Traditional architectural studies were of little help. While there is a considerable body of scholarly writing on architectural materials, most of it deals with structural issues. The development of reinforced concrete and iron and steel for bridges and tall buildings, for example, has received ample study. But few scholars have considered the impact of new technology on the development of ornamental materials. Until now, rockface concrete block, pressed-metal ceilings, and linoleum were considered too ordinary, too common, or in the words of critics from their own day, too "cheap and nasty" for scholarly consideration.

Although there is little modern scholarship on the subject, there is a voluminous trade literature from the 1870–1930 period that advertised and promoted the new materials. Period building magazines, specialized trade journals, and the catalogues manufacturers used to sell their products all proved to be a gold mine of information. Periodicals addressed to the building trades, such as the *National Builder* and *Carpentry and Building,* and trade journals, such as the *Sheet Metal Builder,* the *Upholstery and Carpet Trade Review,* and the *Dry-Goods Economist,* carried reports on new materials, examples of their use, announcements of recently published catalogues, and stories and ads that helped establish a chronology, identify manufacturers, and reveal people's attitudes and experiences.

Trade catalogues, published by manufacturers to place a selection of products before the customer, were also extremely useful. The Library of Congress, the Avery Architectural Library at Columbia University, and the libraries at the Winterthur and Hagley Museums, among others, now actively collect these trade publications, once considered ephemera. Fortunately, several companies involved in the manufacture of the new materials also preserved their records.

Period advertising proved to be a useful tool as well. There are dangers in using advertisements, of course. They cannot always be believed, and they tend to exaggerate. One has to be conscious of who wrote the ad, who the intended audience was, and whose viewpoint is being reflected. Still, advertisements can be useful in telling about larger issues. When the Albert Northrop Company advertised that their metal ceilings "were not shams" but made of real, honest metal, the ads were referring to a contemporary debate about the nature of imitation. When linoleum manufacturers promoted the floor covering as antiseptic, they were reflecting contemporary obsession with hygiene. When metal ceilings were called signs of "progress," the ad writer was citing a fundamental tenet of the period.

Sometimes information on the new imitative architectural materials appears in such unexpected places as period novels. In 1906, in *The Ragged Trousered Philanthropists,* Robert Tresell drew distinctions between a worker whose floor was covered with painted oilcloth and one whose floor had linoleum, and between a poor man's imitation wood-grain wallpaper and a rich man's embossed wall covering. He used the floor and wall coverings to mark class and economic differences, but he also demonstrated the pervasive desire for imitative surface decoration.[2]

Another important source for this study has been the memories of older people who have recounted their personal experiences with the materials. One elderly man in Emporia, Virginia, still runs the Klugel sheet-metal business. His forty years of supplying local builders with ornamental pressed metal and his extended memories through the stories of his first boss, the founder, explained the interaction between manufacturing and local building processes.[3]

Conversations at senior citizen centers also provided help. One gentleman vividly recalled the day in his boyhood when his family put linoleum in their house and he discovered "sock skating": the linoleum was so smooth he didn't have to worry about splinters as he slid across the new floor. He also remembered the difference in comfort, since the linoleum kept the wind from blowing through the floor boards. "It wasn't cheap, either, you know," he said, contradicting common wisdom that devalued linoleum as an inexpensive floor covering.[4]

Another source of information lay in the history of individual buildings. I had started the study of rockface concrete block because there were more than twenty buildings constructed of it in my area of Rockbridge County, Virginia. Documenting these structures provided specific examples of the material's use, its manufacture, construction methods, and remembrances of both patrons and builders. Contacts with architectural historians in various state historic preservation offices produced further examples of well-documented rockface concrete-block buildings, pressed-metal facades and ceilings, linoleum-covered floors, and Lincrusta-Walton–covered walls.

Historians who have explored the development of architectural materials and of industrial production provided context for understanding these new, imitative products. Great Britain, the first industrialized nation, played an important role in the introduction of many of the new materials to America. The history of Canada's building industry is similar to that of the United States in adopting new products. Other European countries and parts of the British Empire offered parallel examples. The focus of my study is primarily the history of the new materials in the United States, but that history includes and is amplified by experiences in other countries.

The approach that underlies this study is commonly called "material culture." Its premise is that objects (material) reveal the history, attitudes, values, beliefs, and experiences of the people who made and used them (culture).[5] This is also a part of the larger tradition of social history. But the most important influence on this study has been the stimulation provided by a group called the Vernacular Architecture Forum (VAF). A professional organization of architectural historians, cultural geographers, folklorists, preservations, architects, and American Studies specialists, the VAF was founded in 1980. In part it was a response to the 1966 Preservation Act, which set up historic preservation offices in all fifty states and sent people into the field to record the nation's surviving architectural heritage.

The early surveys understandably focused on high-style buildings by well-known architects. They were what was deemed most important. Most of the surveyors, including your author, had been trained to think of architectural history as a series of period styles attached to the names of well-known practitioners. Local examples were dutifully plugged into the proper categories: Georgian, Federal, Greek Revival, Gothic Revival, and so on. History was a pattern of linear development, with each style succeeding the next. The local was deemed important by the extent it fit into the national model.

The problem, as most people in the field soon realized, was that not everything fit into those categories. Local chronologies sometimes differed from national ones. Stylistic details sometimes seemed mere decorative trimming on forms that retained consistent plan types over long periods of time. Academic stylistic categories did not explain saddlebag log houses or the collection of agricultural buildings that surrounded a typical farmhouse. Surveyors began to feel that other disciplines, in particular sociology, anthropology, and cultural geography, might contribute as much to their understanding of the vernacular buildings they encountered as traditional architectural studies could. Thus the VAF was formed, dedicated to an interdisciplinary approach to the study of the built environment.

It quickly became apparent that "vernacular" was not so much a type of building to members of this group as it was an approach to how any structure could be studied.[6] First came field work. The building had to be thoroughly studied, recorded, and documented. But rather than stopping there and thinking of the building as a type of three-dimensional sculpture, the vernacular studies approach asked who built it and why. Why did the architect, builder, and patron make the choices they did? What did those choices signify? How did they reflect the larger social, political, and cultural context? How were those choices shaped by a building system that included materials, their production, availability, distribution, and use? What were the ideas represented in the building and how did those ideas change over time?

The vernacular approach not only diminished the importance of style as a sole determinant in a building's value but also invited examination of all parts of the building—the floor plan and structural system as well as the exterior and interior stylistic ornament. All sorts of buildings could be considered—log cabins, house trailers, bungalows, and fast-food chain restaurants. The study of any type of building was valuable because all of it was the material of our culture. Even high-style buildings could be approached with these questions. Whereas traditional architectural histories had relied on biography, description, formal analysis, and style as the primary factors for study, the vernacular approach probed deeper: Why was that particular architect chosen? Who did the choosing? Why that style? Why those materials? How did those choices reflect values of the period? What was the deeper cultural meaning of it all?

Guided by this approach, I could look at concrete block and ask not only how the invention of the modern cast-iron block machine affected local builders in Lexington, Virginia, and Osgoode, Ontario, but also why Frank Lloyd Wright became fascinated with the material in the 1920s. High style and low style, vernacular studies cut across traditional boundaries and revealed them as part of a larger cultural system. That is why this study considers production technology and distribution and communication systems that made the new imitative materials widely available. It is also why so much time is devoted to the question of the propriety of imitation. Broader social, political, and cultural issues emerge in the debate.

I chose to focus on the 1870–1930 period because so much happened then. While this is a conventional periodization, sometimes called the "Second Industrial Revolution,"[7] it is also a date frame that emerged naturally from the study. With post–Civil War industrial expansion on one side and the building slowdown of the Great Depression on the other, it was a time of innovation, rapid development, and broad acceptance for the new ornamental materials.[8]

Historians also note the development in this period of a "consumer culture"—a shift away from a production-oriented society characterized by "tradition and scarcity" toward a consumer society dependent on an abundant supply of store-bought, or catalogue-ordered goods.[9] New consumer products were available in such a variety of type and prices that every need could be met, no matter what size the pocketbook. Ornamental architectural features that at one time had been available only to the wealthy could now be had by the masses. The "democracy of consumption" meant that stonelike concrete block, plasterlike metal ceilings, marble-patterned linoleum, and leatherlike wall coverings were accessible to almost everyone.

The expansion of industry and exploitation of machine potential for duplication and repetition made all this possible. The development of mass production has been thoroughly documented by historians such as David Hounshell, who described the basic elements of the system as including a cycle of technological innovation, diminished prices, effective marketing, massive orders, and mass production.[10] Alfred Chandler, one of the great business historians of our time, coined the term "throughput" to refer to the economies of speed and standardization essential for continuous flow of mass production.[11]

Contemporary historians such as Philip Scranton, however, have attempted to modify our understanding of mass production. Scranton's research has shown that not all consumer goods were produced by a throughput system. That may have been the mode for Ford's motor cars, but it was not the production method for carpets or furniture. In refining the definitions of production, Scranton has identified some slower, smaller-scaled, more individualized systems he calls "custom, batch, and bulk."[12] Most of the architectural materials discussed in this book fall into the latter categories.

"Custom work" was produced to individual special order. "Batch goods" were marketed through jobbers or wholesalers who gathered orders; then a "batch" would be produced to meet the demand. "Bulk" meant that the factory would keep a stock of goods in supply. By contrast, mass production depended on complex systems with dedicated machinery, extensive division of labor, market strategies that ensured control over prices and steady consumer buying. It often led to brand names, heavy advertising, and dependent dealerships.

Scranton claims that the term "mass production" is overused. It evokes an image of a Ford Motor Company assembly line, while in reality many industries depended on smaller-scaled production systems. Stamped-metal ceiling manufacturers, for example, organized departmentally and depended on skilled workers, not an assembly line. Still, when most people use the term "mass production," it is as a general appellation for the abundance of goods available through industrial processes. In the broadest sense, the 1870–1930 period was one of mass production and mass consumption. The unprecedented availability of goods had a profound effect on society.[13]

The development of machine technology and new industrial techniques alone did not bring all these goods to the public. A whole infrastructure of transportation and communication systems was at work as well. Between 1870 and 1900 America's population nearly doubled with much of the growth from immigration. Railroad mileage, fifty-three thousand miles in 1870, had quadrupled by 1890. With railroads came the telegraph and improved mail service. The telegraph system in particular was substantially renewed in 1909, when AT&T bought a controlling interest in Western Union. Rural Free Delivery was instituted in 1896 and Parcel Post in 1912. These were all essential elements for the development of a national market system.[14] Most catalogues for pressed sheet-metal architectural ornament, for example, offered rail express delivery and included a cipher system for customers ordering by telegraph.

Improvements in transportation and communication and the expansion of cities also encouraged the development of new merchandising enterprises such as the department store, the chain store, and the mail-order catalogue. Marshall Field's in Chicago and Wanamaker's in Philadelphia are examples of some of the many department stores that emerged in the late nineteenth century. Woolworth's was one of the early chains. Montgomery Ward and Sears, Roebuck and Company were the leading mail-order catalogue firms. Together they reached millions of new consumers with low-priced goods. Both Montgomery Ward and Sears advertised concrete-block machines, linoleum, and Lincrusta in their catalogues. Marshall Field's and Wanamaker's sold linoleum in their floor-covering departments; and while Woolworth's didn't sell them, they nevertheless proudly boasted elegant pressed-metal ceilings in their "palace of the people" stores.

A revolution in advertising accompanied these rapid changes in industrial practice.[15] Before 1880 there were few national magazines and even fewer national advertisements. But changes in the printing industry, the development of half-tone reproductions, and the dramatic lowering in cost of publication spurred the growth of the magazine and newspaper industry. Advertising rather than subscriptions became the publishers' primary source of revenue.

Advertising itself changed as well. What little advertising there was in the early days was usually done by the retailer in local newspapers. With the expansion of big business in the post-1880 period, however, manufacturers began advertising in national magazines as a means of building a national market.[16] Readers of Chicago's *National Builder*, for example, could see ads for metal ceilings from some forty-five different companies between 1900 and 1925. Armstrong linoleum abandoned the floor-covering industry's tradition of trade-only advertising in 1917, with a campaign of ads in magazines such as *Ladies Home Journal* and the *Saturday Evening Post*. Armstrong developed window-display kits that retailers could place in their stores to connect their business with the national ads consumers were seeing in the popular magazines. This sort of advertising encouraged name recognition, consumer confidence and retail loyalty.

Manufacturers began to join together in professional trade organizations to control markets and prices and ensure standardized quality. They also used national and regional trade shows to promote their products and get new materials before their public. Manufacturers of concrete products had their own exhibitions; pressed-metal companies were usually included at hardware shows. New linoleum patterns were displayed in both the spring and the fall at furniture and home interior exhibits. Embossed wall coverings had special booths at home improvement shows. The miniature temples of pressed-metal or classical porticos of concrete which formed the exhibits also appeared at the international fairs, one of the period's chief means of celebrating the progress of science and industry. But the temples and porticos could be found in the smaller and more frequent trade shows as well. By all these means, manufacturers promoted new products and increased sales.

America became a major manufacturer in this period. Ranked fourth in world production in 1860, by 1894 her goods were nearly equal in value to those of England, France and Germany combined.[17] Production so outstripped consumption that world trade was a necessity. American metal ceilings were sold in Great Britain, as were American-made concrete-block machines. But goods also came to the United States from other countries, and to protect American industries, tariffs were often instituted. There is no doubt that American tariffs helped establish the tinplate industry in this country. They also made British linoleums more expensive than American goods. British embossed wall coverings were so expensive with a 50 percent markup tariff that the products were limited to a very specialized market until American firms took up their manufacture.

The 1870–1930 period also brought a rapid development of new products. As historian John Kasson has noted, a record twenty-three thousand patents were issued in the 1850s, quadruple the amount of the previous ten years, and that number was equaled or excelled during every single year from 1882 to 1900.[18] One producer of pressed metal, L. L. Sagendorph of the Penn Metal Ceiling and Roofing Company of Philadelphia, received ninety-one patents between 1879 and 1907 for improvements in the manufacture of his products. Inventors and entrepreneurs produced a cornucopia of machines and goods that brought American industrial production to a place of world leadership.[19]

It is understandable that in the face of this rapid change, some would view the new industrial culture with unease and even alarm. The debate over the appropriateness of the imitative nature of the new architectural materials, the fears of elite critics that aesthetic standards were being eroded, the moral argument that machines were devaluing honest labor, and the social confusion over mass culture and its implications were all evident in the period as well. But the counterarguments of those who supported and defended the new materials are also revealing of deeper societal issues. The embrace of industrialism, contemporary concerns for hygiene, the belief in modernism, democracy, and progress were also an essential part of the story of the acceptance of the new imitative architectural forms.

This brief summary of some of the developments in the 1870–1930 period in which concrete block, pressed metal, linoleum, and embossed wall coverings were produced is painted with such a broad brush that it leaves little room for detail or subtlety. In the following chapters, individual histories of these materials will expand the story. The cheap, quick, and easy architectural ornament, produced by "unprecedented technological possibilities" and embraced by the "tastelessness" of a new middle-class society willing to accept "substitute gimcrackery," is also the saga of the development of a modern, industrialized society in which machines made ornament available to the masses.

CHAPTER I

Stone for the Masses: Concrete Block in the Early Twentieth Century

In 1908, William Radford, the prolific author of house-pattern books, added a new category to the genre. Like his earlier books, this one was a guide to building modest, inexpensive houses, complete with plans and elevations; but in this book all of the houses were to be built in concrete. In the introduction, Radford explained the need for such a guide: "The history of the human race represents no parallel to that of the marvelous development during the present generation of home architecture by the use of concrete hollow blocks. . . . Home builders the world over are hungry for information about cement houses. The demand for such information is unprecedented in the annals of building. 'Tell us how to build a home of cement' is a popular cry heard throughout the land."[1]

Radford may have exaggerated the extent of the cry for information on cement houses, but his assertion that hollow concrete blocks had quickly become a new and popular building material was correct. In order to understand how that popular acceptance came about, this chapter will explore the history of Portland cement, the origins and development of concrete-block machines, the use of the machines by individuals and by a growing industry, and the debate about the imitative nature of rockface block.

A BRIEF HISTORY OF CONCRETE

Concrete is an ancient building material. Much used by the Romans, probably the best-known classical example is the dome of the Pantheon in Rome. Technically, concrete is formed when cement, the chemically active binder, is mixed with aggregates and water.[2] The Romans had a natural form of hydraulic cement called *pozzolana* which came from a volcanic deposit at Puzzuoli near Vesuvius. This volcanic ash contained both clay and lime, which had been exposed to intense heat in the volcano. The presence of clay and lime and the element of heat were all essential to the making of cement.

At least two other natural forms of cement occurred in Europe. One, called *trass* or *tarras*, came from Germany, the other, *Santorin*, from Greece. Lime, an element in cement, is made by roasting limestone in an oven and has been used by itself for mortar continuously throughout building history. While there were some isolated examples of hydraulic concrete in the Middle Ages, it largely ceased to be employed after the fall of Rome. There were a few experiments in the Renaissance, but it was only in the seventeenth and eighteenth centuries, primarily in France and England, that people began again to discover what would happen when clay and lime were mixed, heated, and then activated by water.

The Industrial Revolution in England spurred the search for a modern form of cement. Commercial producers supplied two kinds in the eighteenth and nineteenth centuries. One was the naturally occurring type, including *trass, pozzolana,* and some newly discovered forms. The other was a manufactured artificial type, the most famous example of which was Portland cement. Natural cements successfully competed with the manufactured type until the 1890s. Historians usually point to John Smeaton's 1756 Eddystone lighthouse as an important modern demonstration of the strength of hydraulic cement. Smeaton mixed a British lime with Italian *pozzolana* to produce a cement which hardened under water. In America, natural cements were widely employed in constructing early-nineteenth-century canals.

In 1796, James Parker, an English clergyman, discovered "nodules of clay" at the seashore which he then ground and burned in a kiln to produce a whitish powdered substance he called Roman cement. He developed a successful business, but when his patent ran out in 1810, others began to make the cement as well. Architects and engineers frequently used Roman cement in the early nineteenth century, but probably the most dramatic demonstration of its strength was in the famous I. K. Brunell tunnel under the Thames in the 1820s.

Despite the popularity of natural cements and their manufactured variants, artificial cements came to prominence by the early twentieth century. One early example is the cement patented by John Liardet in 1773. It is well known because architects Robert and James Adam promoted it as "Adam's New Improved Patent Stucco." The most successful artificial cement, however, and the one that would eventually dominate the industry, was Joseph Aspdin's Portland cement, named for the popular, gray-colored Portland stone which it resembled.

Aspdin, a mason, patented his process in 1824. The story of the origins of Portland cement is such an industrial legend that it is difficult to separate myth from fact, but the secret Aspdin seems to have discovered was the need to fire a clay and lime mixture at a much higher temperature than previously used. In all the earlier cements the firing temperature was too low to fuse the materials. The other fundamental problem was the proper proportion of clay to lime. While Aspdin's formula was better than most, it took the rest of the nineteenth century for manufacturers to eventually establish the modern standardized formulae.[3]

Aspdin's competition included two other artificial cements. One was Medina cement, which began production in 1848; the other was British cement, made by Isaac Johnson, who claimed his product preceded Aspdin's discovery. Most historians, however, give Aspdin credit for making the first reliable, artificial cement.

Great Britain was the major producer of Portland cement for most of the nineteenth century. British imports dominated the American market until 1871, when David O. Saylor of Lehigh Valley, Pennsylvania, started the first Portland cement company in the United States. He was soon joined by others, and by 1897 nearly 50 percent of the Portland cement used in the United States was domestic. Production doubled in the next three years, and plants in the Lehigh Valley area were responsible for three-quarters of it.[4]

The Portland cement industry underwent a series of important changes in the last decade of the nineteenth century and the first decade of the twentieth. The introduction of rotary kilns and tube mills so improved methods of firing and grinding that by 1900, American firms could for the first time undersell British imports. The technological improvements increased production, lowered costs, and improved quality.

Another change in both Britain and America was the consolidation and professionalization of the industry. Fewer companies were making more and better cement. The manufacturers organized into professional groups, the most important of which in the United States was the Portland Cement Association. The industry associations promoted the use of cement with regional workshops, national advertising, trade catalogues, and pattern books. Their aim was to increase the use of Portland cement. By 1905, one of the forms they recommended was concrete block.

The growth and development of the Portland cement industry is an essential element in the popularity of concrete block. In fact, it is unlikely that concrete in any form, reinforced as well as block, would have become such an important building material in the early twentieth century were it not for improvements in the production of Portland cement. In a symbiotic relationship, both the cement industry and the concrete-block industry grew phenomenally in the first two decades of the twentieth century.

CONCRETE BLOCK, INVENTION AND MANUFACTURE

While concrete is an ancient building material, concrete block is essentially a product of the twentieth century. Experiments throughout the nineteenth century with a variety of means of casting concrete into building blocks resulted in a large number of patents for both American and English inventors.[5] Patents granted in the 1870s, in particular, seem to predict the modern system. Earlier scholars writing on this subject sometimes mistakenly came to the conclusion that the concrete-block industry grew gradually over the last thirty years of the nineteenth century and the first few decades of the twentieth.[6] None of the nineteenth century patents, however, led to any widespread production of concrete block. They all were isolated experiments that produced a few buildings and gave impetus for the idea of block, but not to its practical mass production. That development awaited Harmon S. Palmer's invention of a cast-iron machine with removable core and adjustable sides. He had experimented with the machine for ten years and had built several test structures, including six houses in Chicago in 1897, but his U.S. patent came in 1900. Palmer's practical design was the beginning of the modern industry.[7]

If the history of technology teaches anything, it is that inventive genius alone is not enough to ensure the mass production of a product. Success also requires a good deal of luck, capital, and a means to manufacture, distribute, and promote the new material. The general patterns of this supporting network as it developed in the late nineteenth and early twentieth centuries were outlined in the introduction, but the story of how success came about varies with each product. The striking aspect of concrete block's history is the rapidity with which the public accepted it. The seemingly instant popularity of the new concrete block was commented on again and again by contemporary writers. In 1906, one proclaimed, "Concrete blocks were practically unknown in 1900, but is probably safe to say that at the present moment more that a thousand companies and individuals are engaged in their manufacture in the United States."[8]

Fig. 1. Advertisement for Harmon S. Palmer's concrete-block machines. National Builder *34 (Dec. 1903): 2. Hagley Museum and Library.*

Palmer started the Hollow Building Block Company in 1902, making four hundred block machines that year which sold for two hundred dollars each. At the same time, however, competitors began flooding the market with machines that were slight variations on his. Palmer claimed they were all violating his patent and spent years in court trying to protect his invention. He even placed advertisements in builders' journals offering a reward of five dollars to anyone who would help him find illegal imitators (fig. 1). But, as one writer noted, "there are a multitude of machines on the market and new advertisements appear in every issue of the cement journals."[9]

Most of these machines emulated Palmer's basic idea of a metal frame and mold box with a hand release lever that allowed for removal of the sides and cores. The main types of machines were "downface" and "sideface," depending on whether the block face was on the bottom, or on the side. The downface machine was the more popular.

To produce a block, one shoveled a mixture of Portland cement, water, sand, and stone or gravel aggregate into the machine and tamped it down to compress the mix and eliminate voids (fig. 2). Formulas for the cement-sand-aggregate ratio varied in the manuals of the period, but the general recipe was one part cement to two or three parts sand to four or six parts aggregate.[10] Experts recommended that the gravel or stone be sifted through a wire mesh screen to ensure that stones in the aggregate were no larger than one-half inch. The proportions of water to cement varied with the type of mix, but the general recommendation was that the concrete should be as wet as possible, but not so wet that the resulting block stuck to the metal or sagged when removed from the mold box.

The advantage of Palmer's new machine was that the block maker could throw a lever and release the block as soon as it had been made. He then carried the block away on a pallet or board to dry. After a day, the workmen stacked the block in a covered shed, where, with a periodic sprinkling with water, the block dried for at least several weeks. Some advisers recommended that the block "cure" for a month before use. Promoters claimed that two men, one mixing and one tamping, could make some eighty to one hundred blocks in a day.

Because hollow concrete block could be made with a variety of faces, some manufacturers of block machines recommended using a facing mixture of one part cement to three parts sand for the first one-half inch to give a finer texture to the surface. Color could be added as part of this face mixture. Not everyone agreed that the facing refinement was necessary, and, in fact, most block made in this early period contained the same mixture for

Fig. 2. Process of block making, from Sears' Concrete Machinery, Specialty Catalogue, 1917, p. 15. Sears, Roebuck Co.

the whole unit. If the block maker desired color, he could mix pigment into the concrete batch, thus producing solidly colored blocks; but he had to take care that all the blocks needed for a job came out the same tone.

The Woodshed or Backyard Phase of Concrete-Block Manufacture

The first phase of the hollow concrete-block industry, from about 1900 to 1920, was dominated by the use of the Palmer-type hand-tamped, metal machines which made one block at a time. By 1907, over a hundred companies were producing this type of machine or variations on it.[11] A few of the better known were the Miracle Company of Minneapolis, Minnesota; the Dykema Company of Grand Rapids, Michigan; the Winget Company and the Blakeslee Company, both of Columbus, Ohio; the Cement Machinery Company of Jackson, Michigan; the Besser Company of Alpena, Michigan; the Century Cement Machine Company of Rochester, New York; and the Ideal Concrete Machinery Company of Cincinnati, Ohio.

With evocative names like Miracle, Hercules, Eureka, Triumph, and Wizard, Palmer-type downface machines offered a quick and efficient way to make concrete block. There were alternatives, however, such as the Zagelmeyer cast stone block machine, which used a "slush method": a soupy wet mix was poured into metal molds on open rail cars, then rolled into the curing sheds. Each car could carry up to twenty molds, but the block had to dry for a day before it could be released and the mold used again. Dykema also offered a similar wet or slush system.

Concrete block was easy to make, and the cost of the machines rapidly dropped as competition grew. Palmer had sold his first machines in 1902 for $200, but in 1908 Sears advertised the Wizard for $42.50 (fig. 3). In a 1917 specialty catalogue, Sears claimed that concrete block was so easy to make that "no experience was necessary," "anyone could do it," and it was "profitable whether you manufacture for your own use or for sale. If for your own use, you can make them during your spare time, or on rainy days."[12]

The cheapness of the machines and the ease of making the block led to the "backyard," or "woodshed," phase of the industry. Hundreds of people bought the machines and made block for their own use. H. W. Mallery of Moscow, Idaho, was quoted in a Sears advertisement as saying that his house had been "built by amateurs, as my sons and I had never before worked in cement in any way."[13] In Lewis County, Kentucky, Joshua Stamper bought a Sears machine in 1905. Using sand from a nearby creek, he made enough block for a two-story I-house and a small outbuilding. In Williamsburg, Virginia, in 1907, the father of future painter Georgia O'Keeffe constructed a two-story, rockfaced concrete block house for his family, making his blocks in a Sears machine. In 1908 rancher August Kuhlman, frustrated by the loss of two previous houses to fire, built a concrete-block four-square house for his family in the lower Delores River Valley in Colorado (fig. 4).[14]

Further evidence for owner-built houses is offered by the popular Sears home catalogues. They advertised designs for concrete houses as well as for precut wooden ones. But while the latter would be shipped as a complete package, the concrete designs included everything but the concrete block, since, as the catalogue noted, "most of the customers make their own blocks."[15]

Sometimes the experience of home block making led to the creation of a business, as it did for C. K. Harvey of Smithfield, Virginia. He bought a Sears machine in 1905 to build a house for himself. So satisfied was he with the result, Harvey opened a contracting business and built

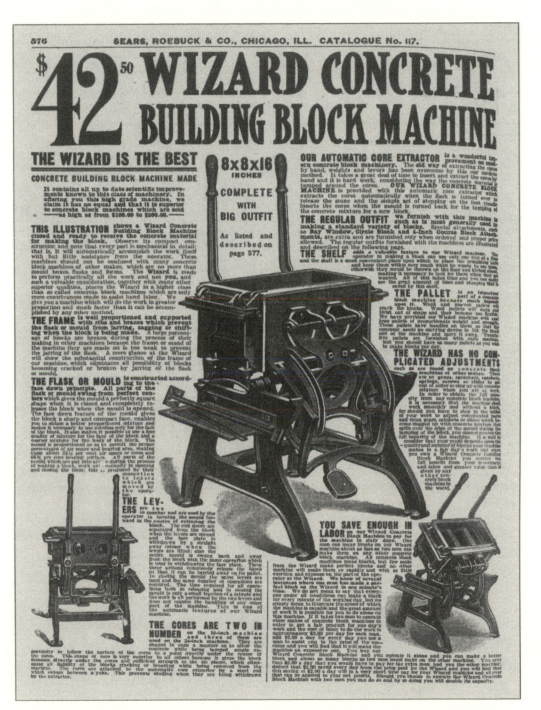

Fig. 3. The Wizard concrete-block machine. Sears Catalogue, No. 117, 1908, p. 576. Sears, Roebuck, Co.

Fig. 4. The rockface concrete-block August Kuhlman House, 1908, lower Delores Valley, Colorado. Historic American Buildings Survey; photograph by Jet Lowe.

seven more concrete-block houses and commercial structures in the area. Later he moved to Murfreesboro, North Carolina, and was responsible for another forty-nine concrete-block homes, churches, and commercial buildings before his death in 1936.[16]

EARLY FACTORY-MADE CONCRETE BLOCK

Harvey was not an exception. By 1910, over a thousand companies were manufacturing concrete block in the United States. In fact, most concrete block was made by people already in the construction or building supply business. National advertising by the Portland Cement Association and by concrete machine manufacturers made the availability of the block machines widely known. With only one machine a whole new industry could begin in any town.

Nels Peterson, a stonecutter in a quarry in Omaha, Nebraska, saw the new concrete block and reportedly said to himself, "Why should I hew these stones when I could make them in a mold?"[17] With his savings, Peterson bought a block machine and started the Ideal Cement Stone Company.

Tom Brenton, a native of Ontario, Canada, opened a brick works in the small Nebraska town of Neligh in the 1890s, but by 1905 had added concrete block to his production line. He used rockface block to build his own house as well as the gates to his supply yard as an advertisement for his products.[18]

In 1921, H. B. Leonard began a concrete-block company in Davidson County, North Carolina. Using first a Sears machine, and later a Besser, he built a block plant along the banks of Brushy Fork Creek, where he found an ample supply of sand and gravel. Leonard built numerous rockface and cobblestone-face block houses in the Winston-Salem, High Point, Lexington, and Midway township areas of North Carolina.[19]

In Lexington, Virginia, local building contractor and quarry operator H. A. Donald was the first to introduce concrete block into his community in 1915. Using a Palmer-type downface machine he built a new livery stable for his friend Frank Brown, the town's blacksmith. Brown had decided to expand his business to accommodate automobiles as well as horses, so he contracted with Donald to build a larger structure (fig. 5). Donald made the blocks on the site so everyone could see this new invention.[20]

During the 1920s, Donald built or supplied the block for twenty more concrete-block structures in the area, including the Bank of Fairfield (fig. 6), finished in 1923 for twenty-four hundred dollars. It may be the only concrete-block building immortalized in poetry. Local poet Ernest Sale wrote a humorous dedicatory verse for the opening of the bank that included this stanza:

> Now for the building, shall it be frame or brick?
> We want something we can build right quick;
> Don't mind the expense, we can sell more stock,
> Then they decided to build it of concrete block![21]

"Don't mind the expense" is a reminder that block was more expensive than wood. Yet it was much cheaper than stone, and as most advertisers noted, would be cheaper even than wood in the long run because it would last "practically forever."

Fig. 5. Frank Brown's rockface concrete-block blacksmith shop, 1915, Lexington, Virginia. Photograph by Delos Hughes.

Fig. 6. The rockface concrete-block Bank of Fairfield, 1926, Fairfield, Virginia.

America's fascination with concrete block was quickly exported. *Concrete and Constructional Engineering,* a journal founded in London in 1906, carried advertisements for concrete-block machines in its first issues. Most of the machines were made by American manufacturers and distributed by British firms. Within a year, however, advertisements for block machines made in Britain were appearing.

British interest in the block had been stimulated by a demonstration cottage erected by the Concrete Machinery Company of Liverpool for the 1905 Exhibition of Cheap Cottages at Letchworth. According to the editors of *Concrete and Constructional Engineering,* "The chief progress since [the exhibit] has taken place in the North of England and in Scotland and Ireland. The economic advantages of concrete-block building are more apparent in districts where it is difficult to obtain bricks, or country places where building materials cannot be obtained without a long cartage. It is so easy to bring a machine on the site and manufacture blocks . . . with any suitable material that is available in the immediate neighborhood."[22] In 1909, the journal reported on concrete-block buildings in Africa including a hospital in Nairobi as well as a church in Cairo.[23]

In North America, the well-documented history of the Boyd Brothers Company of Osgoode, Ontario, is especially instructive. Their papers, preserved in the National Archives of Canada in Ottawa, tell in detail the story of the development and growth of their concrete-block business. Harry and William Boyd were part of a family of carpenters and masons. In 1907, at the suggestion of their father, they decided to try their hand at making concrete block. Harry, the principal organizer of the firm, at first thought of buying a second-hand, side-face machine, but decided the 32-inch block it made was too big to be practical. He looked at a variety of machine makers' catalogues before deciding on the down-face "Ideal," which made an 8-by-8-by-16-inch block. He also liked the strength of the three cross webs in the block design.[24]

The Ideal machine was made by the Ideal Concrete Machinery Company of Cincinnati, Ohio. The first American manufacturer to introduce block machines into Canada, they opened a branch in Ontario in 1902. By 1907, however, when Harry Boyd made his purchase, there were at least nine companies selling block machines in Canada, so he had a variety to choose from.

The Boyd Brothers' cash books show that on May 6, 1907, they leased a gravel pit for $100.00 and the next day bought their Ideal block machine for $123.50. The next week they bought special molds for it in order to make "tile" (pipe) and chimney blocks. The Boyds also ordered two hundred pounds of Lafarge's Canada cement, a Portland cement known for its purity and whiteness. On May 21, two weeks after their initial purchase, Harry wrote, "Made first building block on Ideal machine."[25] The brothers set the machine up in a covered shed on a building site in Ottawa and made the block there. By the fall they had completed a concrete-block "cottage" for George H. Gibson (fig. 7).

While the Boyds initially made only rockface block, they soon purchased other face plates, including a "plain face." By the following year, with the help of the Ideal Concrete Machine Company's Service Department, the Boyds were making bush-hammered block with "Tooled Margin, in white and in sandstone finish," natural color rockface in "several different patterns for the foundations," vertical tooled blocks "for jambs, corners," and "col-

Fig. 7. The George H. Gibson Cottage, Ottawa, Ontario, Canada, constructed by the Boyd Brothers Company in 1907 has various colored and patterned block. National Archives of Canada.

umns in white work."[26] The Boyds also produced a very popular red rockface block, which, combined with the white blocks for quoining, window and door caps, offered an attractive decorative polychromy (fig. 8).

Harry Boyd's notebooks show that he occasionally designed a building, but his normal practice was to refer clients to pattern books. He kept a variety on hand, including several volumes from the William Radford house-pattern series. Boyd's company not only made the block, but his own crew of masons laid them. In the early years they supplied block to other contractors, but after the 1940s, they insisted that only Boyd masons could lay Boyd block.[27]

In 1914, the Boyd Brothers produced a distinctive aggregate finish block using tailings from a lead mine at Galetta. By the 1930s, Harry Boyd had developed a signature style of broken ashlar block patterns employing variously colored and sized blocks. This became the Boyd Brothers' most popular product.

The Boyd company steadily grew; by 1933, it had constructed 186 houses, 9 churches, 9 schools, 28 garages, 5 gas stations, 11 stores, 7 office buildings, 5 cheese factories, 8 silos, and 53 other buildings.[28] They had built so much in the Osgoode–Ottawa area that their material was locally known not as concrete block but as "Boyd block." Harry retired in 1954, but the firm remained in business until 1970.

The examples of the Boyd Brothers and their American counterparts demonstrate a pattern of acceptance of a new technology at the local level. Like the Boyd Brothers, most

Fig. 8. Mrs. William Taylor House, Main Street, Osgoode, Ontario, Canada, constructed by the Boyd Brothers Company in 1910, has rockface walls, ashlar-faced quoins, and lattice-patterned block for the porch face. National Archives of Canada.

block makers were already in the building industry. They started small, often with only one machine, and with relatively little capital investment. Harry Boyd's initial outlay was about three hundred dollars. Boyd, like many early block makers, built several houses for members of his own family and constructed a block factory as a public demonstration of how attractive and reliable concrete block could be. Public interest in the new building material grew from these demonstrations and prompted the next commissions.

The Boyd Brothers' business, like others, depended on trade publications and manufacturers' catalogues for their initial selection of machinery. Later, the Boyds received advice from the Ideal Concrete Machine Company's service department as well as from the Lafarge Company, their Portland cement suppliers. All of these were new forms of advertising and outreach for building material manufacturers.

The success stories of the Boyd Brothers, H. A. Donald, H. B. Leonard, and others, as impressive as they are, can obscure the fact that concrete block did not always enjoy a sterling reputation in its early years. In 1913, Harry Boyd recalled that when he began his business he was "not in favor of the prevailing kind of blocks" and "was of the opinion that we could make something better."[29] William Radford noted in 1909 that many machines had come on the market, and that the "advantages claimed for each had attracted men to the industry" who had "poor knowledge of how to make block."[30] They had been told that anyone could do it. Standards were non-existent. As one manufacturer confessed, sometimes all that was necessary was that "the block held together long enough to get to the site."[31]

Harry Boyd and his fellow manufacturers had to face and overcome the negative reputation of the industry's initial product. Boyd wrote that it was an "uphill fight to convince the trade. The City Architects would not consider concrete building blocks at all. The general public had a prejudice regarding the class of concrete blocks that had been made, and with cause, for those first introduced as building material, had neither strength, stability nor good appearance."[32] Along with the block makers, the machine manufacturers and the Portland cement companies were also eager to improve the reputation of concrete block. It was in everyone's best interest.

CHANGES IN THE CONCRETE-BLOCK INDUSTRY

To overcome its initial negative reputation, the industry began to organize to ensure standards. The National Association of Cement Users and the Concrete Block Machine Manufacturers Association were founded in 1905. The Concrete Producers Association followed in 1918, and the Concrete Block Manufacturers Association formed in 1919. Standardization of block size was an important achievement for these organizations. One drawback of the early block, as Harry Boyd had noted, was its size and weight. It was often large, usually twenty-four or thirty-two inches long. It was also thicker than modern block, making it very heavy. A block might weigh as much as 180 pounds and sometimes had to be laid with a hand-cranked derrick.

The sizes of block varied widely in the early years, but in 1924, the industry organizations agreed on standard units. By the end of the decade, 90 percent of the producers were using the eight-by-eight-by-sixteen-inch block. This standard made block much easier for architects and builders to use. Another industry development promoted by the national organizations was testing to improve the reliability and durability of the block. They published educational pamphlets reporting on the results of the tests which were widely read by block makers and helped institute reliable formulae for concrete mixing and curing.

National organizations also promoted the use of concrete block in trade magazines such as *Cement World,* founded in Chicago in 1907. Catalogues and books addressed to the home-building public offered designs for concrete-block structures. Titles published in the 1920s included *Plans for Concrete Houses* and *Concrete Garages, the Fireproof Home for the Auto-*

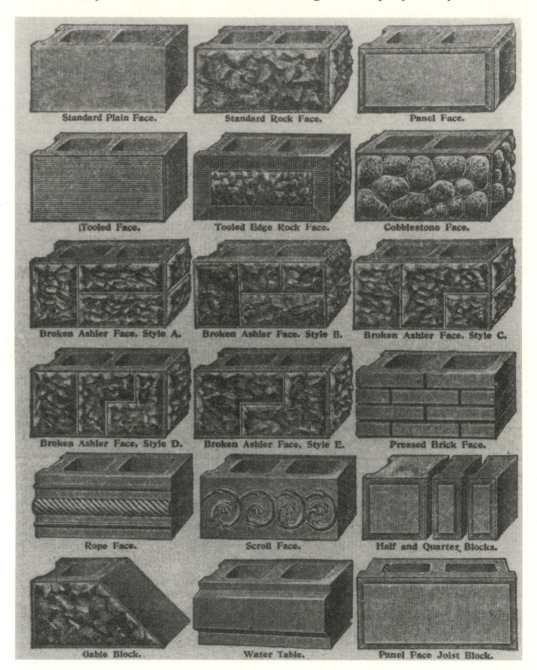

Fig. 9. Types of concrete-block faces available in the Sears, Roebuck Co. Catalogue, *1907, p. 425. Sears, Roebuck, Co.*

mobile. The industry's most audacious promotion was their participation in the Better Homes movement's celebrated *Home Sweet Home* house, which was built on the White House lawn in 1922.[33] This modern version of the house that inspired the song reproduced the colonial wooden original in plainfaced concrete block.

POPULARITY AND CRITICISM OF CONCRETE BLOCK

Its advocates claimed that hollow concrete blocks were a cheap, quick, and easy alternative to more traditional materials. A block cost only between thirteen and twenty cents to make in 1910, and it was cheaper than brick to lay. In the early 1900s, the cost of both wood and brick increased. In 1906, lumber prices rose 64 percent above what they had been in 1898. Brick was up 59 percent. By contrast, cement prices declined 16.5 percent between 1900 and 1906.[34] Pessimists of the day also noted a decreasing supply of lumber. It is no wonder that concrete block seemed a cheap and efficient substitute for traditional materials. Advertisers also pointed out that it was fireproof, required no paint, and needed little care. Its fireproof qualities made it especially appealing for garages and banks. To clinch their argument, manufacturers claimed the block would "last practically forever."[35]

Notwithstanding all these advantages, one of the most important reasons for the popularity of concrete block was its ornamental possibilities. Any number of wreaths, scrolls, or

Fig. 10. Vogl House, 1915, Kent County, Delaware. Mrs. Vogl used a variety of face plates to create a very decorative effect. Delaware State Historic Preservation Office.

cobblestone faces could be produced in concrete block. Sears included a whole page of ornamental plates in its catalogues (fig. 9).

Variety of ornamentation is probably what attracted Mrs. Wilhelmine Vogl when she chose a Sears machine to make her family's house in Kent County, Delaware, in 1915. Vogl, an amateur architect, laid out a plan for their house, designed the ornament, and helped her husband and children make the block and build the structure. She chose a rockface pattern for quoining and window surrounds and plainface block for the walls. Egg and dart molding plates served for the water table, string course, and cornice. Mrs. Vogl cast columns, balusters, and animal statuary to adorn the house and outbuildings, including a barn and milk house (fig. 10).[36]

Not only creative artists like Wilhelmine Vogl but also some manufacturer-builders like the Boyd Brothers exploited the variety of face plates for their buildings, setting the patterns of rockface against white quoins, tooled trim, and lattice-like foundations under porches.

Despite the variety of ornamental faces available for the block, the most widely used form was the rockface, an imitation of quarried stone. This was the standard unit on all Sears machines, and it was the face most in demand from the block makers. A. L. Johnson of the Ideal Cement Stone Company of Omaha recalled that in the early years of his firm, the rockface was a "must" and constituted their largest output.[37] The names, "artificial stone" or "cast stone," commonly used by the manufacturers and builders, emphasized that the block was an imitation of stone. It was cheap and easy and it looked like something more expensive.

However, this imitative quality turned the architectural elite against the material. Oswald Herring, an architect who wrote about concrete houses in 1912, spoke for many when he said, "The sight or mention of concrete block in its present crude form, especially in imitation of 'cut' and 'rockfaced' stone, has been sufficient to band the architectural profession together as a unit in protest and condemnation." He concluded that as a "cheap and vulgar imitation of stone, concrete will never be acceptable in any work of worth."[38]

Many shared his view. In 1907, a special committee of the American Institute of Architects had concluded that while reinforced concrete had much to recommend it, concrete block did not and should be avoided.[39] The committee reached this conclusion, the editors of the *American Architect and Building News* explained, because the "imitations of rockface masonry which are so frequently seen" were so "depressing and distasteful."[40] Even Frank Lloyd Wright, who did a series of experiments with his own version of the block in a group of California houses in the 1920s, condemned the early concrete block. "There never was a more 'inferior' building material than was the old concrete block" he said. "The block was cheap imitation and abominable as material when not downright vicious. Every form it undertook soon relegated it to the backyard of aesthetic oblivion."[41]

Herring and Wright and other architects did not reject concrete block per se; they only rejected the way builders had used it in the early years of the industry and especially its appearance in rockface. Herring devoted his book to the idea that architects could use the new material in tasteful designs. Wright shared this view, although he came into the debate fairly late. Only in 1923 did Wright begin work on his "textile block system." He explained his idea in an essay written that year: "This type is made from the gravel of decayed granite of the hills easily obtained there [California] and mixed with cement and sand in molds or forms to make a fairly solid mass either used in small units or monolithic in construction, or in combination. This is the beginning of a constructive effort to produce a type that would fully utilize standardization and the repetition of appropriate units. This standardization and repetition are essential values in the service rendered by the Machine."[42]

Wright spoke as an industrial architect who saw great potential in the machine. He never admitted to being influenced by the concrete-block industry and had only criticism and contempt for the way others had made and used block, but he echoed the sentiments of many architects and critics of the early twentieth century in asserting that in the right hands, and with artistic attention, concrete block could be a useful modern material.

In 1907, editors of the *American Architect and Building News* had argued that "concrete block which does not pose as anything else may be just as legitimate a structural unit as a block of clay or stone. . . . We have in mind several buildings where these blocks have been used by architects of taste with most satisfactory results."[43] Their point was that there was nothing wrong with machine-produced block if it did not try to imitate something it was not. Herring would have agreed. He argued that "concrete is not quarried, and so it should never be made to imitate rock-faced quarried stone."[44]

The popularity of rockface, however, and the sometimes less than careful use of dirty sand and aggregate, contributed to its negative reputation for cheapness and poor design. James Hobart, an architect writing in *Building Age* in 1910, advised readers to "avoid 'rock-faced' blocks as you would a pestilence."[45] Harvey Whipple, an expert on concrete, wrote in 1918 that the rockface block had been "responsible for more prejudice against concrete block" than "any other feature." He called it "lifeless in color" and severely criticized its monotonous and repetitive texture. He also pointed out that it showed moisture disagreeably, and was frequently poorly set. But his chief objection was that rockface block was "stiff, unnatural and ugly—not because it is an imitation, but because it *fails* to imitate."[46]

Given this condemnation of the rockface block, why was it so popular and ubiquitous? While architects and critics rejected the idea of block imitating quarried stone, ordinary people seemed to think it was fine. Americans built thousands of rockfaced buildings all across the country in the first three decades of the twentieth century. Twenty houses went up in the middle-class suburban development called Oakherst Place in St. Louis, Missouri, in 1906; fifty in the 1909 working-class company town of Mineville, New York.[47] No state is without such examples.

In Artesia, New Mexico, John Hodges opened the Hollow Stone Manufacturing Company in 1904, only a year after the town had been laid out. The editor of the local newspaper, the *Artesia Advocate,* enthusiastically reported on his progress:

When a factory was established in Artesia a few months ago for the making of hollow concrete building blocks, no one realized the importance of the move, nor how much it meant to the town. This substantial and beautiful substitute for stone has revolutionized building in the West. The first house to be built was the Crouch livery stable . . . then the two-story Baskin building. . . . The appearance of these two was so attractive and so substantial that the factory has been deluged with contracts. . . . The two-story residences are about to be completed and a half-dozen cottages are under construction, as is also the Methodist Church. . . . A large force

of workmen is employed. . . . Mr. Hodges informs us that additional machinery has been installed this week and the demand for stone will be supplied.

Hodges was so successful, he opened two more plants. Meanwhile, Charles and Joe Clayton, Hodges's rival contractors, bought a portable cast-iron machine that they hauled in a wagon to make block at the site.

Artesia may have had a higher percentage of concrete-block buildings than most towns because of the scarcity of other building materials in their area, but concrete block was accepted and admired as a new material in its own right (fig. 11). The editor's phrase "substantial and beautiful substitute for stone" revealed the reason for its appeal. He did not see it as a disagreeable makeshift or a sham. He found it a wholly satisfactory alternative for stone, better than what it imitated because it was less expensive and more readily available. He thought the appearance of the block was "attractive." To him, this "substitute stone" was not what Whipple had called failed imitation; it was successful allusion. Elite critics of the period might have agreed with Ada Louise Huxtable's later assessment that such acceptance was evidence of the "tastelessness of the middle class," but for the editor of the *Advocate* and the citizens of Artesia, like thousands of people everywhere, the beholder's eye found beauty in the rock faces of the concrete block.

Examples like Artesia argue for the democratic appeal of the material. In 1906, Louis H. Gibson wrote, "The cement block machine is a great art democrat. It may produce and reproduce artistic forms for the masses. It may give us beautifully decorated structures at minimum cost."[48] This argument would eventually be used in support of many of the new materials of the 1870–1930 period. People unable to afford expensive "real things" could, nevertheless, have substitute materials that offered the same rich effects. New technology made the substitutes inexpensive and widely available. The editor of the *Advocate* could see that concrete block had democratically, and dramatically, transformed his town.

The Demise of Rockface Block

Between 1900 and 1930, thousands of the rockfaced concrete-block buildings were built, many of which survive today on the mainstreets and backstreets of America. The hand-tamped, cast-iron, moveable-side machines helped to build garages, homes, commercial buildings, farm buildings, even fence posts.

Why did rockface block fall out of favor? A combination of changes in both taste and technology in the 1930s led the industry to shift production to the more utilitarian and less decorative plainface block. As to taste, the rise of modernism and its preferences for smooth-faced surfaces was one factor. The sleek, "modern" look of 1930s gas stations is a case in point. If the station were built of concrete block, it was the smooth, plainfaced variety, not the rusticated rockface.

As to the impact of technology on the demise of rockface block, this requires a more detailed answer.

Development of Cinder Block

One major change in the concrete-block industry in the 1920s was the introduction of light-weight aggregates. A number of experimenters had grappled with the problem of the weight of the sand-and-gravel block. The successful solution was developed by F. J. Straub, who patented a lightweight cinder block in 1917. At the plant he opened in Lancaster, Pennsylvania, in 1919, he promoted his product with demonstrations such as setting a "Straublox" building on fire while local fire chiefs witnessed the event. He then invited his guests to write testimonials to the cinder blocks' fireproof qualities. Straub made twenty-five thousand cinder blocks in this first year of production; by 1926, he was making seventy million block units annually. Straub also promoted the idea of cinder block as a cheap, lightweight structural frame that could be faced with more traditional materials such as brick.[49]

Literally made with lightweight coal cinders as the aggregate, cinder block was strong. One could hammer a nail into it, and it was much easier to lay than the older, heavier concrete block. Like Palmer, Straub had to fight to prevent imitators from infringing his patent rights. Unlike Palmer, he did it more successfully. Straublox was licensed and produced throughout the 1920s and 1930s.

In the 1930s, and especially in the 1940s, however, many other lightweight aggregates were introduced. Some, such as pumice, were natural. Others, like cinders and slag, were by-products, and still others, such as expanded shale, clay, and slate, were manufactured. The latter have been particularly popular since the 1940s. Expanded shale, clay, and slate aggregates are made by rapid firing, which bloats the raw material with expanded gases. The product is then quickly cooled to retain a cellular structure. Haydite, one of the earliest of the expanded shale products, was patented in 1919 but first used for block in 1923. Pottsco, introduced about 1930 and later called Celocrete, was blast furnace slag treated with water.

Fig. 12. The McQueen AME Chapel in Lee County, North Carolina, was built of block made on an old, hand-tamped machine by the congregation's minister in 1943. Courtesy of the North Carolina Division of Archives and History; photograph by Dan Pezzoni.

Later in the 1930s, Waylite, a slag expanded with steam, was introduced. The expanded aggregates were all lightweight, strong, and had a pleasing light color.[50]

Changes in Machinery

Improvements in the machines also changed the concrete-block industry. In the 1920s power tamping and "stripper" machines replaced the earlier hand-tamped, downface forms. The stripper had rigid sides, and the block was extruded from the mold rather than released through movable sides. Most of the manufacturing process, including the tamping, was automated. The Boyd Brothers adopted the new automatic machines in the mid-1920s.

The industry introduced two major changes in the 1930s: automatic vibrators that eliminated tamping and machines that could make multiple blocks. Louis Gelbman and the Stearns Manufacturing Company of Adrian, Michigan, started to develop what would be called the Joltcrete machine in 1934. It could make three standard blocks at once and nine blocks a minute. Other vibrating block machines appeared in the late 1930s and 1940s, including the popular Besser Vibrapac. Automatic vibrating machines dramatically increased productivity and also encouraged the use of lightweight aggregates because they could handle that mixture better than the tamp machines had. By 1940 most aspects of making block, from mixing to curing, had been automated. The use of steam to cure blocks, first suggested in 1908, became standard by the 1940s and was an important factor in producing a finished block quickly.[51]

The backyard phase of the history of concrete block was over by the end of the 1930s. In its place was a fully automated and expanding industry. The same factors that had given rise to the early production of concrete block—the ease of assembly, the advantages of repetition, standardization, rapidity of production, cost-cutting practicality—now meant that ornamental forms were no longer economically feasible. The automated system was geared to producing the plainface, lightweight block we know today.

There were survivals, of course. The single-block molding machines were still on the farms and in the backyards of people who had purchased them. Sometimes the relics became useful again. In Lee County, North Carolina, in 1943, war shortages and racial prejudice combined to stymie the efforts of McQueen Chapel's African American congregation to build a new church. Their minister, Jake Stewart, solved the problem by reviving an old block machine to make the rockface blocks for the Methodist chapel himself (fig. 12).[52]

Block companies with old machines on hand still sometimes used them. In Lexington, Virginia, the H. A. Donald Company had now become the Charles W. Barger and Son Company, but the old Zagelmeyer molds were still at the quarry. The foreman recalled that when the trucks came in with leftover ready-mix, workers would fill the old machines "just for the fun of it." They kept a supply of rockfaced block on hand for "ornamental and specialized work" until the late 1960s. Many rockface foundations and chimneys in Lexington confirm the accuracy of his account.[53]

While the later examples are interesting, this study is about the early history of concrete block. It demonstrates the popular acceptance of a material that was a cheap, quick and easy substitute for more traditional building forms. The concrete-block industry developed rapidly in the early twentieth century with the aid of new technology in materials and machines. In the first two decades of the century, the backyard phase, individuals frequently bought the inexpensive machines for their own use. But most people who bought the block machines already were in the construction business. Gradually, the industry consolidated and professionalized ensuring reliable, standardized materials.

The popularity of concrete block was also clearly tied to its ornamental and imitative qualities, and especially to its appearance in rockface. That may be difficult to understand today when rockface concrete-block buildings are usually considered "ugly." Nonetheless, their one-time popularity is evident in the countless examples that survive from the 1900–1930 period.

CHAPTER 2

Embossed Facades:
Ornamental Sheet Metal

One of the marvels of the 1876 Philadelphia Centennial Exhibition was the Sheet Metal Pavilion erected by the Kittredge Cornice and Ornament Company of Salem, Ohio (fig. 13). Constructed of leaded and galvanized sheet iron with pressed-zinc ornament, it was intended as a "practical illustration of the adaptability of sheet metals to architectural and general building purposes." The official exhibition newspaper claimed that the advantages of this "comparatively new" material were such that everyone who saw it would be impressed by its durability, architectural effects, and low cost.[1]

Though many were impressed, some, like the editors of the *American Architect and Building News,* objected to the imitative nature of sheet metal and called the pavilion the "most offensive building on the grounds."[2] Others hailed the pavilion as the portent of things to come, as indeed it was. The use of sheet metal for architectural ornament was comparatively new in the 1870s, but in the next several decades, a major sheet-metal industry developed that helped to change the face of buildings across the continent. This

Fig. 13. Sheet Metal Pavilion, Philadelphia Centennial Exhibition, 1876. Metal Worker 6 (30 Sept. 1876): 2. Hagley Museum and Library.

chapter covers the history of sheet metal for building, its widespread popularity from 1870 to 1930, its various ornamental forms, the manufacturers who made it, and the debate that surrounded its use.

History of Sheet Metal

Since ancient times, people have beaten metal into sheets and used them for architectural purposes ranging from roof covering to sewer pipes. In the late seventeenth century, water-powered rolling mills replaced the earlier hand-hammering process. Large rotating iron cylinders pressed pieces of metal into flattened sheets that were more uniform and much thinner than the hammered ones. The metals best suited to this process were lead, copper, zinc, iron, and, by the second half of the nineteenth century, steel. Tin was another important architectural metal, but it was too soft to be used by itself. Its nontarnishing nature made it an ideal coating for sheet iron, however. A brief examination of each of these materials offers a useful background for understanding the popularity of sheet-metal ornament in the second half of the nineteenth century.[3]

Lead and Copper

Soft and not subject to rust, lead was one of the first metals to be hammered into a sheet form for architectural use. The Romans covered roofs and lined baths and aqueducts with it. In the middle ages, it protected church spires, roofs, and domes. From the sixteenth century, in northern Europe, lead appeared as roofing, gutters, and downspouts. In the eighteenth century, important buildings in America, such as the Governor's Palace in Williamsburg, had lead roofs. The severe extremes of North American temperature fluctuations, however, eventually made builders realize that lead was far less suitable in the New World than the Old. Constant expansion and contraction caused the sheets to tear easily.

Despite this failure, in the early nineteenth century, lead became an important roofing material in North America, but not in its sheet form. Instead, it was melted and mixed with tin to form an alloy coating for sheet iron. The resulting product, known as terneplate, became a popular roof covering, much prized for its fireproof and noncorrodable qualities. It competed with and eventually supplanted tinplate for roof work in the United States. Both will be discussed in further detail later in this chapter.

Copper is extremely durable and much lighter than lead, qualities that made it an important architectural material, but it was also the most expensive of the sheet metals and thus required a major investment. First rolled into sheets in England and France in the seventeenth century, copper was widely used in important public buildings for roof covering and for ornamental details. Once British-imposed restrictions on the manufacturing of finished metals were lifted with the Revolution, American entrepreneurs almost immediately built rolling mills to produce both sheet copper and iron. Paul Revere's newly opened mill supplied the copper sheathing for Bulfinch's Massachusetts State House in 1802. Old Christ Church in Philadelphia was roofed in copper in the 1830s.

Although copper was expensive compared to other roofing metals, its reputation for durability and longevity made it a good investment for the long run. It could cost more than twice as much as an iron roof, but it would last three times as long. When copper weathered, a patina of copper sulfate formed on its surface, which acted as a protective coating preventing corrosion. The green patina also provided a distinctive color accent.

Because sheet copper was so expensive, it was usually used for roofing only on major buildings, but it can be found in smaller quantities as decorative details, guttering, downspouts, and weather vanes in more modest commercial and domestic structures. In the late nineteenth and early twentieth centuries, architectural components such as stamped ceilings, sidewalls, roof crestings, and finials were sometimes offered in copper; but because of its cost, copper never competed well with iron and steel. Sheet-metal manufacturer W. H. Mullins commented on this fact in his 1894 trade catalogue when he noted, "The cost of copper entering into these ornaments is so great, and the demand for Copper Ornaments as yet comparatively so limited, I have not felt justified in carrying them in stock, and therefore have not listed them in my Catalogue, but will be pleased to quote prices at any time my customers may desire."[4]

Iron and Steel

Iron is another metal with a long history, yet it was not until the Industrial Revolution that it became an important architectural material. In the late eighteenth and early nineteenth centuries, iron appeared in cast form for doors, columns, stairs, and whole building facades. In its wrought form it was important for ornamental fences, gates, railings, and balconies. As rolled sheets, however, iron was most often employed for roofing and guttering in the late eighteenth and early nineteenth centuries. English-born American architect Benjamin-Henry Latrobe owned part interest in a Philadelphia mill that produced the sheet iron for the 1804 roofs on the White House and the U.S. Capitol wings. In 1814, he recommended sheet iron to a friend, citing the roof on Princeton's Nassau Hall as an example of iron's durability.[5] One of the problems with sheet iron, however, was that when exposed to the atmosphere it formed a crust of iron oxide commonly called "rust." Corrosion could eat away at the surface, eventually destroying the metal. To prevent this, sheet-iron roofing was usually painted and had to be regularly repainted.

In the late eighteenth and early nineteenth centuries another solution to the problem of rust was provided by the development of tinplate. Small sheets of iron were dipped in molten tin. The tin coating alloyed with the iron and protected it from corrosion. Tinplate became a very popular roofing material. It also accounts for the term "tin roof." Even though the material was iron with a tin plating, most people simply called it "tin."

One of tinplate's most famous early advocates was Thomas Jefferson, who used it for roofs at Monticello, Poplar Forest, and the University of Virginia. In a letter to Charles Yancey in 1821, Jefferson wrote, "I would advise you to cover with tin instead of shingles. It is the lightest and most durable cover in the world."[6] Tinplate was not only light and durable but also noncombustible, and its fireproof qualities were considered one of its chief recommendations. Even with its tin covering, however, the abrasions that came with the normal wear and tear of roofing could lead to rust, so most people recommended painting tinplate roofs every few years.

Some scholars claim tinplate may have originated as early as the twelfth century, but it was only in the mid-eighteenth century with the development of rolling mills that the mass production of tinplate was possible. With its abundant natural deposits of tin, Wales became a thriving center for the British tinplate industry in the early nineteenth century. Tinsmiths in America bought the Welsh tinplate sheets and made them into roof coverings and guttering, as well as lanterns, candlesticks, coffee pots, stoves, and household utensils. By the mid-nineteenth century, probably the most frequent use of tinplate was for "tin" cans.[7]

Terneplate, the lead-tin alloy already mentioned in the earlier discussion of lead, was tinplate's chief competition. Its origins are more obscure and less well documented than those for tinplate, but the manufacturing process was nearly the same. The only difference was that the sheets of rolled iron were dipped in a mixture in which lead, a much cheaper and more plentiful ore than tin, was the chief ingredient. The proportions of lead to tin varied, but usually tin constituted only 15 to 20 percent of the terneplate alloy. Some authorities cite the British 1844 and 1858 patents for terneplate as the beginnings of its industrial history, but other sources indicate that companies in both Britain and the United States manufactured early versions of it in the 1830s, and it was mentioned in U.S. tariff legislation in 1842.

The word "terne" derives from the French for "dull," probably a reference to the dull appearance of lead. By contrast, nineteenth-century catalogues often called tinplate "bright tin" because of its shiny surface. The confusion over tinplate and terneplate is heightened by the fact that with weathering, these surface differences are minimized and the two are difficult to tell apart. This is even more true when they are painted. Adding to all this is the fact that in common parlance, roofers apparently called both materials "tinplate," even when they knew the difference. Terneplate was cheaper, however, and in America, was the preferred roofing material by the end of the nineteenth century. In fact, terneplate was sometimes called simply "roofing plate." By the 1890s both tin and terneplate were applied as protective coatings to steel as well as sheet iron.[8]

In the first half of the nineteenth century, tinplate and terneplate roofing sheets were relatively small, usually ten by fourteen inches, and were soldered into flat sheets or laid as overlapping shingles. By the 1870s there were ten standard sizes, the largest being forty by eighty-four inches, but most roofing plates came in sizes of fourteen by twenty inches or twenty by twenty-eight inches and in several varieties of weights. The standing-seam method of roofing, in which the sheets were joined in an overlapping, raised ridge that followed the slope of the roof, was in practice by the early nineteenth century but became much more common after 1870, when the larger sheets were available.

As widespread as the use of tinplate and terneplate was in the United States, throughout most of the nineteenth century these materials were imported from Britain. The 1890 McKinley Tariff Act changed that situation dramatically by imposing a very high tariff on imported tinplate. This gave the infant American tinplate companies a chance to compete. By 1896, they were making 98 percent of the domestic supply and eventually supplanted Britain as the world's leading producer.[9]

In celebration of American production, the U.S. Iron and Tin Plate Manufacturing Company of Demmler Station, Pennsylvania, erected a temporary, ceremonial city gate in rockfaced patterned tinplate with castlelated towers and a crowning eagle for the McKeesport, Pennsylvania, centennial in 1894. William McKinley, then governor of Ohio, was the honored guest. City officials presented the visiting dignitaries with souvenir tinplate keys and badges. Speeches proclaimed that just as these gates opened to the city, so too had McKinley's tariff opened the gates for the tinplate industry in the United States (fig. 14)[10]

Another improvement in sheet-iron manufacturing in the mid-nineteenth century, equally as important as tinplate and terneplate, was galvanizing. Again, the purpose of galvanizing was to provide a protective coating for the iron to prevent rust. In this case the coating was zinc. Although named for an Italian scientist who had been the first to discover electricity could be produced by chemical action, it was French and British chemists who developed the technique for coating iron in the late 1830s. By the 1840s, the process had been introduced into the United States, and by the mid-1850s, galvanized iron sheets were widely available. Because of differences in manufacturing, galvanized iron could be produced in sheets measuring twenty-four by seventy-two inches, much longer than those of tinplate. Sheets of this length were especially suitable for cornice work. Another improvement at the same period was corrugation, which greatly increased the strength of the sheet iron and made it more useful for roofing.

Sheet steel was produced in the United States from the late 1860s, but dramatic improvements in the open-hearth process in the 1880s made possible its production in much larger quantities. It became cheaper, more widely available and gradually replaced sheet iron for most architectural work. One of steel's major advantages was that it was stronger than iron, which meant that it could be die-pressed into fairly large ornamental sheets. By the end of the century, steel had replaced iron for cornices, building fronts, and other architectural features. Its strength also gave impetus to the development of new lines of architectural ornament including decorative roofing shingles and exterior and interior cladding.[11]

Sheet-Metal Cornices and Zinc Ornament

While decorative architectural elements made of sheet iron and steel were most common in the last half of the nineteenth century, one of its most popular forms, the sheet-metal cornice, originated in the 1830s. There is a legend that the first sheet-metal cornice was made in Cincinnati in 1834 by a tinsmith who witnessed a construction accident in which a stone cornice crushed two workmen.[12] Horrified by the event, he decided to find a better and safer alternative to heavy stone and applied his tinsmith skills to making a lighter substitute. The first cornice brakes—machines which bent sheet metal into decorative profiles (fig. 15)—were patented in the late 1830s, so the story may have some validity, but the use of sheet iron for cornice work was not widespread until the 1850s and later. Like most origin myths, the story may not be factual, but does contain an element of truth. Sheet metal was a safer, lighter building material than stone. It was also cheaper.

Galvanized sheet iron could be bent, cut, and soldered until it emulated all the elements of a classical cornice, or any other architectural fashion as well. The popularity of the commercial Italianate style corresponded with the growth and development of the sheet-metal cornice industry. In fact, some have argued that the sheet-metal cornice was an essential feature of the style.[13] That may be true, but sheet-metal cornices can also be found in every style popular in the late nineteenth and early twentieth centuries (fig. 16). Moldings, dentils, pediments, and brackets could all be made by a tinsmith's skill with the aid of a brake, tinsnips, tongs, mallets, seamers, and solder.

Galvanized sheet iron stood up well to the cutting and bending necessary for cornice work, but it was too brittle for deep embossing. Zinc, a softer and more malleable metal, provided the qualities needed for high-relief decoration. Sheet zinc had been popular in Germany and Belgium since the eighteenth century for roof covering, and there is some evidence it was used in the United States as well, but it had the same problems as lead: it was too soft to hold up to the extremes of the North American climate. Zinc was well suited, however, to the stamping of decorative ornament. In the second half of the nineteenth century it was die-stamped into swags, rosettes, fleur-de-lis, and acanthus leaves to provide decorative adornment for sheet-iron cornices, window hoods, pilasters, and window bays. On interiors it provided elaborate ceiling centerpieces, which were promoted as practical substitutes for those usually made of cast plaster. The importance of stamped-zinc ornament in the origin of the metal-ceiling industry will be more fully discussed in the next chapter.

Sheet-Metal Shingles

The earliest references to stamped sheet-metal shingles appear in the 1870s, but widespread production came only in the 1880s and 1890s.[14] The individual units were usually seven by ten inches, ten by fourteen inches, or fourteen by twenty inches and could imitate one or more shingles within a single plate. In the early twentieth century, sizes as large as sixteen by twenty inches or twenty-four by twenty-four inches with multiple shingle patterns were available, but they were recommended only for large roof expanses such as barns or churches. Like most roofing material, the metal shingles were sold as "squares," with one hundred square feet equaling one square. The shingles were made in iron and steel tinplate, terneplate, and galvanized sheets.

A pioneering North American manufacturer of the shingles was the Metallic Roofing

Fig. 15. "Niagara cornice break" advertised in L. D. Berger Company's Tinner's and Roofer's Supplies catalogue, 1895, p. 88. Hagley Museum and Library.

No. 1 Niagara Cornice Brake.

This brake is made entirely of iron and steel. By distributing the metal on correct principles, we succeeded in constructing a brake lighter than other iron brakes, and yet perfectly adapted to the ordinary work of cornice makers.   We avoided surplus stock, which only adds to the cost and transportation charges and makes a brake unhandy.   And, on the other hand, we did not have recourse to materials susceptible to changes of temperature and dampness.

Will bend No. 22 iron with the angle iron on bending bar.

Will bend No. 24 iron without the angle iron.

No. 1—8-foot Niagara Cornice Brake, shipping weight, 1,800 lbs. $150 00
Beading Attachment, including one rod (state diameter wanted), extra......... 22 00

Company of Toronto. Levi Montross, one of its founders, took a patent on a metal shingle in 1884. He followed that with three additional patents in 1885, 1886 and 1887. His Eastlake metal shingle, a square with side locks and either a maple leaf or star pattern proved to be one of the firm's best selling items both in Canada and the United States. The embossed ornament formed a kind of corrugation which strengthened the thin metal sheet (fig. 17). It was laid diagonally as a diamond pattern; each plate overlapped the next to hide the nail holes and provide waterproofing. The shingles were not recommended unless the roof had a fairly steep pitch.[15]

One of the earliest American manufacturers of metal shingles was the Iron Clad Company of Brooklyn, New York, which advertised their Metallic Shingles in 1879 as "handsomer and far

Fig. 16. Sheet-metal cornices, blocking, and signs in the J. S. Thorn Sheet Metal Works *catalogue, 1890, p. 17. Hagley Museum and Library.*

superior to Slate, Tin or Wood; they are Fire-proof and will last a life-time; anyone can put them on."[16] Between 1883 and 1889, the building journal *Carpentry and Building* regularly carried stories on "novelties" in metal shingle designs, including advertisements for the Garry Iron Roofing Company of Cleveland, Ohio, and their "new Metallic Roofing Tile"; the New York National Sheet Metal Roofing Company's "Walter's Metallic Shingle"; and the Philadelphia Cortright Metal Roofing Company's "Cortright-Darlington metallic tile" among others.[17] Promoted as easier to put on, more decorative and less vulnerable to wind damage than standing-seam and flat-seam tinplate sheets, the shingles were a "new form of metal roof."[18]

The popularity of metal shingles brought many competitors into the market. In Canada, the Metallic Roofing Company's chief rival was the Pedlar People, a firm founded in Oshawa, Ontario, in 1861 as a tin shop and hardware business. In 1892, they opened a plant specifically to make stamped shingles, ceilings, and cladding. Their advertising proclaimed: "The steel shingle has sounded the death knell of the wood shingle. It not only makes a better roof, but a cheaper roof. It is not only more durable, but it is more artistic and more easily put on. Pedlar Perfect Steel Shingles have created the perfect metal roofing that is not only proof against fire and lightning, but against rain and tempest and snow."[19]

Popular for Mansard roofs, towers, gables, and porches, the metal shingles were available in a wide variety of patterns. Their chief appeal was that they looked like slate, but were lighter

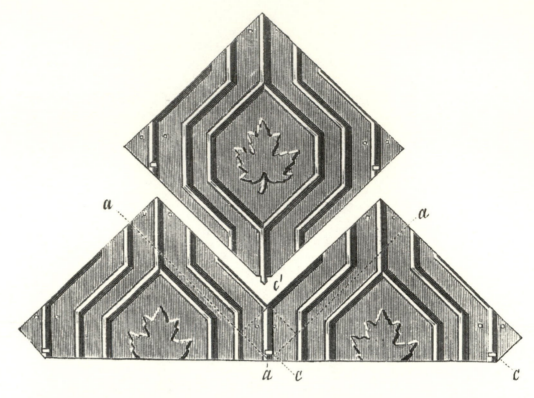

and cheaper. The Metallic Roofing Company celebrated this imitative quality in an 1890 advertisement that boasted their Eastlake shingle was indistinguishable from "Best Blue Welsh Slate if painted a dark color."[20] By the late 1890s, the shingles also appeared in Spanish tile patterns. As the Pedlar People claimed, they had "all the artistic features of terra cotta . . . with none of its disadvantages." The metal tiles were lighter, required less roof framing, were easy to lay, did not crack, and had no cement joints which could open and leak.[21]

Manufacturing metal shingles was not an elaborate process. The companies bought prepared iron or steel sheets which had been rolled and either galvanized, or coated with tinplate or terneplate. At the factory the thin sheets were then cut into plates of the appropriate size. These were stamped in a press to provide their decorative embossed patterns, sheared true, painted, and then packed and shipped. From the 1880s through the 1920s they were a ready form of ornament for mass consumption.

Sheet-Metal Facades

Stamped sheet-metal facades began to compete with the older cast-iron versions in the 1880s and 1890s, though often the two were found in combination. A cast-iron ground floor facade would accompany a galvanized sheet-metal cornice and window hoods. The wear and tear of street activity demanded the sturdy cast iron on the first level, but at the upper reaches, sheet iron or steel was lighter, easier to use, and cheaper.

That was the solution chosen by James H. Slater in 1891 in La Grande, Oregon, when he selected his building's facade from the St. Louis Mesker Brothers Company catalogue. The ground level columns were cast iron, but the rest of the details were galvanized sheet

Fig. 18. The Josephine B. Leary Building in Edenton, North Carolina, constructed in 1894 is a Mesker Brothers cast-iron and sheet-metal facade. Courtesy of the North Carolina Division of Archives and History.

Fig. 19. The "cheap galvanized steel front" of a building illustrated in George L. Mesker and Company's Architectural Iron Works Catalogue, *1902, p. 2. Hagley Museum and Library.*

steel.[22] In 1894, Josephine Napoleon Leary, an African American business woman, replaced her fire-damaged building in Edenton, North Carolina, with a brick structure and also chose a Mesker Brothers cast-iron and galvanized sheet-metal front (fig. 18).[23] In 1902, D. L. Gaskell, a Salisbury, North Carolina, contractor, wrote to the rival firm of George Mesker in Evansville, Indiana, praising the eighteen building fronts they had supplied to his town.[24] Like the La Grande and Edenton buildings, the Salisbury metal fronts, many of which still survive, were a combination of cast iron and sheet metal.

Eventually, sheet-metal companies offered whole facades of sheet steel (fig. 19), although at first with an acknowledged apology for their thinness. W. H. Mullins Company of Salem, Ohio, for example, advertised "Cheap Sheet Metal Ornaments" in their 1894 catalogue and claimed that to "meet a class of competition which has recently arisen in the west" they had developed a line of relief building facades in "light gauges of sheet metal." They did not advise using them for "the best work," but "when cheap work to meet the competition is wanted, they are just the thing."[25]

Fig. 20. Unidentified building with elaborate sheet-metal cornice, window caps, and rockface siding. Penn Metal Ceiling and Roofing Company *catalogue, 1906. Hagley Museum and Library.*

Fig. 21. Metal garages in
Edwards Manufacturing
Company Catalogue
No. 68 *1923, p. 217.*
Hagley Museum and
Library.

In the late 1880s, improvements in sheet-steel production and drop presses made possible the stamping of larger decorative panels. Customers could now purchase not only building fronts but also cladding for the whole building in imitation of rockface stone or pressed brick. The sheet-metal companies recommended it for covering old buildings with deteriorating facing as well as for new structures. Easily nailed over a wooden frame, the pressed panels could instantly produce the appearance of a substantial masonry building (fig. 20). The illusion might be further enhanced by covering the sheet metal with a paint mixed with sand. Later, in 1911, sheet-metal manufacturers also advertised prefabricated, fireproof garages with rockface metal siding (fig. 21). Interestingly, the rockface pattern, an imitative form so popular for concrete, was also a staple for sheet metal, appearing as early as 1887.[26]

Sheet-metal ornament reached the peak of its popularity in the last decade of the nineteenth and the first decade of the twentieth centuries throughout North America. If anything, its success as interior cladding for ceilings and walls was even greater than for exterior work, a story told in the next chapter. In order to understand how all this came about, it is necessary to look more closely at some of the companies that made the sheet-metal building materials and to examine their methods of production and distribution.

The Manufacturers

In the mid-nineteenth century, small tin shops did most architectural sheet-metal work, largely by hand-craft methods. That situation began to change in the mid-1870s, when several midwestern firms introduced large scale factory techniques to the production of both stamped-zinc ornaments and sheet-metal cornices. The Kittredge Cornice and Ornament Company of Salem, Ohio, was one of the earliest and largest. Founded in 1872, the company actively promoted the industry and even supported a trade journal, the *Sheet Metal Builder*.[27] It was Kittredge who built the Sheet Metal Pavilion at the Philadelphia Centennial Exposition in 1876.

Other companies came into the business in the late 1870s to meet the growing demand for architectural sheet metal. Many of the early firms were clustered near the centers of the iron industry and nearby major rail lines in Ohio, Indiana, West Virginia, Pennsylvania, and New York. But there were also important manufacturers in more outlying areas such as Boston; Milwaukee; St. Louis; Dubuque, Iowa; St. Paul, Minnesota; and even Nevada, Missouri. In fact, between 1870 and 1930, there were at least forty-five major sheet-metal companies with national distribution operating in ten different states. All of them depended on the railroad for their raw materials and for distribution of their finished products.

Probably the most famous of all the sheet-metal building materials companies were the two firms owned by the Mesker brothers. Their father, who had emigrated from Germany as a boy, settled in Cincinnati, where he trained as a "tinner," a craftsman who worked with tinplate and made and repaired everything from cooking pots to stoves. In 1844, the elder

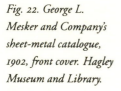

Fig. 22. George L. Mesker and Company's sheet-metal catalogue, 1902, front cover. Hagley Museum and Library.

1902

GEO. L. MESKER & CO.
ARCHITECTURAL
IRON WORKS

THE LARGEST AND MOST COMPLETE
ESTABLISHMENT IN THE UNITED STATES.

MODERN STORE FRONTS — HANDSOME DESIGNS.
CAST IRON, WROUGHT IRON, GALV. IRON, WOOD WORK
AND GLASS FOR STORE FRONTS.

·EVANSVILLE·IND·U·S·A·

Mesker opened his own business and plied his wares up and down the Ohio and Mississippi Rivers. He moved to Evansville, Indiana, in 1850, and founded a company to produce stoves and copper, tin, and sheet-iron ware. When he retired in 1876, the elder Mesker left the business to his sons. One of them, George, took over and built the business into the largest architectural ironworks in the United States (fig. 22). Meanwhile, two of George's brothers, Ben and Frank, settled in St. Louis and started the Mesker and Brother Company in 1879. The firms were always fierce competitors. Between them they made thousands of sheet metal building fronts like those already mentioned in Oregon and North Carolina (fig. 18) and, through their catalogues, sold them all over the country.[28]

The career of W. H. Mullins offers another instructive example of the rise of one of the major sheet metal firms. As a twenty-five-year-old Pittsburgh railroad clerk in 1882, Mullins scraped together enough to buy a wrecked locomotive, which he disassembled and sold for parts and scrap, earning a thousand dollars' profit. That was enough to buy into a firm in Canton, Ohio, that became Bakewell and Mullins. Thomas H. Bakewell had earlier bought out the remains of the Kittredge Cornice and Ornament Company. Bakewell and Mullins soon became one of the largest manufacturers in the Midwest.

While the firm produced an extensive line of architectural ornament, including capitals, moldings, cresting, cornices, and building fronts, they were best known for their metal statuary. Augustus Saint-Gauden's *Diana* was probably their most famous piece. The statue of the running huntress with a drawn bow stood atop McKim, Meade and White's Madison Square Garden in New York from 1895 until the building's destruction in 1925. She now resides in the main hall of the Philadelphia Museum of Art. Mullins received the contract for the *Diana* (including both the eighteen foot high original and the thirteen foot high final version) because he had developed an innovative system of die stamping the copper sections of the statue. This was much more efficient that the older hand-hammering methods which had been common for earlier copper sculpture such as the Statue of Liberty.

Despite their success, Mullins and Bakewell differed in their views on the future direction of the company. In 1890, Bakewell offered to buy out Mullins for fifty thousand dollars or to sell the company to him for the same amount. Much to Bakewell's surprise, Mullins was able to secure a loan to buy the company, changed its name to W. H. Mullins, and continued to expand the firm and diversify its products. In the early twentieth century, he added automobile parts and metal boats. The Mullins company eventually became too large to be a single proprietorship, so it reorganized into a corporation in 1904. Mullins still held the majority of the stock and remained as president.[29]

The examples of the Meskers and Mullins illustrate the rise of the large manufacturers of architectural sheet metal ornament. But there is also the story of the smaller manufacturer and the local tinsmith, who played important roles in the production and distribution of the material.

In 1893, William Franklin Norman was a traveling salesman for the Wheeling Corrugating Company of Wheeling, West Virginia. He received $166.67 a month to sell the firm's steel roofing, ceilings, sidewalls and other products. Covering primarily a western territory, Norman settled in Nevada, Missouri. He became convinced there was a local demand for pressed metal, so in 1898 he and tinner John Berghauser founded the W. F. Norman Sheet Metal Manufacturing Company.

They started in a small shop making roof crestings and cornices. Though large firms dominated the business, reductions in the cost of cornice brakes (the machines that bent sheet metal into decorative profiles) in the 1890s encouraged smaller shops like Norman's to compete for local business.[30] An 1891 article in the *Metal Worker* commented on this phenomenon: "The time was when the industry was summed up by mentioning the names of a few manufacturers, but now almost every sheet metal establishment does cornice work." Norman was among them. He still acted as an agent for the Wheeling Company and bought pressed ornament from them until 1905. Then he expanded his business, built a new factory and began to produce his own pressed-metal ceiling and roofing line, advertised regionally as "Made in the West—They are the Best!"[31] Compared to his former employer, the Wheeling Corrugating Company, or to the huge Meskers or Mullins operations, Norman was a fairly small manufacturer with a largely southwestern regional trade.

Smaller still was the local tin shop, such as the H. T. Klugel Architectural Sheet Metal Company of Emporia, Virginia. In 1902, Klugel left his native Danville, Illinois, where he had been trained as a tinner by his father, to strike out on his own. Unlike many young men of his time who went west, he headed east to settle in Emporia, a town at the intersection of two major rail lines. There Klugel opened his architectural sheet metal shop. Like many small sheet metal businesses, Klugel bought the rolled metal sheets from the big foundries and then manufactured cornices, stove flues, gutters, and drain pipes in the local shop. When pressed ornament was needed, they ordered it from the big firms. If a local store owner wanted a pressed-metal ceiling, Klugel showed the customer a catalogue selection, ordered the ceiling plates, and installed them. He kept a variety of pressed-metal ornaments on hand for use when putting together a decorative marquee for the town's bank or a cornice for the hotel. Thus, at the local level, a combination of bought manufactured items and local tinner's skills supplied the needs of the community. Klugel worked for contractors throughout his region. A creative advertiser, he used the facade of his 1914 headquarters building as a spectacular display of the possible uses of sheet metal ornament (fig. 23).[32]

These examples, whether large, middling, or small, show a pattern of capital investment in new industrialization in the second half of the nineteenth century. Many of the entrepreneurs had been trained in the handcraft of sheet-metal work, but turned those skills to industrial production techniques. Responding to improvements in equipment, such as drop presses and cornice brakes, and in materials, such as the larger sized sheets of steel, they rapidly expanded their businesses. In almost every case, their companies also offered innovations, taking out new patents for both machinery and products. Located near rail lines, the sheet-metal firms depended on the country's improved transportation and communications systems to get their raw materials and to ship their finished products. All of them employed a system of telegraph ciphers for placing orders. Large scale productivity, manufacturer-controlled distribution, and advertising were all part of their success.

Distribution of Sheet-Metal Products

One of the major changes which occurred in business practice in the second half of the nineteenth century was the gradual elimination of the wholesaler, or "jobber." Rather than relying on regional distribution centers which stockpiled products and sought retail outlets, manufacturers took advantage of the expanded rail service to ship their products directly

Fig. 23. H. T. Klugel's Architectural Sheet Metal shop, Emporia, Virginia, 1914. Virginia Department of Historic Resources.

to local retailers.[33] Jobbers continued to play important roles in some industries, such as the linoleum trade, but they largely disappeared from the sheet-metal business.

The Edwards Metal Roofing, Siding and Ceiling Company proudly and typically boasted of the advantages of the new direct sales system when they announced in their 1912 catalogue, "We are not merchants or jobbers, but manufacturers and make everything we sell. In this way we give you rock-bottom prices and assure you only first class goods." They also pointed out that their plant in Cincinnati was on a "special switch-line," so they only had to load the materials onto the rail cars and "ship it directly to you."[34]

Advertising Sheet-Metal Ornament

In the early nineteenth century, when the sales stream had flowed from manufacturer to jobber to retailer to consumer, the retailer had been largely responsible for advertising. Most of it was local and in newspapers. In fact, with the exception of patent medicine and sewing machines, little advertising appeared in national magazines before the 1880s. But with the elimination of the jobber and the consolidation of capital in larger companies, there was a revolution in advertising practices. Manufacturers now took responsibility for the investment in promoting their products.[35]

Improvements in printing, the development of half-tone illustrations, and the lower cost of production all contributed to a boom in the magazine industry in the last two decades of the nineteenth century. Journals directed to the building trades multiplied and the manufacturers' advertising filled their pages (fig. 24). A 1910 ad in the *National Builder* underscored the advantages of the system. Addressing their comments to the building contractor, the Northrop, Coburn and Dodge sheet-metal company boasted, "Hundreds of inquiries are received by us every week from our magazine advertising. Those from your town we'll turn over to you if you want them. Let us know at once. It makes no difference where you are—in Maine or California, you can reap the benefits of advertising."[36]

Another means of marketing new products was the trade show. Inspired in part by manufacturing displays at world's fairs, and by the organization of industries into associated groups, the trade fair became a regular event. The sheet-metal industry, too, realized the trade fair was a means to display new products, to attract attention, solicit orders, and distribute advertising literature. Building magazines enthusiastically reported on trade shows such as the Wisconsin Hardware Association exhibition held in Milwaukee in 1912. They were delighted to publish photographs of display stands like that of the Milwaukee Corrugating Company, a miniature temple constructed of various sheet-metal products (fig. 25).[37]

The chief marketing tool for the sheet-metal manufacturer, however, was the trade catalogue. It became the prime link with the consumer.[38] The manufacturer's goal was to put the catalogues in the hands of builders and contractors. Regional agents like W. F. Norman helped them to do so. As Norman traveled his western territory, representing the Wheeling Corrugating Company, he presented the latest catalogues to local builders and encouraged their orders. Manufacturers also sent catalogues to the building trade press, who regularly reported on the new publications. For example, in 1905 the *National Builder* noted that they had just received a "new ninety page catalogue bound in attractive canvas" from the Wheeling Corrugating Company.[39] In their national advertising the manufacturers also promised to

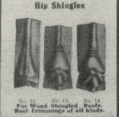

Fig. 24. Examples of advertising for sheet-metal products. National Builder 40 (June 1909): 74. Hagley Museum and Library.

mail the new catalogues at no charge to anyone who wanted one. The smart contractor usually had a whole library of manufacturers' trade catalogues to show his customers.

Contractors may have been the intended recipients of the catalogues, but consumers were the target audience. Manufacturers designed their catalogues to attract consumers' attention and impress them with the quality of the products. Although the two Mesker companies produced their catalogues on cheap paper with line engravings for illustrations, they were the exception. By 1900, most sheet-metal companies were competing with each other for ever more elaborate presentations (fig. 26). Artist-designed decorative covers encased booklike publications that were sometimes one hundred or more pages in length and filled with half-tone illustrations of the products and photographs of buildings where the material had been used.

Manufacturers established their authority and earned consumer trust with catalogue copy that boasted of how big their plants were, and how long they had been in business. The photographs of the plants that sometimes accompanied these statements are surprising to the present-day reader who might consider them images of industrial blight. But the fact that the pictures are presented with such pride suggests a different contemporary meaning. In a 1912 catalogue, the Edwards Company of Cincinnati, Ohio, noted, "The pictures here shown may give you some idea of the magnitude of our big plant."[40] What followed

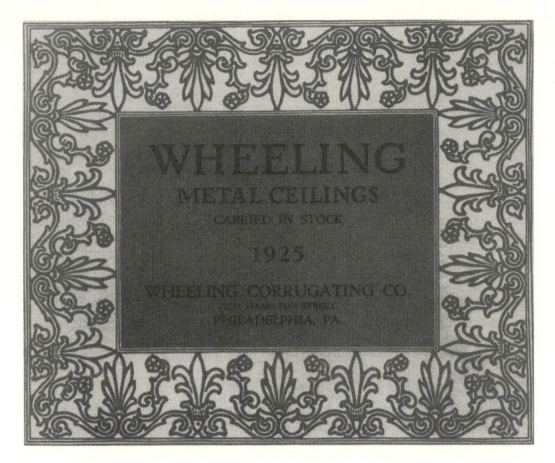

Fig. 26. Cover of the Wheeling Metal Ceiling catalogue, 1925. Hagley Museum and Library.

were images of large buildings with nearby rail lines, busy workers operating machines, and smoke stacks bellowing out smoke. Surely these were images of progress. This was the industrial revolution that would bring new sheet-metal products to people everywhere.

Catalogue copy also testified to how happy customers were. Letters were often reproduced such as that of John Ward of Qu'Appelle Station in the Northwest Territory, which appeared in the Metallic Roofing Company of Canada's 1894 catalogue: "I can very heartily recommend your Metallic Roofing for any one in the northwest. A poor man taking up land out here can build his house, and by using your metallic roofing have, at a comparatively small cost, a perfectly safe roof over his head, free from fire, rain and wind."[41] The catalogues also carried information on how to order the materials and usually included a telegraph cipher code. Thus, the sheet-metal industry took advantage of the whole infrastructure of mass communication and transportation that had transformed business practice in the second half of the nineteenth century.

Advantages and Disadvantages of Sheet Metal

One of the chief selling points for all the architectural sheet-metal products was that they were an economical means of ornamentation. The George L. Mesker and Company 1902 catalogue, for example, advertised the advantages of its steel building fronts: "Old frame buildings can be fitted with handsome fronts at a very low price. Don't use weatherboarding when you can get these handsome fronts so cheap. Send us dimensions of your building and see how cheap we can make a fine front of it—equal in appearance to a fine brick building."[42]

Sheet metal was also promoted as better than the products it replaced because it was more durable and fire-resistant. The fire-resistant qualities of sheet metal were often promoted by scientific test demonstrations such as the one reported in the *New York Record and Guide* in 1914. The Association of Metal Ceiling Contractors of Greater New York pitted metal against plaster and wood in a test conducted at the Columbia Testing Station by Professor James S. McGregor. The results, showing the superiority of metal, were proudly published in the sheet-metal industry's catalogues.[43] The companies also pointed to the fact that insurance rates were lower with sheet-metal products, so consumers could save money as well as have peace of mind about the safety of their buildings.

There were some disadvantages to sheet metal, however, especially in exterior use. Its fire-resistant qualities were much exaggerated as several disastrous urban fires proved. Metal might be incombustible, but at high temperatures, it lost its strength and could not be relied upon. Even with galvanizing and plating, abrasions could still cause rust, and regular repainting was necessary. Air pollution from coal burning fires attacked the protective coatings as well and limited the life of metal roofing in large cities.

These problems could be avoided with proper maintenance, and even if sheet metal was not entirely fireproof, it was still more so than wood. A different and more philosophically troubling problem for the industry was the aesthetic issue of sheet metal's appearance and the imitative forms in which it was produced.

The "Servile Imitation" Debate

The term "servile imitation" had been used as early as 1874 to describe sheet-metal ornament, and it appeared repeatedly in a thirty-year debate conducted vigorously in the building press.[44] An 1885 article in the *Metal Worker* described the problem: "One of the most serious objections to galvanized iron work . . . is that it is simply a servile imitation of other materials. . . . [The] boast of those who have manufactured this class of work has often been that it . . . so successfully imitated stone and wood as to be scarcely detected by careful observers."[45]

One of the most notable expressions of the controversy was played out in the pages of the *American Architect and Building News (AABN)* in 1876 over the appropriateness of Kittredge's Sheet Metal Pavilion at the Philadelphia Centennial. The *AABN* editors called it "perhaps the most offensive building on the grounds" with "coarse ornament of the most pretentious kind." They also condemned the sheet metal on the dome of Memorial Hall as "mean" and the zinc statuary on the roof as "clumsy." Their conclusion was that galvanized iron might be a "very valuable material for its uses, and its uses are many" but there is "no need of pressing it into the place of other materials."[46]

A defender of sheet metal who identified himself only as "Quaker" from Philadelphia, wrote a series of letters to the *AABN* objecting to their "uncalled-for denunciations" and arguing that imitation in and of itself was not a bad thing. He cited historical examples from the Greeks and Romans, who used stucco to imitate stone. He also pointed out, "We cannot all expect to possess an original Angelo, Raphael or Rubens, but we may enjoy a good copy. . . . Shall we be so bigoted as to discard the art teachings of such masters . . . because we are not able to possess the originals? . . . It may do for a Ruskin, who would roll the world back a century, but not for this enlightened and progressive age."[47]

Quaker's argument, one others would also take up, was that metal was a modern material and architecture should exploit all of its potentials, one of which was imitation. He also raised the question of what was imitation and what was not. The sheet metal in the dome on Memorial Hall, for example, far from being "mean," was instead, Quaker claimed, an "honest use of architectural sheet-metal work in positions requiring lightness coupled with strength and durability," while cut ashlar stone facing of buildings throughout the world was an attempt to "cheat the masses into the belief that the walls are of such material."[48]

The editors of the *AABN* countered that comparing stone ashlar facing to sheet metal was like comparing "clothing to a mask." Moreover, they declared, "if a man has not a natural disgust for shams, it is difficult to argue him into it."[49] They claimed to "simply refer to established facts when we say that hollow forms of thin metal . . . are to a trained eye at once and always distinguishable by their inferior look. . . . They are universally acknowledged to be so inferior to the things they imitate that hardly any one would think of substituting them if they were not very much cheaper."[50]

Quaker asked, "Must the fact that these forms can be produced so as to be within the reach of almost our entire building-community . . . be the sole reason why so fierce an onslaught shall be sustained?"[51] He also argued that while there might be some merit to the claim that "building for future ages" should be in stone, most of the structures that employed sheet metal were not meant to stand "but fifty to seventy-five years," and that it "savors strongly of wanton waste of the people's money to insist that the costlier embellishments must be in stone" when there were materials available that were "equally good and appropriate."[52] The *AABN* editors had the last word, however, summarizing their objections to sheet-metal ornament: "That it is superfluous, that it is weak, that it is ugly, and that it is a sham."[53]

The controversy over the centennial buildings took place in 1876, but the debate went on. Writing in *Carpentry and Building* in 1891, architect T. Claxton Fidler declared, "Such things as entablatures of iron and cornices . . . are 'hollow shams,' and constitute an offense against good taste."[54] Even Frank Lloyd Wright, a 1928 latecomer to the debate, suggested that there could be a serious modern application for sheet metal. The problem, Wright thought, was that because of the way it had been used, the material was so degraded that architects seemed to despise it. He called it "the prime makeshift to his highness the American jerry-builder."[55]

An analysis of the arguments in the "servile imitation" debate reveals three major points. One was about the appropriateness or inappropriateness of imitation; the second was about the success or failure of that imitation; and the third was about the "cheapness" and universality of mass-produced, repetitious sheet-metal ornament.

These points recall Ada Louise Huxtable's contention that the American desire for cheap, quick, and easy ornament was fueled by the "tastelessness of a new middle class society that accepted substitute gimcrackery for traditional materials."[56] Huxtable, who was writing in 1960, expressed the same point of view the editors of the *AABN* had taken in 1876 when she referred to the "tastelessness of the new middle class." Implied in her statement, however, is a suggestion that "Quaker" would have agreed with—there was a new middle-class society to whom sheet-metal materials were wholly satisfactory. Was it tastelessness or was it simply a different taste? The new middle-class society might have joined Quaker in saying, "You will allow me to be as strong in my belief as you are in yours, of course."[57]

AABN's editors claimed that the "trained eye" could always identify sheet metal by "its inferior look." It wasn't so much that it imitated stone and wood (though that was bad enough); the problem was that it failed to convincingly imitate stone and wood. Yet the new middle class would have agreed with a writer in *Carpentry and Building,* who, in 1879, said that "probably no amount of argument is sufficient to dispel this objection [to repetitious, common, imitative ornament] from the mind of the architect" but "To the ordinary mind, however, this objection counts for little."[58] The suggestion of class difference in attitudes toward acceptance implied in this statement had also been commented on by Quaker when he asked, "Must the fact that these forms can be produced so as to be within the reach of almost our entire building-community . . . be the sole reason why so fierce an onslaught shall be sustained?" The point was that the elite rejected mass culture not because it was inferior but because it was common.

To the ordinary people who bought the cornices, shingles, and building fronts, sheet metal was not so much imitation as allusion. The 1879 *Carpentry and Building* writer cited above suggested this when he characterized stamped ornament as holding the same "position which the chromo holds relative to the costly painting of which it is a faithful reproduction."[59] Whether or not sheet metal actually fooled anyone into thinking it was stone or wood was irrelevant. What mattered was that it was successful ornament in its own right. The editor of the *Sheet Metal Builder* made the same argument in 1874 when he wrote that good sheet-metal ornament was "neither mock-wood nor mock-stone" but something that while "possessing all the essential elements of beauty and taste peculiar to either," was nonetheless "adapted to the material of which it is constructed—sheet metal."[60] Sheet-metal ornament was a substitute, a faithful reproduction, but also a material possessing its own unique qualities, and these qualities deserved to be admired.

Moreover, sheet metal represented modernity and progress. Quaker referred to "this enlightened and progressive age" in which new products had been shaped by new technology. These were products that were better than the stone and wood they replaced. They supplied rich ornament, durability, and fire resistance at a price the masses could afford. This point was underscored in a E. E. Souther Iron Company of St. Louis catalogue which proclaimed, "This is the age of steel and there is scarcely a purpose heretofore served by a construction of wood, which cannot now be replaced by steel to better advantages." It was, they said, "a vastly superior" material for "all building purposes."[61]

The use of architectural ornament in sheet metal was part of the industrial expansion of the second half of the nineteenth century. Decorative shingles, cornices, and facades were widely marketed in the post-1870 period and were especially popular in the American West. By the 1890s, when steel began to replace sheet iron, new products such as pressed-metal ceilings and cladding gained in acceptance. Their heyday was in the first two decades of the twentieth century.

In the late 1920s, however, the popularity of sheet-metal ornament began to decline, in part because of a change in aesthetic ideas. Metal facades and cornices had been most popular in the Italianate and various ornate eclectic styles; when those went out of fashion, so did the facades and cornices. A combination of the economic disaster of the Great Depression in the 1930s, and the diversion of metal into military uses in the 1940s, all but ended the architectural sheet-metal ornament business. Companies like W. H. Mullins gave it up altogether and after the war turned to heating and air-conditioning ducts, kitchen cabinets, and automobile parts.

A few sheet-metal firms survived, and with the revival of interest in architectural ornament brought on by the preservation movement in the 1960s and 1970s, continued to make cornices, wall plates, pressed ceilings, and roofing tiles.[62] Pressed-steel siding, especially in its rockface form, has remained available for inexpensive building. Today it can most commonly be seen in foundation surrounds for trailer homes.

The aesthetic debates over the appropriateness of sheet metal's imitative qualities reflects criticism faced by many new materials in the 1870–1930 period. Was pressed metal a dishonest sham, inferior and unattractive? Or was it an economical, durable and safe substitute that expressed modern, progressive values? These issues and their social implications will be more fully discussed in chapter 7, but the most popular form of pressed-metal ornament at the turn of the century—ceiling and wall decoration—is the subject of the next chapter.

CHAPTER 3

Artful Interiors:
Metal Ceilings and Walls

In 1915, the *Metal Worker* published a story about Dan Casey, a small-town building contractor. When the plaster over the desk in his own office fell, Casey seized the opportunity to try a metal ceiling. Soon it was the talk of the town:

> News travels rapidly in towns of two thousand, and before nightfall every villager who could find time had looked over the job, and held his own private opinion as to the merits of metal ceiling versus plaster. Holding one's private opinion in a small town is generally good for much publicity, and the new ceiling was well advertised. There was an artistic effect about it that had never been seen in the village before, and a month later, when a blast of dynamite shot a stubborn old pine stump out of the vacant lot alongside Jansmer's grocery, it broke a window and loosened most of the plaster, and the owner placed with Casey the first real order for a metal ceiling.[1]

That was the beginning. Next Casey supplied a metal ceiling for the courtroom, then the drugstore, the city hall, the restaurant, the new high school, the barbershop, the dry goods store, and the Bijou Moving Picture Theater. The climax came when the wealthiest man in town, J. Wetmore Craig, ordered a metal ceiling for his dining room.

The author of this story confessed that some of the characters in it were fictitious, but insisted Dan Casey was real, and so was his metal-ceiling business. Enterprising builders should follow his example and "send out some boys with a catalogue and samples" because "business was ripe" and "the chances for profit were good."[2]

This apocryphal tale of the grass-roots discovery and instant embrace of a new building form is an appropriate introduction to the story of the metal-ceiling business. Chapter 2 covered the general background to the sheet-metal industry; this chapter will explore the particular history of pressed-metal ceilings and walls. They were some of the most widely used, profitable, and long-lasting sheet-metal products of the 1870–1930 period.[3]

ORIGINS OF THE METAL CEILING

The earliest references to ceilings made of metal appeared in the 1870s. These ceilings were simply corrugated iron meant to provide a fireproof separation between floors in buildings such as

CURVED CORRUGATED IRON.

FIG. 13.

Curved to any specified radius, for roofs and ceilings.

FIG. 14.

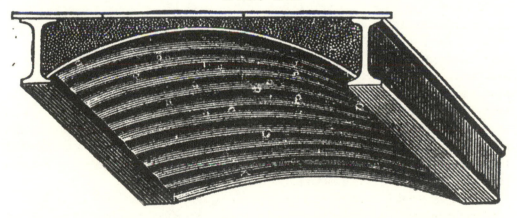

Curved, as applied on iron beams for ceilings in fire-proof buildings. When ordered, the exact distance between the body of beams must be carefully specified, also the rise in the arch.

Price for curving, ½ cent per square foot extra. Furnished only on sufficient time to get iron made to length required.

Fig. 27. A simple corrugated-iron ceiling for fireproofing. Ceilings of this type appeared as early as 1872. Canton Iron Roofing Company, Illustrated Catalogue, 1888, p. 24. Hagley Museum and Library.

Fig. 28. A Northrop-type corrugated-iron ceiling. Carpentry and Building *11 (Mar. 1889): 53. University of Delaware.*

Fig. 29. A German company's design for a corrugated-iron ceiling with embossed zinc ornament. Carpentry and Building *8 (Oct. 1886): 188. University of Delaware.*

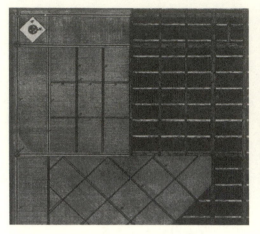
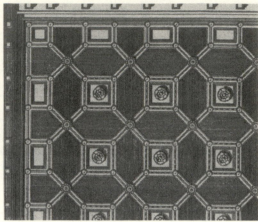

jails or factories (fig. 27).[4] Although one Henry Adler of Pittsburgh took out a patent in 1875 for a "sheet metal ceiling consisting of panels secured in position by concealed fastenings, cap pieces and ornamental corner pieces,"[5] the earliest successful commercial patents were those issued to Albert Northrop of Pittsburgh in 1884 (fig. 28).[6] Northrop's ceilings were small panels of corrugated iron laid against furring strips over the ceiling joists. Seams between the panels were covered with metal molding strips.

Northrop suggested that his customers could create a decorative pattern by varying the direction of the corrugation or adding embossed rosettes to mark the corners. Despite such attempts at ornamentation, the corrugated ceilings were criticized for looking "unfinished."[7] Perhaps in response to this criticism, in 1889 Northrop offered embossed tinplate panels as decorative borders for the corrugated-iron ceilings.[8] The panels were probably similar to the embossed shingles that had been on the market since the early 1880s.

In 1886, *Carpentry and Building* reported on a more decorative alternative. A German company offered a ceiling of small diamond-shaped corrugated panels, enhanced with deeply molded overlapping ribs and embossed center panels (fig. 29). The reporter did not say what the ribs and center panels were made of, but they were probably stamped zinc. An 1889 article in the same magazine reported that the iron-with-zinc ornamented ceilings had "been extensively used in Europe."[9] Such metal ceilings were used in Germany and France, but they were not common in Britain until well after their introduction in the United States, Canada, and Australia.

Sheet-metal manufacturer Alfred E. Bowers Jr. offered another example of an early metal ceiling in a 1934 article in which he described how his father, an interior decorator, teamed with a plasterer named William Dunn and a wood lather named George Pettit to make a ceiling of tinplate panels in Bowers's Brooklyn house in about 1884.[10] They used real rope and wooden rosettes to cover the seams and joints. Bowers Sr. and his partners eventually formed the Brooklyn Metal Ceiling Company. Their early ceiling attempt may have become a sort of origin myth for the company, but there is no evidence for Alfred Bowers Jr.'s claims that their isolated experiment was the foundation for the American metal-ceiling industry.

Instead, it is evident from period literature that the American metal-ceiling business grew from experimentation with the German-inspired iron-and-zinc forms in the 1880s.[11] Firms such as Bakewell and Mullins of Salem, Ohio, machine-pressed sheets of zinc into decorative elements

and bolted them to a corrugated-iron base.[12] The results could sometimes be very elaborate, in fact far more elaborate than the German prototypes, as the 1889 Council Bluffs, Iowa, courthouse ceilings demonstrate (fig. 30). Praised as being "almost entirely new and original and quite different from those usually made from plaster or stucco," the metal ceilings were also fireproof, lighter, easier to install, more durable, and cheaper than cast plaster.[13]

STEEL CEILINGS

German iron-and-zinc ceilings inspired the beginnings of the American metal-ceiling industry, but American innovation brought the production of metal ceilings to a maturity that would eventually dominate the world market.

American companies introduced a major technological change in the 1890s, when they began to replace the corrugated-iron base and embossed zinc ornament with panels of stamped sheet steel. Steel could be produced in larger and thinner panels than iron and stood up better to the stamping process. The W. R. Kinnear Company was the first to patent this new kind of ceiling in 1888. The key difference between the new steel ceilings and the old iron ones was that panels of 28- to 30-gauge steel were die-pressed as a single unit. Instead of assembling the various bits of zinc ornament and bolting them to an iron base, the Kinnear Company stamped the ornament into a single steel panel. The panels were twenty-four inches wide, but their length varied from one to two to four feet. Later, by the 1910s, panels as long as seven or eight feet were produced, but the two-by-four-foot panel was the most common. By the 1890s other sheet-metal companies had adopted Kinnear's stamped steel system or had devised their own variations of it.

One advantage of steel over other available materials was that a much higher relief could be formed and the overall patterns could be far more elaborate. The editors of *Architecture and Building* acknowledged this virtue in 1890 when they compared the "crude corrugated shapes" of ceilings of the past with the new "substantial artistic style" of the present.[14] By the end of the century, stamped steel ceilings were the standard in the industry.

Technological changes in the 1880s had reduced the cost of steel and made it more widely available. Additional improvements in drop press machines and the consolidation of capital into larger companies meant that the manufacturers could meet the growing demand for metal ceilings and provide them quickly and cheaply. Many companies founded in the 1870s to make sheet-metal roofing, cornices, and storefronts were, by the 1890s, also making steel ceilings and sidewalls. Some, like the Mesker Brothers of St. Louis and George Mesker of Evansville, Indiana, simply added ceilings as a minor part of their already extensive business in architectural sheet-metal ornament. In a 1902 catalogue, George Mesker boasted that while some manufacturers spent time and money producing many designs for steel ceilings and side walls, his company only made three types, and thus theirs were cheaper.[15]

Other companies, however, such as Longley Lewis Sagendorph's Penn Metal Roofing and Ceiling Company of Philadelphia, made the ceilings and walls their major line. Sagendorph (1842–1909) was born in Hudson, New York, and grew up in Providence, Rhode Island. After fighting in the Civil War, he packed up his inheritance in a carpet bag and headed south to start his first fabricating plant in Staunton, Virginia, in 1869. Ten years later he moved the business to Cincinnati to be nearer the center of the iron industry and the rail lines. His Sagendorph

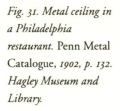

Fig. 31. Metal ceiling in a Philadelphia restaurant. Penn Metal Catalogue, *1902, p. 132. Hagley Museum and Library.*

Iron Roofing and Corrugating Company grew rapidly as he took out over thirty patents on sheet-metal products and the machinery and tools to produce them. By the 1880s he had expanded his business to include outlets in Chicago, St. Louis, Birmingham, Jersey City, and Philadelphia. In 1889, he sold the company, moved to Philadelphia, and started over again with a new firm, the Penn Metal Ceiling and Roofing Company.

Taking advantage of the new technologies for stamping steel, Sagendorph built a plant in Philadelphia and began buying up other factories, eventually expanding to Boston; Camden, New Jersey; and Parkersburg, West Virginia. Between 1889 and 1907, Sagendorph took out another sixty-one patents, including thirteen specifically for improvements in the production of metal ceilings. The Penn Metal Roofing and Ceiling Company continued to make ventilators, guttering, and metal lath as well as roofing, siding, shingles, and cornices, but stamped steel ceilings were their leading product. Sagendorph even included them in the name of his new company.[16]

While few if any companies devoted themselves solely to making metal ceilings, many like Penn Metal, found the ceilings to be such a popular form of sheet-metal ornament that they marketed them separately from other products, devoting whole catalogues to ceilings and walls and boasting about their high quality and the varieties of their artistic styles (fig. 31).

The Manufacturing Process

In 1912, the *National Builder* reported on a visit to the Berger Manufacturing Company's plant in Canton, Ohio. Their detailed account described "the entire process that transforms the raw material into the artistic panels, scrolls and patterns of wonderful design," which, they declared, "when properly assembled, make ceilings that are better in every way than the old form of plaster and wood."[17]

The process had two parts. One was to prepare the designs, the other was to stamp the steel panels. First the designs for the stamping dies had to be made. Companies as large as Berger's employed their own design departments, where staff artists created full-scale charcoal drawings of proposed patterns. Once company managers selected and approved the designs, the artist transferred them from the drawing paper onto a slab of wet modeling clay and sculpted the pattern into three dimensions. The modeler put every aspect of the design into the clay, including each "figure, line or scroll," which were "worked true and distinct" with the help of compass, level, and square.

When the clay model was complete, the artist cast it in plaster, first in a shell cast which made a negative, and then from that into a plaster positive which was a faithful reproduction of the clay. "Much careful attention is given this last cast by the modeler, every line and impression being gone over, trued, leveled and smoothed, after which it is given two coats of liquid shellac." This plaster cast was the source for the metal dies.

Next, Berger's workmen melted iron in the "moulding room" and poured it over the plaster to make a negative of the design. The workmen took this cooled iron die to the machine shop, where "the entire cast [was] milled and smoothed." The metal die, a negative image of the design, was called the "female" or bottom section. The workers next made the "male" or top part by pouring molten zinc over the bottom die. They then raised the cooled top section and fastened it to the hammer head of the press. Thus there were two dies, one the heavy, strong iron bottom, the other the more malleable, softer top.

The two dies could be attached to either a "draw press," which worked by mechanical pressure, or to a "drop hammer press," which worked by the force of a dropping hammer. The Berger Company preferred the latter, since it gave a more even, overall clarity to the pattern. Meanwhile, other workers prepared the steel sheets for stamping, painting them first with a "ceilcoat," a light gray primer. Next they were sent to the press operator for the actual stamping. He regulated the force of the blow and was also responsible for accurately placing the sheet in the press in order to bring "the plate home and true."

After the pressman die-stamped the metal sheets into their decorative patterns, the shearsman trimmed them over a "templet." Every sheet had to be sheared alike to make a perfect fit, so the shearsman's eye and skill were important. In the final step, workmen in the shipping room crated the stamped and sheared panels and made them ready for shipment.

This account of the making of steel ceilings reveals a departmental production system. Each unit had specialized tasks to perform. They prepared the sheets and stockpiled them before sending them on to the next department. Highly skilled workers, even artists, were involved whose careful attention to detail was essential for making the ceilings the quality product they were touted to be. The creation of the design was the most labor-intensive aspect. Once the dies were prepared, skilled workers painted, stamped, and sheared, and less-skilled workers packed and shipped.

This was far from the popular notion of a Ford Motor Company-type assembly line for mass production. Instead, the company's departmental system was best suited to what modern business historians call the "batch" or "bulk system." Rather than a continuous flow of production, with workers making single, uniform products for mass consumption, manufacturers usually produced to order (batch) or to anticipated order (bulk). Which dies were placed in the presses to make which ceiling plates depended on what orders had been received or were anticipated based on market history. Continuous orders were important to keep the plant busy. For that, the companies depended on their agents, their advertising, and their catalogues.

INTERIOR WALLS

While the history of metal ceilings can be traced with some certainty, that of decorative stamped-metal walls is more obscure, although generally, the two seem to have paralleled each other. The 1876 Sheet Metal Pavilion at the Philadelphia Centennial Exhibition (discussed in chapter 2) had an interior wainscot of corrugated terneplate and cornice moldings of galvanized iron with pressed-zinc ornaments. Just as ceilings of iron and zinc became available in the 1880s, so too did cornice friezes and wainscoting of the same material.

In the 1890s, when the industry developed the technology for producing larger sheets of steel for stamping, manufacturers applied these processes to materials for both interiors and exteriors. On the exterior, cladding came in masonry patterns; on the interior, the panels reflected contemporary design ideas of treating the wall as a tripartite system of frieze, field, and wainscot (fig. 32). By 1897, manufacturers were offering such whole-wall treatments, though consumers could also purchase the panels separately, mix and match, or combine them with more

Fig. 32. Stamped-metal sidewall designs. Penn Metal Catalogue, *1902, p. 91. Hagley Museum and Library.*

traditional wallpaper. Manufacturers employed the same techniques for walls as they had for ceilings.

Advertisers often linked metal ceilings with walls, as in the 1905 Northrop, Coburn and Dodge Company catalogue, which claimed, "The favor with which Northrop's Stamped Steel Ceilings and Walls have been received in this country and abroad has stimulated us to higher artistic effects than ever before attained and we know will be appreciated by the fastidious and discriminating class who desire the most artistic architectural finish for interior decoration."[18]

Wall and ceiling designs were also linked in the trade catalogues, where they were co-ordinated under similar stylistic period names and layout arrangements. But it is also evident from period advertising and from modern architectural surveys that while sidewalls reflected the same high-style, up-market ambitions as metal ceilings, the walls were never quite as popular. Metal ceilings were clearly the market leader.

MARKETING METAL CEILINGS AND WALLS

The growth of the metal-ceiling industry is reflected in the number of advertisements that appeared in trade journals. The earliest was Albert Northrop's in 1884, but within five years advertisements for metal ceilings were common in all the builders magazines. Whole pages of ads appeared in the 1910s, and, while there was a decline in advertising in the later 1920s,

some continued even into the 1930s.[19] Metal ceilings were advertised and marketed as a separate category from other sheet-metal products. While ads for metal shingles might mention crestings and exterior cladding, ads for ceilings usually concentrated on them alone, often with photographs of buildings in which the ceilings had been installed (fig. 33).

Manufacturers employed the same techniques to promote metal ceilings and walls as they had used for other sheet-metal products. Advertisements in trade journals, the publication of trade catalogues, and participation in trade shows all played a part. Trade catalogues were particularly important, however, and their presentation of metal ceilings and walls reflected the changes that occurred in the printing and advertising industries. Volumes from the 1890s were usually small in size and printed on cheap paper with line engravings for reproductions. They included large selections of sheet-metal products with ceilings and walls in a small section in the back. By 1900, the paper was slick, the illustrations were half-tone photographs, and the catalogues looked like books, sometimes with multicolored, decorative, hard-bound covers. Moreover, whole catalogues were devoted to ceilings and sidewalls as the primary product. Other items such as shingles or exterior cladding might have a small section in the back, but most of the one hundred or so pages featured ceilings.

With the same boosterish tone the *Metal Worker* used to tell Dan Casey's story, advertising in trade journals and catalogues urged everyone to come on board. "Here's your chance! Carpenters, contractors, and builders here is a chance for you to build up an independent profitable business for yourself right at home. Many agents are now devoting their entire time to selling Edwards Metal Ceilings."[20] The Berger Company similarly proclaimed, "The rapid increase in building has created an enormous demand for Berger's Classik Steel Ceilings and no ambitious dealer can afford to overlook this profitable opportunity."[21] Others touted the metal-ceiling and metal-wall business because it would provide indoor work in the winter, but above all, contractors were urged to jump at the chance because "there is Money for you in Steel Ceiling Work."[22]

ADVANTAGES OF METAL CEILINGS

The advantages of metal ceilings and walls, proclaimed again and again in the advertising literature, can be summarized in five key points: The ceilings and walls were (1) fire resistant, (2) sanitary in that they did not promote dust, could be easily cleaned, and were "vermin proof," (3) permanent, being resistant to moisture and needing little care, (4) cheap compared with other alternatives, and (5) decorative. An examination of each of these claims offers evidence of the appeal of metal ceilings to consumers.

Fire Resistance

Nonflammability was a chief selling point in the advertising literature. It also had more merit than fireproof claims made for exterior sheet-metal products. Metal was noncombustible, but probably the chief fire resisting quality of the ceilings was the insulation caused by the dead air space between the ceilings and the joists. They were even more fireproof when there was an older plaster ceiling behind the new metal ceiling. Pictures and accounts of buildings that caught fire but were saved when a metal ceiling confined the flames to one floor were often reported in the building magazines.[23] Official fire tests such as one conducted by the Association of Metal Ceiling Contractors of Greater New York in 1914 proved that metal ceilings were more fire resistant than wood or plaster.[24] Manufacturers proudly boasted that metal ceilings meant lower insurance premiums.

Sanitation

Metal ceilings produced less dust than plaster and could be more easily cleaned. The fact that soap and water could be used made the ceilings especially appealing for hospitals. Metal tiling effects for walls in bathrooms and kitchens were also recommended for the same reason. The ceilings could also be put up over a cracked plaster ceiling without the mess of taking the old one down.

The claim that interior metal coverings were "vermin proof" probably reflected contemporary fears of insects and worms eating wallpaper or wood. One Texas contractor, however, interpreted "vermin" as something larger. He wrote to the *Metal Worker* in 1912 that metal ceilings must have a tight seal between the panels and never should be put up against unsheathed ceiling joists, because without a wood backing, one lone mouse could "make as much racket as a jackass in a tin stable."[25]

Permanence

A recurring theme in promotional literature was the advantage of metal ceilings over falling plaster. Dan Casey's office ceiling was not the only one to fall. The *Metal Worker* recorded an 1895 visit to a local metal-ceiling plant where an anxious customer interrupted the reporter's conversation with the manager. Just that morning the plaster had fallen in the customer's bedroom only minutes after he had gotten out of bed. He was determined to replace not only that ceiling but also the one in his dining room "as the ceiling there gave promise of demolishing his china."[26] O. O. Shackleton of Hackensack expressed the same sentiment in 1890: "The ceilings recently put up in my house . . . are in every respect all that we could wish—neat, beautiful, attractive, clean—and we are not afraid to sit under them."[27] Even as late as 1931, an article in the *Sheet Metal Worker* suggested that contractors use newspaper headlines such as, "Near Panic as Ceiling Falls at the Medford Prom!" to emphasize the dangers of falling plaster in contrast to the safety of metal ceilings.[28]

Low Cost

All the advertising literature for metal ceilings promoted them as an economical alternative to plaster or any other ornamental material. In fact, many advertisements noted that even though the initial price might be more than plain wood or plaster, the low cost of upkeep and the virtual permanence of metal ceilings would save money in the long run.

The actual cost of the ceilings varied from year to year and with the elaborateness of the design. In 1895 Berger's steel ceilings were priced at 7 to 10 cents a square foot. The ceilings and walls were usually sold as "squares," however, just as roofing was, with one hundred square feet equaling a "square," which could cost $7.00 including the furring strips and nails.[29] In 1910, Sears, Roebuck and Company claimed to be able to sell their metal ceilings at half the cost of other manufacturers and advertised some designs for as little as $2.60 a square.[30] By contrast, plain wood and plaster could be had for about $2.20 a square. Metal ceilings were, however, the cheapest form of ornamental work.

Decorative Possibilities

The decorative effects of metal ceilings and walls were one of their most important features. The claim to "art" separated them from other sheet-metal products. The Berger Company advertised that they were the first to classify their designs by proper art historical style in about 1902. Earlier efforts by other manufacturers were "but a conglomerate mixture of incongruous styles," while Berger's "Art in Steel Ceilings" categories were "correct, harmonious and appropriate."[31]

The Berger Company may have been the first, but others soon followed with trade catalogues that presented ceilings and walls under such stylistic headings as Greek, Gothic, French Renaissance, Rococo, and Colonial. Manufacturers claimed the styles were "architecturally correct," and on the whole, they seemed to be just that.[32] A 1920s *Pedlar Art Steel Ceilings* catalogue demonstrated a sophisticated understanding of design history. It described "L' Art Nouveau" as an "effort to ignore the so-called historic styles and produce harmony, rhythm, balance and contrast of decoration by means of novel combination of flowing lines and swaying curves, with occasional recourse to natural forms; also known as Art Moderne, Secession Art, etc."

The language manufacturers employed in advertising the ceilings frequently referred to "high class decoration" and "artistic and beautiful effects."[33] This sense of high art was in part due to the fact that many company designers were trained in art schools. Some companies even named their products Art Metal and Art Kraft and pointed out the "high-class" status of the buildings in which their ceilings had been installed.

TYPES OF BUILDINGS

Today, metal ceilings are most often associated with commercial establishments, partly because that is where most have survived. Thousands of them still exist in downtown businesses across the country. The four-square-block central business district of Lexington, Virginia, for example, contains fifteen such ceilings. The two-block main street of Clifton Forge, Virginia, has thirteen metal ceilings. Half a continent away, the Lawrence, Kansas, main street has twenty. The ubiquity of metal ceilings is testimony to the manufacturers' claims for their everlasting qualities.

One important example of pressed-metal interiors survives at Canterbury Shaker Village in New Hampshire. Irving Greenwood, who kept a journal on work at the community, reported in 1906, "North office has steel ceiling and walls, packing room has steel ceiling, walls half steel and half sheathing. Bought for us by Mr. Head of the

Fig. 34. Cornice and frieze from the Canterbury Shaker Village dining room. Curiously, the swags were installed upside down. Canterbury Shaker Village, Canterbury, New Hampshire.

Kinnear and Gager Co., Columbus, Ohio, cost $68.91."[34] The Shaker community ordered another set of ceilings and sidewalls from a Penn Metal Company catalogue for their Trustees' Office in 1913.

Fortunately, the original catalogues survive in the Canterbury Shaker Village archives. They show, for example, that nine different patterns were used in the Trustees' dining room. The ceiling's main field panels were placed around a separate center panel and bordered by frets. Below the ceiling was a cornice, a frieze, sidewalls, chair rail, wainscot, and baseboard. Oddly, some of the parts, most noticeably the cornice featuring classical swags, were installed upside down (fig. 34), either by accident or whimsy.

Metal ceilings are most likely to have survived in commercial buildings, but period building literature indicates that they were used in a surprising variety of building types—churches, hospitals, schools, theaters, hotels, restaurants, banks, lodge halls, amusement parks, and residences. The sale of metal ceilings for homes was, however, the most difficult and least successful of the sheet-metal manufacturer's promotions.

Part of the problem was expense. Plain wood or plaster was much cheaper, as were decorative wall and ceiling papers. Another problem was simply the tradition that ordinary houses did not have elaborate decorative ceilings. The type of house that did usually had an owner who could afford ornamental plaster. For the wealthy patron, metal ceilings, despite all the claims to high art, were usually associated with common, commercial building types. Manufacturers tried vigorously to break into the home market, however, as their advertising shows. The 1915 catalogue of the Canton Steel Ceiling Company tried subtlety: "The harmonious decorative and beautiful effects possible in Steel Ceilings help to make for happy and contented homes."[35] The 1923 Edwards Company catalogue continued the theme more insistently: "Metal Ceilings are no longer a luxury—they can almost be said to be a necessity. Where formerly they were used almost exclusively on churches, stores, halls and other buildings, they are now also extensively used in private residences. There are a number of excellent reasons for this rapidly growing popularity. From every view point the metal ceiling is the ideal ceiling."[36]

There were some domestic successes. In Radford, Virginia, Philadelphia architect Frank Miles Day had designed an impressive Queen Anne–style residence for a local family in 1901. The house sat empty for several years after its construction. When the Harvey family purchased it in 1905, they found that water leaks had damaged the original plain plaster ceilings. Their response was to install decorative, pressed-steel ceilings in all the major downstairs rooms. This practical solution cost less than removing the old ceilings and installing new ones. The metal ceilings are still in excellent condition.

Although manufacturers were least successful in selling their metal ceilings for domestic installations, these were the most coveted in the hierarchy of potential uses. Even the apocryphal story of Dan Casey's metal ceiling business incorporated this ranking. The first installation was in Casey's construction company's office, the second in a grocery store, next were public and commercial buildings, a high school and a movie house. The "climax came" when J. Wetmore Craig, the wealthiest man in town, ordered a metal ceiling for his dining room. A rich man's house epitomized acceptance. It was something aimed for, but a rare and prized achievement.

Installing the Metal Ceiling

For all the advantages of metal ceilings, there were some problems, most of which came from faulty installation. The process required workmen of some experience and skill. Customers supplied the measurements of the ceiling to be covered, and the manufacturer provided the appropriate number of panels to fit the space. The installer needed a hammer, saw, chalk line, punch, nail set, and trimmer's shears.

The workman began with the furring strips laying them over the ceiling joists, or the old plaster on twelve- or twenty-four-inch centers starting from a center chalk line. That damaged plaster did not have to be removed was a major advantage of the metal ceilings, but in installing the furring strips over old plaster, one had to be sure the nails were hitting the joists. For new ceilings some manufacturers recommended sheathing the joists with cheap wood or builder's paper for insulation. New ceiling or old, it was important that the furring strips were level, and sometimes shimming wedges were necessary to ensure that. Next the metal panels were nailed to the furring strips (fig. 35).

Edges of the panels were usually stamped with a bead that allowed them to overlap or interlock. Some manufacturers precut nail holes to avoid stress on the panel, and provided decorative nail heads which became part of the design. Others used a bent lap joint, but whatever the joining system, the decorative design was usually incorporated into the edges to mask the joints.

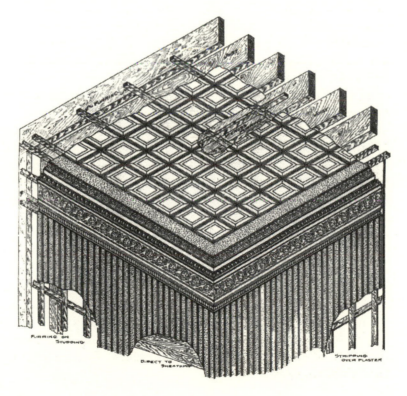

Fig. 35. Diagram of metal ceiling installation process. Penn Metal Company Penco Metal Ceiling Catalogue, *1927, p. 4. Hagley Museum and Library.*

As simple as the installation process sounds, problems could occur, especially if an amateur were doing the work. If the furring strips were not level, the new ceiling might buckle. Seams might separate. If the measurement of the room was not professionally exact, there might be too much or too little at the corners or edges. Mortising the corner joint took special skill.

Who was capable of properly installing a metal ceiling was debated in the trade press. In 1911, Sears, Roebuck and Company advertised that putting up a steel ceiling was so easy anyone could do it, especially if the ceiling was from Sears.[37] These ads were misleading, however. Most manufacturers admitted that professionals were necessary. In fact, the V. Moeslein Company of New York, noted in 1894 that "all ceilings in the vicinity of New York, we prefer to put up ourselves and paint or decorate them also."[38] The company offered to arrange for competent contractors outside of their local region, but said encouragingly that "a painstaking carpenter, tinner or decorator, can usually do a very satisfactory job."[39]

Other manufacturers offered to recommend contractors. To fulfill their promise, the Willis Manufacturing Company of Galesburg, Illinois, in a 1901 advertisement pleaded for mechanics to help install the company's orders.[40] W. A. Slagle, the sheet-metal contractor from Emporia, Virginia, said in a 1991 interview that after fifty years of experience he did not think any amateur could put up a metal ceiling, and that even local carpenters and builders usually asked his firm to do the work when a metal ceiling was required.[41]

Advertising literature frequently claimed that putting up a metal ceiling was "easy." It was certainly easier than putting up a decorative plaster one, but the weight of evidence suggests that experience and skill were necessary for proper installation.

INTERNATIONAL TRADE

The metal-ceiling business, begun in the 1880s, was booming by 1900. Firms such as the Willis Manufacturing Company in Galesburg, Ohio, were not only "making shipments to every state in the Union" but had a large export trade as well. The Berger Company of Canton, Ohio, had agents in New York, Boston, Philadelphia, St. Louis, Minneapolis, and San Francisco, and by 1911 were supplying ceilings to Argentina. Several American manufacturers published trade catalogues in Spanish probably for this South American market. In 1915, a note in the *Metal Worker* reported that several large moving picture theaters in Buenos Aires had recently installed metal ceilings, though the manufacturer was not identified. The *Metal Worker* also claimed that a few Brazilian factories had begun to stamp their own ceilings from imported American and English steel.[42]

Many other countries also began to manufacture metal ceilings. Canada had two major manufacturers, the Metallic Roofing Company of Toronto and the Pedlar People of Ontario, both of which are especially well documented.[43] The Metallic Roofing Company began in 1884 as a general manufacturer of sheet-metal products. As noted in chapter 2, one of the firm's best-selling items was a patented metal shingle, but they also began to produce ceilings and sidewalls in 1895. The company's 1902 showroom, an architect-designed, all-metal building in front of their factory in Toronto, displayed examples of all their architectural sheet-metal products, including several types of decorative interior ceilings and walls. One of the largest companies in Canada, the Metallic Roofing Company had an extensive overseas trade. Order books for 1897 to 1902 included ceilings sales to customers in Japan, India, Scotland, England, Norway, Denmark, Holland, and South Africa.[44]

The other major Canadian firm was the Pedlar People. Henry Pedlar had opened a hardware store in Oshawa, Ontario, in 1861, where he used his tinner's skills to make kitchen utensils in the back room. His son, George Pedlar, eventually took over the business and in 1892 expanded it by opening a stamping plant to make roofing, siding, and ceilings. In 1900 the business adopted the name Pedlar Metal Roofing Company, and in 1911 incorporated as the Pedlar People. By the 1920s the firm claimed to be "the largest plant in the British Empire for the exclusive production of sheet metal building materials."[45] Pedlar produced a full line of sheet-metal architectural products but gave special attention to their "Pedlar Art Steel Ceilings." By 1930 they were supplying metal ceilings for most of the F. W. Woolworth stores in Canada.[46]

Pedlar's was not the only metal-ceiling business in the British Empire. In Australia, German immigrants Ernst and Alfred Wunderlich began a business in Sydney in 1887 importing zinc ornamental roofing materials from Germany. In 1888 Alfred Wunderlich patented a pressed-zinc ceiling that was described in *Builder and Contractor's News* as realizing "every requirement that human ingenuity can suggest; it improves on all old methods, and . . . enables a ceiling to be made far more tasty and decorative than formerly, whilst being beyond suspicion in regard to safety."[47]

Wunderlich imported German workers to teach the stamping process to his Australian journeymen in a small plant near Sydney. By 1900, he had converted his operations to using steel imported from England. With agents covering all the Australian colonies and New Zealand, Wunderlich continued to expand his operations, establishing a branch factory in Perth in 1909 to specialize in "Art Metal Ceilings."[48] In terms of both technology and production, Wunderlich's success parallels that of the larger American and Canadian firms.

The story is a little different in England. Metal ceilings had some early successes there, but they never achieved the level of popularity they did in America and elsewhere. American manufacturer Albert Northrop exported his ceilings to England as early as 1890, but the British consul in Philadelphia seemed unaware of this transatlantic trade when in 1900, he "strongly suggested [metal ceilings] for export to Great Britain." The consul also expressed the hope that "before these American walls and ceilings can be placed on the market in Great Britain some enterprising British firm may be equal to supplying the requirements of the British public."[49]

One British firm already had been experimenting with stamped metal since 1894. The Emdeca Company of London offered sheets of stamped and brightly enameled zinc which they promoted as a cheap and practical substitute for bathroom tile. By 1904 the British Stamped Metal Ceiling Company had formed and was boasting that it had installed over one hundred steel ceilings in the new Savoy Hotel.[50] The *Decorator* praised the ceilings, saying, "Sheet metal ceilings have been used for many years in the United States with great success and there is no doubt they will soon become popular here. Not that these [the Savoy ceilings] are made in America, they are distinctly of British manufacture, the factory being in Bristol."[51]

The British Stamped Metal Ceiling Company eventually bought up the Emdeca Com-

Fig. 36. Metal ceiling in the saloon at Erddig, Clwyd, Wales. National Trust Photographic Library; photograph by Algernon Smith.

pany and continued to sell the distinctive wall tiles along with their Steleonite stamped-steel ceilings. Although she misspelled the name, these were the ceilings Mrs. L. M. Yorke, last chatelaine of the great Welsh house, Erddig, referred to in 1924 when she wrote, "The ceilings of Steelorite (thin plates of steel, much used in America and Africa) in the Chapel, Saloon, Tapestry Room, Chinese Room, Red Bedroom and part of the Nursery Passage were put up after a fire in 1907 when £120 worth of damage was done to the roof." Five of the six ceilings mentioned are still in place at the house, which is now owned by the National Trust (fig. 36).[52] But in spite of such grand examples as Erddig, or the occasional survival in a more modest house or store, the evidence for the metal-ceiling industry in Britain is mostly documentary.[53] The ceilings were certainly used, but not many seem to have survived and they were never as widespread in Britain as they were in other countries.[54]

DECLINE IN POPULARITY

With all its popularity, why did the use of metal ceilings decline? The reason seems to be the same in the United States, Canada, and Australia. The combination of a building slowdown in the Great Depression, the diversion of sheet metal into military purposes during World War II, and a change in taste in the postwar period, when smooth surfaces and dropped acoustical-tile ceilings became popular, helped spell the end to the widespread use of metal ceilings.

Yet even with the decline, some companies never stopped making metal ceilings, and recent interest in preservation has spurred a mini-boom of popularity. The metal ceilings are still considered fire-resistant, clean, durable, and the easiest and quickest way to ornament at the best price. At least five companies in the United States continue to produce them.[55] Several, like the W. F. Norman Corporation of Nevada, Missouri, are survivors of the turn-of-the-century period and even use their original dies. The Norman Corporation, which will reproduce almost any item in its 1902 catalogue, is very proud to have furnished metal ceilings for Donald Trump's Taj Mahal Casino in Atlantic City.

WHY "TIN" CEILINGS?

Without doubt the major reason for the popularity of metal ceilings and walls was that they met a need. They were a practical, durable and economical means of achieving a decorative effect. Why then do metal ceilings have a reputation for being a "cheap" material? Even the popular term "tin ceiling" reflects this attitude. With the exception of Albert Northrop's experiments with tinplate for borders in the 1880s, the ceilings were never tin, and none of the period literature used that term. In the 1880s and 1890s the ceilings were iron and zinc; by 1900, they were steel.

There are several possible explanations for the term "tin ceiling." One is that it is a survival from the nineteenth-century "tinner" or "tin knocker," or "tin smith," a craftsmen who worked with tinplate—sheet iron covered with a thin protective layer of tin. Even when other metals were used, this business was still called a "tin shop." In popular parlance, it seems, any thin sheet metal was called "tin" even when it was zinc, copper, iron, or steel.[56]

There is another aspect to this explanation, however. The term "tin ceiling" also reflects slang that has been used since the nineteenth century to disparage metal building materials. In the mid-nineteenth century a railroad town with cast-iron fronts was often called a "tin town." The British term "tin chapel" for a Methodist chapel and the American terms "Tin Lizzie" and "tin horn" link thin metal with the idea of cheapness, and according to the Oxford English Dictionary imply that the object is a base imitation of something else.[57] Probably "Tin Lizzie," the slang term for Henry Ford's relatively inexpensive, mass-produced motor cars, is the most revealing, since it was applied to a manufactured item that had great popular appeal. In that context, both "Tin Lizzie" and "tin ceiling" suggest a common recognition of the cheap, quick, and easy qualities of the mass-produced items.

The Debate over Imitation

The "servile imitation" debate over the propriety of sheet metal's imitation of other materials that received so much attention in the building press in the 1870s and 1880s was inherited by the metal-ceiling trade in the 1890s. Manufacturers' sensitivity to the issue was reflected in Albert Northrop's 1890 protest that his ceilings were "not an imitation of anything." They "were not a sham" but "real panels, real moldings, real rosettes," not "painted ones" of "crumbling plaster or inflammable wood" but made of "real imperishable iron."[58]

Other metal-ceiling manufacturers, however, were frank to admit that metal ceilings were a substitute for decorative plaster. Metal ceilings should never be painted with a "glossy surface" which would look like metal, cautioned a writer in *Carpentry and Building* in 1912; instead, the ceilings should be a dead, flat white "giving the effect of molded plaster or stucco." During the heyday of the Spanish mission style, in the 1920s, ceiling manufactur-

Fig. 37. "Spanish texture" metal ceiling. Milwaukee Corrugating Company, Revised Net Prices on Mikor Sheet Metal Building Products, *1924, p. 117. Hagley Museum and Library.*

ers even introduced lines called "stucco" and "Spanish texture" (fig. 37). In 1931, the pastor of the newly remodeled St. Paul's Lutheran Church in Waterloo, Wisconsin, proudly announced that at the dedication ceremonies, "not one [of the congregation] was able to realize that the ceiling was steel."[59]

Metal ceilings could imitate wood as well as plaster. An 1913 advertisement in *House Beautiful* offered a "craftsman beam ceiling" in metal (fig. 38). "Why put up an inflammable wood ceiling when an incombustible one of equal appearance can be obtained?" asked the Northrop, Coburn and Dodge Company of New York. They also offered "stamped steel ceilings in Tudor, Jacobean designs—different from the usual and superior to stucco in appearance and durability."[60]

Such advertisements outraged the architectural elite. The idea that a "craftsman beam ceiling" could be imitated in machine-made metal countered the very principles of the Arts

Fig. 38. "A Craftsman-style beam ceiling," Northrop, Coburn and Dodge Company advertisement. House Beautiful *33 (Apr. 1913): iv.*

and Crafts Movement's philosophy of hand craft. Competitors as well as aesthetes were scornful of metal imitating wood. The Grand Rapids Carved Moulding Company advertised that their wood moldings were "not pressed, mashed or burned. They are cut in solid wood, not pressed metal. They are the real thing!"[61]

Critics objected not only to sheet metal's imitation of other materials, but also to the very nature of its mass-produced, mechanical-looking qualities. An Australian critic, Hardy Wilson, in 1905, dismissed the "mechanical textureless surface" of the metal ceilings that "would not have been appreciated at any period earlier than the commercial-Victorian."[62]

An article in the English journal *Carpenter and Builder* in 1900 sounded a note of apology for the imitative qualities of metal ceilings even while intending to praise them: "A metal ceiling, while not so nearly artistic as a paneled ceiling in oak, cherry or birch or as a properly decorated ceiling in plaster, has a beauty of its own . . . and is less costly than any other ceiling having any claim to artistic beauty and being fireproof, light and easily applied, it is sure to become quite popular as soon as its good qualities are known, and the prejudices of old fashioned workmen are removed."[63]

To counter claims that mass production made the ceilings "mechanical" or not as "proper" or as "artistic" as more traditional wood and plaster ceilings, proponents argued that mass production was the way of the future, and that metal ceilings were the "modern" solution to building problems. A writer in the *Sheet Metal Worker,* in 1936, observed that "steel ceilings and sidewalls were never intended for the pretentious buildings in which expensive decorative treatments are the mode."[64] But he thought them perfect for any "progressive contractor" smart enough to recognize the value of this modern material.

There is ample evidence that to the thousands of ordinary people who chose metal ceilings and walls they were a practical and aesthetically attractive material. In 1889 an article in the *Zion Herald* in Whitinsville, Massachusetts, rhapsodized that the new Methodist Church ceilings were "an ornament to the Village" and "a joy to all lovers of Zion."[65] The new People's Bank ceiling, according to the editor of the *Lexington (Va.) Gazette* in 1915, was "handsomely paneled in metal" denoting the "progressive spirit of this enterprising and successful bank."[66] In 1917 the Hirscheimer Brothers of Canton, Ohio, wrote the Berger Company that the new ceilings in their store made it "one of the most attractive in the city."[67]

While part of the larger sheet-metal industry discussed in chapter 2, pressed-metal ceilings and walls were a specialized product and marketed separately as "artistic" ornament. New technology in the late 1880s, with improved drop presses and the production of larger sheets of sheet steel, made possible the stamping of decorative panels. But it was their fireproof, sanitary, and economical supply of attractive, durable, modern ornament that made metal ceilings and walls so popular in the first two decades of the twentieth century.

This discussion of metal ceilings and walls brings the examination of cheap, quick, and easy materials from the exterior to the interior, where, curiously, imitative ornament seemed more acceptable. As the following chapters will demonstrate, there were still critics who objected to imitation wherever it occurred, but their rhetoric was not nearly so virulent when it came to interior floors, walls, and ceilings.

CHAPTER 4

Fashion Floors:
Linoleum, Its Predecessors and Rivals

In 1925, Frederick Walton (1837–1928), the inventor of linoleum, published a small booklet entitled *The Infancy and Development of Linoleum Floorcloth* (fig. 39). He acknowledged that the invention of linoleum might not rank with James Watt's steam engine, but nevertheless, he claimed "to have done a useful work. Every householder can vouch for the utility and sanitary value of linoleum, and many house wives will, I hope, bless my memory in the future, although my name may be forgotten."[1]

Walton was correct in his assessment. It had been a useful work, and while housewives may not have known his name, they certainly have made use of his floor covering. From the time of Walton's initial patents in the 1860s to the 1960s, when linoleum was replaced by vinyl, his invention was probably the most widely used floor covering in the world. It became so accepted that today the term "linoleum" still applies to most kinds of hard-surface floor covering. This chapter on the history and development of linoleum starts with its predecessor, floor oilcloth, and includes the development of the linoleum industry, the process for linoleum's manufacture, methods of marketing, and attitudes toward design.

FLOOR OILCLOTH

Linoleum's predecessor was a material called floor oilcloth or painted floorcloth. Frequently it was simply referred to as floorcloth, and sometimes as oilcloth or waxcloth. No one can pinpoint the exact origins of this waterproof, decorative floor covering. While references to painted cloth and to "oyl" cloth appear in the fifteenth and sixteenth centuries, there is no clear evidence for its use on floors until the early eighteenth century.[2]

The 1728 estate inventory for Massachusetts Governor William Burnet included "two old checquered canvas' to lay under a table" and a "large painted Canvas Square as the Room," suggesting the floorcloths had been in the house long before 1728.[3] In 1738, the *Encyclopedia of Architecture* warned against the practice of using painted floorcloths as a waterproof covering for hallways because moisture could be trapped underneath and rot the wooden flooring. Floorcloth must have been in use long enough for someone to notice the problem. In 1750, Samuel Johnson, a man not known for his social graces, recorded his disdain at efforts to impress him with a painted floorcloth. He wrote that his host "ordered his servant to lift up a corner that I might contemplate the brightness of the colours and the elegance of the texture, and asked me whether I had

Fig. 39. Frederick Walton, the inventor of linoleum. Reproduced from Industrial and Engineering Chemical News *12, no. 7 (10 Apr. 1934): 119. Roanoke College, Salem, Virginia.*

ever seen anything so fine before. I did not gratify his folly with any outcries of admiration, but coldly bade the footman let down the cloth."[4] In 1760, John Winters advertised in the *Maryland Gazette* that he could "paint floorcloths as neat as any imported from Britain," suggesting that there was an established import trade.[5]

References like these indicate that painted floorcloths were common by the eighteenth century. Frequently used under dining tables for protection of more expensive carpet, and in passages and on stairs as a waterproof covering for wood, floorcloths were usually made in two- to three-yard squares of linen, hemp, or cotton, seamed together into larger sections. Craftsmen sized the cloth and waterproofed it by hand with successive layers of paint, adding decorative patterns with either stencil or freehand painting.

Nathan Smith established the earliest recorded factory for making floorcloth in Knightsbridge, London, in 1763. His patent referred to a commercial trade in floor oilcloth, but asserted his intention to introduce a new process for its manufacture. Scholars credit Smith not only with the first factory but also with the first printing block for applying designs to the floorcloth. By the end of the eighteenth century, there were at least twenty oilcloth factories in England, and by the end of the first decade of the nineteenth century, there were several in the United States as well.[6]

The Industrial Revolution had a critical impact on the production of oil floorcloth. The introduction of the fly shuttle for power looms in the early nineteenth century made wider lengths of canvas available. In sail-making centers such as Dundee and Kirkcaldy in Scotland, weaving factories began to produce heavy canvases in widths of eighteen to twenty-four feet specifically for the floorcloth trade. Now seamless wall-to-wall floorcloths could be produced.

One of the important Scottish manufacturers, Michael Nairn, established a canvas weaving factory near Kirkcaldy in 1828. By the 1840s he was producing eight-yard-wide canvas to supply nearly two dozen English floorcloth firms, two-thirds of those in existence.[7] Nairn, worried that his traditional market in sailcloth would suffer with the advent of steam ships, saw the floorcloth industry as a ready alternative. In 1847, he established his own floorcloth factory, the first in Scotland. Skeptical neighbors called it "Nairn's Folly," but they would eventually use the name with ironic humor as the company grew to be one of the leading floorcloth manufacturers in Britain.

In 1849, a visitor to Nairn's floorcloth factory described the manufacturing process in detail.[8] Canvas, eight yards wide and twenty-five yards long, was stretched and nailed onto large vertical frames. Working on scaffolding, men brushed and troweled both sides of the canvas with sizing (fig. 40). When it was dry, the workers rubbed it with a pumice stone, cut the loose threads, and added a second coat of sizing, which was allowed to dry and then pumiced again. The workers next troweled on successive layers of thick paint, waiting for each layer to dry before smoothing it with the pumice stone. After each layer was dry and smooth, the next layer of paint was added. The number of coats determined the thickness and quality grade of floorcloth. This part of the production process could take two to three months.[9]

The floorcloth was next laid on long tables in the printing loft. In a manner similar to wallpaper printing, workers used wooden printing blocks, usually eighteen inches square, to apply patterns. Each color required a separate block. In more elaborate designs, a dozen blocks might be necessary to complete the pattern. Two men on each side of the table were assisted by boys who spread paint on printing pads. The printer pressed the block onto the

pad to pick up the color, and then carefully placed it on the cloth where he hit it with a large mallet to impress the color onto the cloth. Covering a full-sized floorcloth required six hundred squares. Depending on how many blocks made up a pattern, two or three thousand placements of the square and blows with the mallet might be necessary.

Floorcloth designs usually imitated tile, marble, or carpet. One result of the printing process was that the patterns looked like they were based on a dot matrix. This was because in order to cover large color areas, a checkerboard pattern of small indentations was cut into the wood blocks to give the blocks "teeth" to hold the ink. The resulting pointillist pattern resembled the woven texture of carpet. In 1851 at the Great Exhibition, the judges' criticism of this effect led Nairn to create blocks with a much smaller grid of indentations. When all the color blocks had been printed on the floorcloth, the workers then used a "mash block" to obscure the grid pattern and give an overall even coverage. Finally, they used a block with metal strips to outline the different color sections and give them more definition.[10]

In the final step, the floorcloth was hung from great cross beams in the drying room. When full, the room could hold one hundred tons of floorcloth in a variety of colorful patterns. One awed visitor described it as a "rare and gorgeous sight."[11] With a final "seasoning," or "curing" in the drying room of six months or more, the entire process from loom to shipment required nearly ten months.

Manufacturers made significant improvements to this laborious process in the second half of the nineteenth century. Nairn himself was responsible for several of them. In the 1860s he introduced steam heat, which greatly reduced the time needed for "seasoning." Along with other firms in the 1880s, Nairn also began to use new flat-bed printing machines and an automated system of calenders, or rollers, for applying the sizing and paint.

While eighteenth-century floorcloth had been made largely by hand and was restricted to the homes of the wealthy, nineteenth-century industrialization made floorcloth more affordable to the middle class by reducing labor costs. Charles Dickens observed in the 1830s that floorcloth was a feature of up-to-date chemists' shops and new city offices.[12] Several prominent advisors on home matters recommended floorcloth to their readers in 1869. In England, Mrs. Beeton provided two recipes for its care,[13] while in America, Catherine Beecher and her sister, Harriet Beecher Stowe, thought it appropriate for kitchens.[14]

By the end of the century, reduction in the cost of floorcloth made it common even in working-class dwellings. Robert Tressell described a workman's house in his 1906 novel *The Ragged Trousered Philanthropists:* "The front door opened into a passage about two feet six inches wide and ten feet in length, covered with oilcloth." In the front sitting room, "the floor was covered with oilcloth of a tile pattern in yellow and red." He also commented that the workman's floorcloth had been "obtained on the hire system" and was not yet paid for.[15]

Floorcloth was not the only product made by the large oilcloth companies. In Lancaster, the firm of James Williamson and Son had begun making table-baize oilcloth in the mid-1840s. Produced by a method similar to that of floorcloth manufacture, table oilcloth had a cotton backing coated with "kivver," a thin paste made of china clay, chalk, white lead, potato flour, umber, lac, and resin to which was added linseed oil and a dryer. Only two coatings were required. It was trowelled, pumiced, printed, and dried much the same as floorcloth, but the average widths were forty-five to fifty-four inches.

Besides table covering, homemakers used table-baize oilcloth for mantel and shelf covering and borders, as well as "splashers" around sinks and wash basins and as a waterproof dado for hallways and entrance areas. In addition, oilcloth was popular for window blinds and furniture covering. "American cloth" was oilcloth that imitated the grain of leather and was much used as an inexpensive upholstery for carriages. By the 1870s, Williamson also made floor oilcloth and Nairn had begun making table-baize. Diversification of product line characterized the industry throughout its history.[16]

KAMPTULICAN AND OTHER EARLY FLOOR COVERINGS

Floorcloth, much prized as an inexpensive, practical waterproof covering, was not problem-free. It didn't wear very well, it was cold to the feet, and had an unpleasant smell when new. Various experimenters in the mid-nineteenth century attempted to find more practical alternatives. In 1844, Englishman Elijah Galloway patented a floor covering called Kamptulican, a name taken from two Greek words meaning elastic covering. It consisted of a compound of India rubber, gutta percha (a tree sap derivative), and cork. It enjoyed some success: architect Sir Charles Barry chose it for the corridors of the new Houses of Parliament in the late 1840s, and by the 1860s, ten companies in London alone were manufacturing it.[17] Compared to floorcloth, however, Kamptulican was expensive. While it was available well into the twentieth century, it never achieved the widespread acceptance that linoleum was to have.

Corticine, later called cork carpet, was patented in 1871.[18] Made with a polymerized oil and cork dust, it was noted for softness and resiliency. William Morris patented a design for an African marigold pattern for printed Corticine floorcloth in 1875, but we do not know which company manufactured it for him. The pattern was still available in the Morris and Company catalogue in 1900.[19] The British Trade Register listed the Corticine Floorcloth Company from 1884 to 1908, but Corticine was produced by other oilcloth companies as well.

Two other resilient floor coverings made brief appearances in the 1870s. One was Suberium, which was advertised in 1874, and the other Boulinikon. Nothing more is known of the former, but the latter was described in 1879 as being made of "buffalo hide torn to fine shreds . . . wool and hair, all elastic and extremely durable substances." They were mixed with an oil and compressed.[20]

The Invention and Early Development of Linoleum

The variety of experimental floor covering produced in the mid-nineteenth century reflects the contemporary obsession with novel materials. The most successful of them all, however, was linoleum.

It is a commonplace that commercial success often inspires legends about a product's origins. Such legends usually focus on the single, heroic inventor who may have made his discovery by accident but struggled against great hardships to find fame and fortune. Reflecting a nineteenth-century deterministic philosophy, these myths present technological innovation as good and their development into commercial products as inevitable. Linoleum is no exception. The story repeated in all the literature about linoleum is that one day the young Frederick Walton noticed a skin of oxidized linseed oil on the top of a paint jar. He peeled it off and began playing with the rubberlike piece, thinking of ways to use it. He undertook a series of experiments, and after many trials and tribulations, in 1860, received the first of the patents that would be the basis for linoleum.[21]

Like most myths, there is a core of truth to this tale; still, it ignores the crucial context for Walton's invention. No poor, struggling, unappreciated inventor, Walton came from a background that nurtured experimentation. He was the son of a Manchester engineer and manufacturer who had done his own experiments with elastic materials and had patented an India-rubber wire card for carding cotton. The elder Walton initially encouraged his son in his experiments, provided him a laboratory within his factory, and helped finance the young man's attempt to use India rubber as a base for wire brushes.

Rather than leaping from paint pot to linoleum as the legend implies, Walton first tried, unsuccessfully, to make a fast-drying varnish for book covers. Rather than being a solitary, heroic inventor, he was one of many who were experimenting with substitutes for rubber. Materials like Kamptulican probably gave him the idea for applying his discovery to floor covering. None of this detracts from the importance of what Walton did; it simply places Walton's experiments in the fuller context of nineteenth-century fascination with practical invention.

Walton sold his share in his father's business, borrowed more money from his family, and set up a factory in Chiswick, where in 1863 he made and patented his first piece of linoleum.[22] In need of further capital, he formed a partnership with William. J. Taylor and several other investors. They established a new factory at Staines, just west of London, in 1864. In its first annual report in December 1865, the Linoleum Manufacturing Company, Ltd. noted that it had been in business eleven months, and in actual production only a few months, "as much time was occupied in erecting and adapting the machinery, buildings, etc. commenced by Messers Walton, Taylor and Co."

Walton later claimed that the new company made 53,133 square yards of linoleum in their first year.[23] For several years the steadily growing profits were put back into the business to finance expansion. In 1865, the firm reported a profit of £1,564.11, and in the following year, £7,361.12, with the note that "sales nearly reached production." Their goal was to make 5,000 square yards of linoleum each week. In 1868 the profit was £11,096.17, and for the first time the company paid a dividend.[24]

Walton's memories may have been a bit vague in 1925 when he claimed that for four or five of these early years the company had showed a loss—an assertion not supported by the record books. He wrote in his history of linoleum that only when the company started advertising and opened a shop in a "good location" in London did things begin to change: "The total result was that after several weeks the trade awoke to the fact that the public wanted linoleum and we opened 200 new accounts during that year."[25] Walton did not say what year this happened and the record books make no mention of it. Instead, they show a sure and steady climb in profits and production, continued expansion of the factory and of overseas sales.

Walton was not the controlling partner in the Linoleum Manufacturing Company. He received a salary as manager, had a seat on the board and a significant number of shares, but in order to put his creation into production, he had to give control of it to others. Perhaps that is why, unlike James Williamson of Lancaster and Michael B. Nairn of Kirkcaldy, Walton never received a peerage. He was an inventor, not a captain of industry.

Still, linoleum was Walton's invention. His name was on the patents and it appeared in all the advertising. Some might argue that his creation of the name "linoleum" was almost as important as the product itself. Like so many of the names for inventions in this period, linoleum had a classical source; it came from Latin—*linum* for "flax," from which linseed oil is made, and *oleum* for "oil." Thus, literally, "linoleum" means "linseed oil."[26] It was such a satisfactory name that it was used in every language of every county where linoleum was sold and even applied to successor materials.

PROCESS OF MANUFACTURE

Essentially linoleum is oxidized linseed oil mixed with ground cork dust, rosin, gum and pigments that are pressed between heavy rollers onto a canvas backing. As simple as this may sound, the actual production process was complicated and lengthy.

The first step was to oxidize the linseed oil. A difficult and time-consuming process, it was absolutely essential to gain the resilient, waterproof qualities that made linoleum so special. The workers boiled the linseed oil in large vats to remove impurities, then cooled it and piped it to the oxidizing shed, where long sheets of thin, cotton scrim hung. Poured into perforated troughs at the ceiling level, the oil was allowed to flow over the scrim twice a day for six to ten weeks in the heated shed. At the end of this period, the scrim had a tough, elastic, inch-thick skin of oxidized linseed oil (fig. 41). This was the key ingredient. At this stage the oxidized oil looked very much like linoleum, but further processing was necessary to ensure its hard-wearing endurance as a floor covering.

The sheets were taken down and fed into machines which ground them to a pulp. In the next step, making the linoleum "cement," workmen mixed the pulp with rosin and Kauri gum (fossilized tree sap from New Zealand) in huge, heated kettles. They poured the "cement" out onto the floor and dusted it with white powder (fig. 42). Then they chopped the rubbery substance into foot square chunks, aged it for three weeks and put it through a machine that looked like a meat grinder. Workers mixed the resulting shredded cement with ground cork dust and pigments. Some later formulas called for wood flour at this stage as

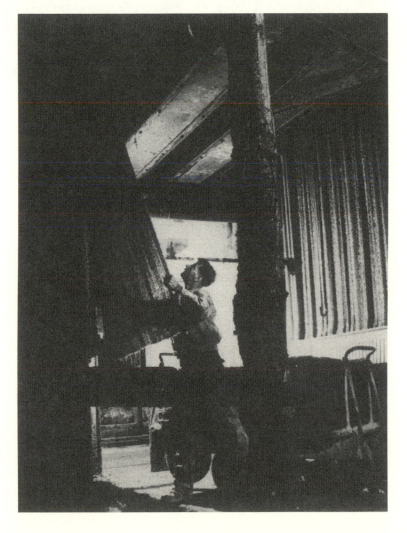

Fig. 41. Scrim sheets with oxidized linseed oil. Kirkcaldy Museum and Art Gallery, Kirkcaldy, Scotland.

well. Remixing the cement, cork dust, and pigments several times produced a substance resembling a thick, oily sawdust.

The granulated mixture was then pressed between heated calenders onto a canvas or burlap backing. The distance between the rollers determined the thickness or grade of the linoleum (fig. 43). In the final stage, workers hung the linoleum in a large heated room called a "stove" (fig. 44). Festoons of linoleum, thirty yards long, dried in the stove from two to eight weeks depending on their thickness. The heating further oxidized and hardened the material.

That was the method for making a basic, one-color linoleum. For printed material, manufacturers used a process similar to that for floorcloth. Before the 1880s, the printing was done by hand with wooden blocks, but later, both flat-bed printing machines and rotary devices were standard (fig. 45). Printed linoleum was put back into the drying stoves for six or seven more days to harden the paint. The last step was trimming the selvage and inspecting the surface (fig. 46). If satisfactory, it was measured, cut into sixty-square-yard sections, rolled, crated, and put in the warehouse for shipment.

All linoleum companies used this Walton system. Many had their own variations, which they guarded as trade secrets, but these were only slight modifications; the basic process remained much as Walton had created it. The most significant improvement came in the 1890s, when Walton introduced a new system for oxidizing the oil. Called the "showerbath and smacker" process, the oil was sprayed on the scrim rather than poured (the "showerbath"), and then mixed in a machine that forced air into it (the "smacker"). This greatly speeded the oxidizing of the

Fig. 43. Linoleum calenders. Armstrong's "Production of Linoleum," lantern slide set, c. 1915. Hagley Museum and Library.

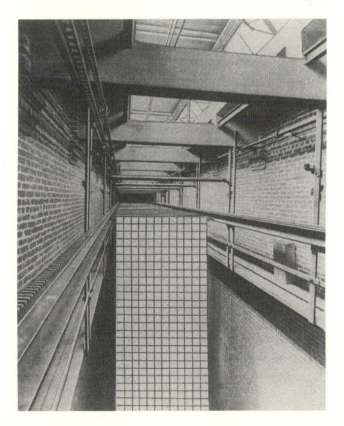

Fig. 44. The stove room, where festoons of linoleum were hung to "season." Armstrong's "Production of Linoleum," lantern slide set, c. 1915. Hagley Museum and Library.

Fig. 45. Interior of Armstrong's block shop, where patterns for printed linoleum were carved into wooden blocks and rollers. Armstrong's "Production of Linoleum," lantern slide set, c. 1915. Hagley Museum and Library.

Fig. 46. Inspection of finished linoleum, Armstrong's "Production of Linoleum," lantern slide set, c. 1915. Hagley Museum and Library.

linseed oil, reducing the time needed from several weeks to several days. Other changes included the development in 1880 of calenders, or rollers capable of taking four yard widths instead of the original two yard standard, new machines to mix the ground cork dust and linoleum cement, and the painting of the canvas or burlap backing to help waterproof it.

WALTON'S COMPETITION

Advertised as "warm, soft and durable," Frederick Walton's linoleum was superior to floor oilcloth because it was thicker, more waterproof, resilient, and much longer-wearing.[27] Even though its printed designs might wear, the ground was a dark color rather than floorcloth's white, so it showed less. Solid-color linoleums showed no wear at all.

Linoleum was so popular that as soon as Walton's patents expired in 1877, older oilcloth firms began to imitate it. Walton sued Michael Nairn and Company for infringement of his trademark when they began to manufacture and sell their own brand of linoleum. But in 1878, the British courts ruled against Walton, largely because he had failed to register "linoleum" as his trade name. The courts declared that the word "linoleum" was now public property because it was in such widespread use. Walton claimed it was so widely known only because he had spent ten thousand pounds advertising it through W. H. Smith in all London railway stations. Unpersuaded, Mr. Justice Fry ruled that "linoleum" merely described the floor covering Walton had invented; now that the patents had expired and others were making it, there was no other name to call it. The opinion offers clear evidence of how widespread and commonplace linoleum had become in its brief, fourteen-year history.[28]

Nairn's company was the first to compete with Walton's, but by the 1880s there were others. In Kirkcaldy, a center for the developing linoleum business, Barry, Ostelere and Shepherd

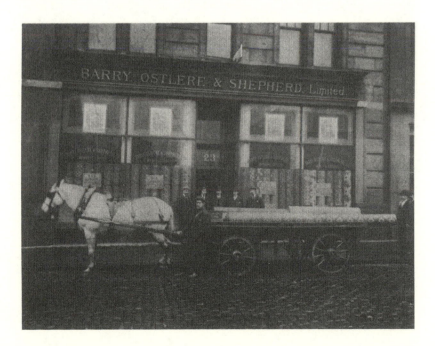

Fig. 47. Barry, Ostlere and Shepherd's linoleum outlet store in Glasgow, Scotland, c. 1912. Kirkcaldy Museum and Art Gallery, Kirkcaldy, Scotland.

(fig. 47) and the Fife Linoleum Company prospered alongside Nairn. Fife supported two other firms, and Dundee still another. In 1887, James Williamson and Son in Lancaster added linoleum to its product line. Several smaller linoleum firms also sprang up near London.

Walton's Linoleum Manufacturing Company continued to expand its markets, took out foreign patents, and sold rights to firms in Germany, France, and America. In 1872 Walton arrived in New York to help Joseph Wild establish the American Linoleum Manufacturing Company. For two years, Walton supervised the building of the factory and company town on Staten Island. He named the village Linoleumville.[29] In 1879 the journal *Carpet Trade* reported, "The manufacture of sheet oilcloth has been considerably interfered with as of late . . . by the introduction of linoleum" and cited, as one reason, the popularity of the new American company.[30]

INLAID LINOLEUM

The next major technological improvement in linoleum was Frederick Walton's introduction of "straight-line inlaid linoleum." In early linoleum, pigment was mixed with the ground so the material was a solid color. Designs, when used, were printed on the surface, just as on oilcloth. Walton and other firms wanted a way to make the patterns just as permanent and long-wearing as the linoleum base.

Fig. 48. Workers hand piecing the inlaid linoleum design. Nairn Company, Kirkcaldy, Scotland, c. 1950. Kirkcaldy Museum and Art Gallery, Kirkcaldy, Scotland.

Walton's 1863 patent included a proposal for inlaid linoleum but gave no mechanism for its production. In 1879, Walton patented a "Granite" linoleum: various colors were put through the calender at the granular stage to produce a streaked pattern which penetrated through to the back. He produced marble, granite, and jaspé (mottled and striated) effects with this system.

C. F. Leake patented another type of inlaid linoleum called "molded" in 1880.[31] Leake, an employee of Walton's Linoleum Manufacturing Company, developed a version of inlaid linoleum that involved forcing various colored linoleum mixtures still in the granulated stage through a slotted tray or stencil. That could produce multicolored patterns called "molded," or "granulated" inlay, but the colors tended to overlap and could not reproduce the precision of a tile design. Leake had developed his inlay during the time when Walton was in America. The company put it into production in 1882; by the mid-1890s, several other firms, including Nairn were using variations on this method.

Walton complained that in manufacturing Leake's molded inlay, the Linoleum Manufacturing Company had violated their contract agreement to develop Walton's system. In settlement, he received a release from agreements to give them his future linoleum-related inventions.

In 1882, Walton took out his own patent on straight-line inlay, but his were not the only experiments with the material. In America, Wild's plant manager, David Melvin, patented a method for producing straight-line inlaid linoleum in 1889.[32] Melvin's and Walton's systems involved sheets of colored linoleum which were rolled out like cookie dough and cut into patterns. Workers then hand-pieced the various colored linoleum sections together into a design over the canvas backing (fig. 48). The roll was heated and re-calendered fusing it into one piece. Straight-line inlay was much more precise than the molded version. It proved so satisfactory that some manufacturers like Nairn continued to use the hand-piece method into the 1950s.[33]

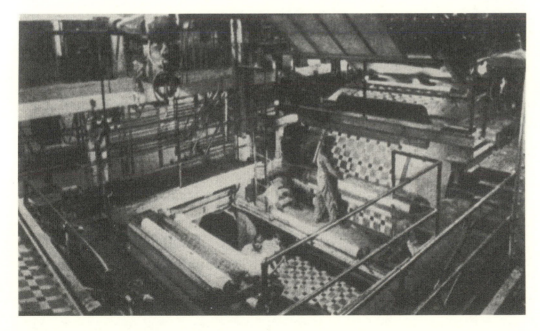

Fig. 49. Walton's giant rotary press for straight-line inlaid linoleum. Reproduced from Scientific American 143 (Oct. 1930): 312. Leyburn Library, Washington and Lee University.

Fig. 50. Printed linoleum, c. 1920, left, from a house in College Park, Pennsylvania, and right, inlaid linoleum, c. 1910, from a house in Lawrence, Kansas.

Walton, however, was determined to find a way of doing all this with a machine. It took nearly fourteen years to complete the task. In 1890, he patented the first continuous inlaying machine and in 1895, organized the Greenwich Inlaid Linoleum Company to begin production. Not until 1904, however, did he feel that he had finally perfected the automatic, straight-line, inlaying machine (fig. 49).[34] Walton's inlaid linoleum was of such quality that other manufacturers eventually bought his machines. Both the hand-pieced and the machine-made inlaid linoleum would wear indefinitely, since "the colors went straight through to the back" (fig. 50). Inlaid linoleum was the top of the product line and expensive compared to the plain and printed forms. In 1911, inlaid sold in the United States for $1.07 to $1.64 per square yard, depending on the grade and design. By contrast, plain and printed linoleum could be had for 50 to 55 cents per square yard. The cheaper forms continued to be produced.

AMERICAN LINOLEUM COMPANIES

By the early twentieth century, at least five firms were manufacturing linoleum in the United States. Joseph Wild's American Linoleum Manufacturing Company employed seven hundred workers in 1905, making ninety thousand square yards of linoleum a week. Wild continued in business until the Depression forced him to close in the mid-1930s.[35]

Two large and important firms, George Blabon and Thomas Potter, operated in Philadelphia. George Washington Blabon had begun as a jobber for other oilcloth companies in

1851, but in 1865 he opened his own factory to make table, floor, and carriage oilcloth and window blinds. After deciding to add linoleum to his line in 1885, he toured plants in England and Scotland and hired British engineers to help him set up his plant. Under their guidance, an American foundry produced the first linoleum calender to be built in the United States in 1886. Blabon also introduced flat-bed printing of linoleum in 1886, when his firm bought George W. Williams's machine and later his patent from a Long Island oilcloth company. In June 1887, George W. Blabon and Son produced their first linoleum for the market. They remained a leading producer well into the 1930s.[36]

Thomas Potter bought an already established oilcloth business in Philadelphia in 1837. He built a new factory and became one of America's largest oilcloth producers. He began to make linoleum in the early 1890s and in 1892, developed a nine-color, high-speed printing machine that could cover twenty-four square yards a minute. Contemporaries claimed that it could do the work of one hundred men.[37] The American flat-bed printing machines were much admired in Europe, and firms like Nairn eventually imported them.

Fearing that new American tariffs would eventually hurt their export business, Michael B. Nairn joined with the New York decorating firm of W. and J. Sloane in 1886 to form an American branch of the Nairn Company. The Sloane Company had been the main wholesaler of Nairn linoleums for some time and became the sole selling agent for the new firm as well. Even though fear of American tariffs had spurred Nairn to found an American branch, once the new plant in Kearny, New Jersey, was completed, Nairn and Sloane had the audacity to lobby for protective American tariffs. Whether their efforts had anything to do with it or not, several tariffs were imposed on imported linoleums in the 1890s, the most important being the Dingley tariff bill of 1897. In 1889, John Sloane wrote to Nairn that their new plant was making thirty-two thousand yards of linoleum daily and selling at a rate that was "quite disconcerting." He predicted that "Nairn Linoleum will soon be as familiar a household word on this Coast as Pear's Soap." In 1892, the company did well enough to declare its first dividend.[38]

Wild, Blabon, Potter, and Nairn founded successful businesses, but the manufacturer who would eventually dominate them all was Charles D. Armstrong of the Armstrong Cork and Tile Company of Lancaster, Pennsylvania. Established in Pittsburgh in 1860, Armstrong's company first produced cork stoppers for bottles and jars. By the turn of the century, Armstrong, the founder's son, worried that the national prohibition movement would hurt the business, decided to diversify the product line. In 1902, Armstrong bought the patent rights of a German firm for the production of cork insulation. They produced corkboard for cold storage and food processing plants and in 1904 began making cork floor tile.

The company's most important venture, however, began in 1907 when Charles Armstrong convinced his board the firm should make linoleum. It was a logical strategy since ground cork dust was the chief binder in linoleum. Since the 1880s, Armstrong had sold its cork debris to Wild and other linoleum manufacturers. With so much of the raw product readily available, it made sense for them to start making linoleum. They already owned a cork plant in Lancaster, Pennsylvania, so they opened their new linoleum operation there in 1908. John J. Evans, the first supervisor, recruited engineers and employees from Scotland and Germany. He started with 170; by the 1920s there were nearly 2,000 workers at the plant. Armstrong was an innovative company, both in product development and in advertising techniques, an aspect that will be further discussed later in this chapter. By the end of the 1920s, Armstrong's linoleum dominated the American industry.[39]

These examples illustrate several important points about the rise of the linoleum industry in the United States. The invention of the material and the initial technology came from Britain. But American development of new machinery, such as the flat-bed printing devices, eventually influenced European production. Another point is that firms which made linoleum usually already had a vested interest in either oilcloth or, in Armstrong's case, cork. Wild's was the exception, being the only company to start from the ground up, but it had the same advantage Nairn's New Jersey branch would later have—a parent company that could supply expertise. The overall development pattern was one of a gradual, incremental buildup of the industry and an interdependence between companies and countries as linoleum came to eventually replace floor oilcloth as the most popular hard-surface flooring. In spite of protective tariffs, linoleum was a worldwide industry.

WORLD TRADE

The number of companies producing linoleum continued to expand in the early twentieth century. Britain led in export production, but Germany soon began to rival it. There were several firms in Germany, the most important of which was the Deutsche Linoleum Werke Hansa in Delmenhorst, which had bought the original Walton patents in 1882. Like Armstrong, they too had started as a cork company. In Canada there was the Dominion Company, and there were also factories in Australia, France, Belgium, Austria, Italy, Sweden, and Russia.

Linoleum was a worldwide product, as were its raw materials. The linseed oil came primarily from South America and the United States as well as the Ukraine, the cork came from Portugal and Spain, the jute for the canvas backing came from India and Pakistan and was processed into burlap in Scotland. Linoleum was also used all over the world, especially where European colonial powers had established themselves. World War I greatly disrupted this network, especially when burlap became essential for making sandbags for the trenches, but the trade quickly reestablished itself in the postwar period.[40]

FELT-BASE FLOOR COVERING

A new hard-surface floor covering that would eventually outsell linoleum appeared in 1910. Called "felt-base," it was first made by two American roofing firms, the Barrett Company of Pennsylvania and the Bird and Son Company of Massachusetts. They simply took roofing felt, coated and painted it, and presented it as a floor covering. As others adopted and developed the idea, the product evolved. A rag or paper felt base was saturated with a petroleum derivative or a bituminous composition to waterproof and harden it. The surface received first a seal coat, then an enameled wearing coat containing a linseed oil composition, and finally a painted pattern. Printing for this decorative finish was done in the same manner as oilcloth or printed linoleum. The back of the felt was also coated and the assemblage was heated in stove rooms to dry.[41] A much cheaper product than linoleum, it also required less time to produce (fig. 51).

By the early 1910s, a number of companies were making the felt-based floor covering, and they all had their own ingenious trade names for it. In 1915, Potter's introduced Floortex, and Cooks, a New Jersey firm, Feltoleum. Armstrong presented Fiberlin, "a new line to meet competition in cheap floorcovering."[42] Congoleum, another company making felt-based floor coverings, took over Barrett in 1918 and then, in 1924, merged with Nairn's American branch. One reason many companies added felt-based floor covering to their product lines in the 1914–19 period was the wartime shortage of raw materials for linoleum.[43]

While felt-base did not replace linoleum, it did create some identity problems. The older linoleum companies were careful in their advertising to point out the differences between felt-base and linoleum. Potter called Floortex a "cheap grade of floorcovering" and said, "We do not claim that Floortex is equal to printed linoleum, and if anyone were to sell it as such it would not only mislead the customer but might help destroy confidence in the genuine article."[44] The worry was not misplaced. At a quick glance, felt-based flooring looked like linoleum, but it was not resilient, had no cork or burlap, and its thin coating of paint could easily wear through. Armstrong regularly warned its customers against mistaking felt-base for linoleum and recommended that people look at the back for the burlap and try to tear the material. If it tore, it was felt-base.[45]

As a result of its own investigation of companies selling felt-base as a linoleum product, the Federal Trade Commission ruled in 1919 that linoleum was a distinctive material, based on the Walton patents and no other floor covering could be sold under its name.[46]

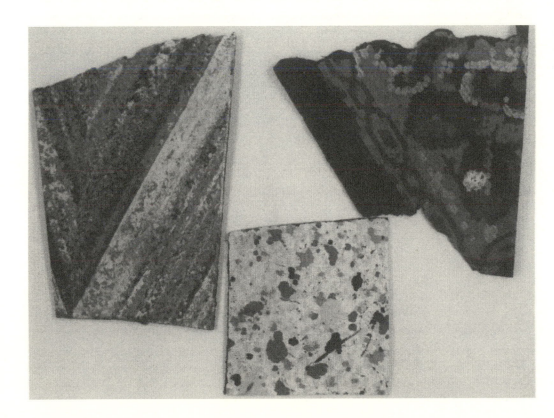

Fig. 51. Felt-base examples from homes in Lexington and Buena Vista, Virginia.

Still, with companies selling products called Congoleum and Feltoleum, the connection was made in the public's mind. Rockbridge County, Virginia, resident Troy Weimer recalled when his family put Congoleum in their house in the 1930s: "It tore easily and people thought it was linoleum, so it made them think badly of it."[47] An industry writer warned, "The fact is that those who buy the substitute are so dissatisfied with it that they never again think of buying any kind of linoleum whatever."[48] Armstrong was so concerned about the problem, they dropped their Fiberlin line right after the war and did not make felt-based flooring again until 1925, when competition from Nairn's Gold Seal Congoleum spurred them to develop "Quaker Rugs."[49]

By the end of the 1920s, almost all of the large, American floor-covering firms were offering a felt-based floor covering. It surpassed linoleum in volume of production in 1923, and never lost its advantage. During the Depression years in the United States, five times as much felt-base was made as linoleum. In 1935, a little over 24 million square yards of linoleum were produced in the United States, valued at $18 million, while 128 million square yards of felt-base were produced, valued at about $31 million.[50] In other words, the higher priced, better quality linoleums still commanded a significant market share even while more and more of the felt-base was produced. The trend extended to other markets as well. The British firms of Nairn and Williamson began making felt-base in the 1930s. It was especially popular in rug-like widths and in patterns that imitated carpet.

While felt-base did not replace linoleum, two other products eventually did. Vinyl was the most important and best-selling of the two. The first patents for vinyl floor covering were taken in 1934, and experimental production began in 1947. Armstrong introduced its first commercial vinyl flooring in 1951, and other firms soon followed.[51] Vinyl looked like linoleum, wore almost as well, was resilient, and took pressure without denting (important in the heyday of the stiletto heel).

Asphalt tile, the other floor covering, was initially developed by a roofing firm in the 1920s but did not receive widespread production until the 1940s. Ironically, while its first formulae included asphalt as a binder, by 1947, there was no asphalt in what continued to be called asphalt tile. The binder was instead a synthetic resin and the filler was asbestos. Very popular for commercial buildings, asphalt tile, like vinyl, looked like linoleum, but could be made cheaper and faster. While linoleum still took several months' production time, vinyl and asphalt flooring could be made in one day.[52] Small wonder that by the 1960s vinyl and asphalt tile replaced linoleum. Still, linoleum had been one of the most popular and widely used floor coverings from the 1870s to the 1960s, a period of over ninety years.

ARMSTRONG'S NATIONAL ADVERTISING CAMPAIGN

Advertising was essential for companies of all sorts to get their products known. In the early years, however, most linoleum advertising was addressed to the trade, not to the general public. Walton's efforts to make linoleum a household name by advertising in London railway stations in the early 1870s was a unique and isolated example of a floorcloth company presenting its product directly to the public. The more common practice in both England and America was to advertise only to the trade. Thus publications like the American *Carpet and Upholstery Trade Review,* or the British *Cabinet Maker and Complete House Furnisher* regularly carried ads for various oilcloth and linoleum producers in the late nineteenth and early twentieth centuries. In the late 1910s, however, Armstrong broke with industry tradition and began advertising directly to the consumer; they were the first American flooring company to do so.

Their marketing innovation was the brainchild of Henning W. Prentis Jr., a 1903 Phi Beta Kappa graduate of the University of Missouri. Prentis had been hired by Armstrong as a bright, young prospect for their insulation sales department. When the company president, Charles D. Armstrong, decided to offer a pamphlet explaining what cork was, Prentis was asked to produce it. His flair for writing thus established, he began to help with the company's modest trade advertisements. His supervisor came to feel that Prentis was spending too much time with advertising and not enough with sales. At a showdown, the boss asked, "What is more important, advertising or sales?" and was taken aback by Prentis's unequivocal declaration, "Advertising!"[53]

Neither Prentis's supervisor nor Charles Armstrong was totally convinced that advertising deserved any one man's full-time attention, but in 1911 they gave him a small budget and allowed him to try. Prentis thought that the manufacturer should help the wholesaler and retailer sell the product to the customer, so he developed four booklets called *Selling Helps*. Meant for the retailer, they covered newspaper advertising, window displays, streetcar advertising, and lantern slide demonstrations. He also developed a series called *Told in the Store* on successful sales techniques. Skeptics within the company were still not convinced, even when orders for the booklets quickly exhausted the supply.

Prentis next undertook a study of the potential for national magazine advertising. He hired an outside agency to do the research and then convinced the board to give him the unprecedented sum of fifty thousand dollars for a three-year experiment. The first advertisement, "Armstrong Linoleum for Every Room in the House," appeared in *The Saturday Evening Post* in September 1917. Soon Armstrong had ads in *McCalls,* the *Delineator, Ladies Home Journal, Woman's Home Companion,* and *Designer.* Armstrong would later tell retailers, "Right in your town, these magazines are going into the homes of approximately three out of every five literate white families."[54] Despite such racist assumptions, the campaign was a success with an immediate increase in orders. Learning quickly, other companies began to advertise nationally as well.[55]

British companies thought the Americans were foolishly spending millions of dollars competing with each other in advertising. By contrast, they had formed a cartel called the British Linoleum Manufacturers Association to fix prices and divide markets among themselves. On the continent, another cartel did the same. In America, while there is some evidence that the linoleum manufacturers may have colluded on price trends, their chief marketing weapon was advertising.[56] The social and cultural implications of this will be further discussed in chapter 7.

ADVERTISING LINOLEUM'S ADVANTAGES

When Armstrong, Blabon, Congoleum, and others began national advertising in the late 1910s, they appealed directly to the woman consumer. Ads like "The Story of a Woman and a Floor" (fig. 52) addressed women as household managers, concerned about cleanliness and time-

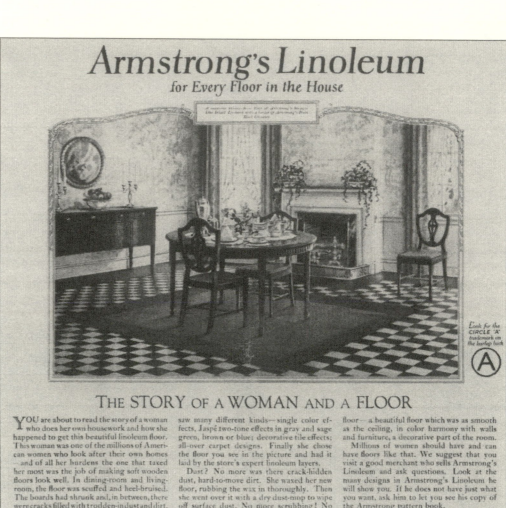

Armstrong's Linoleum
for Every Floor in the House

THE STORY OF A WOMAN AND A FLOOR

YOU are about to read the story of a woman who does her own housework and how she happened to get this beautiful linoleum floor. This woman was one of the millions of American women who look after their own homes — and of all her burdens the one that taxed her most was the job of making soft wooden floors look well. In dining-room and living-room, the floor was scuffed and heel-bruised. The boards had shrunk and, in between, there were cracks filled with trodden-in dust and dirt.

Every time the woman looked at that wooden floor, she sighed. The dining-room was the gathering place of the family. Three times a day their shoe soles rubbed the paint from its surface. Three times a day little feet bounded over it and hammered in more dirt and scuffed and battered and shabbied it.

That wooden floor meant work, work, work for her — a constant demand for repainting, revarnishing, or refinishing. Then one day she heard of floors of Armstrong's Linoleum — smooth, unbroken floors, practically one-piece floors. She went to her merchant and she saw many different kinds — single color effects, Jaspé two-tone effects in gray and sage green, brown or blue; decorative tile effects; all-over carpet designs. Finally she chose the floor you see in the picture and had it laid by the store's expert linoleum layers.

Dust? No more was there crack-hidden dust, hard-to-move dirt. She waxed her new floor, rubbing the wax in thoroughly. Then she went over it with a dry dust-mop to wipe off surface dust. No more scrubbing! No more grubbing! Glory be!

That floor did not get progressively shabby-looking. It became progressively better-looking. It gave that woman a chance for some pride, when callers came. It was moreover a sound-deadening floor; a glowing, smiling floor; an easy-on-the-nerves-and-feet floor — a beautiful floor which was as smooth as the ceiling, in color harmony with walls and furniture, a decorative part of the room.

Millions of women should have and can have floors like that. We suggest that you visit a good merchant who sells Armstrong's Linoleum and ask questions. Look at the many designs in Armstrong's Linoleum he will show you. If he does not have just what you want, ask him to let you see his copy of the Armstrong pattern book.

Write to us. Our Bureau of Interior Decoration will be glad to advise you on the subject of linoleum patterns and colors for different rooms. No charge.

"FLOORS, FURNITURE *and* COLOR"
By Agnes Foster Wright

Mrs. Wright, a former President of the Interior Decorators' League of New York, has written a book which tells how to use color effectively in home furnishing and decoration. This book is well illustrated and will give real help in planning individual rooms. For twenty-five cents we will mail you a copy, postage prepaid. All Armstrong's Linoleum, plain, printed, or inlaid, can be identified by the Circle "A" trademark on the burlap back.

ARMSTRONG CORK COMPANY
Linoleum Division
1924 Mary Street, Lancaster, Pa.

management as well as the beauty of their homes. Armstrong hired Hazel Dell Brown as director of its new Bureau of Interior Design in 1922. She appeared in ads offering advice, ran a design department to help consumers select colors and patterns, and authored several books on using linoleum in decorating the home or business. In all of this, linoleum was promoted as a modern, clean, safe, durable material that was far superior to any other floor-covering alternatives.

Part of linoleum's claim to superiority was its resiliency. As one ad noted, "Linoleum is, par excellence, a comfortable floor. Cork and oxidized linseed oil are naturally elastic and combine to make a sort of cushion that absorbs the shock of footsteps."[57] Moreover, "linoleum is always warm as contrasted to the coldness of tile and marble."[58]

Another advantage of linoleum was its cleanliness. A waterproof, nonskid surface, it was easy to wash. There were even claims that it had antiseptic qualities. In 1913, a German scientist reported experiments that suggested the oxidizing linseed oil gave off a germicidal gas. Advertising literature often repeated this claim making linoleum seem especially ideal for kitchens, bathrooms, nurseries, and hospitals (fig. 53).[59]

Linoleum was prized as well for its durability. Unlike the earlier floor cloth, linoleum was thick enough to wear well. Reportedly it might last sixty years or more. Armstrong eventually concluded it would "last as long as the house,"[60] provided it was installed properly. The earliest linoleum had been simply tacked down like a carpet, but Armstrong advocated cementing the linoleum over a felt base to avoid cracking. This made the linoleum a permanent flooring, not a temporary floor covering.[61]

Because of its waterproof, durable qualities, linoleum was sometimes used in unexpected places. The navies of Britain, Germany, and the United States found linoleum to be a practical, nonslip, nonsplintering, waterproof covering for ship decks in the period from the Spanish-

Fig. 53. Armstrong linoleum for the kitchen. Helpful Hints for Linoleum Salesmen, 1918, p. 35. Courtesy, the Winterthur Library: Printed Book and Periodical Collection.

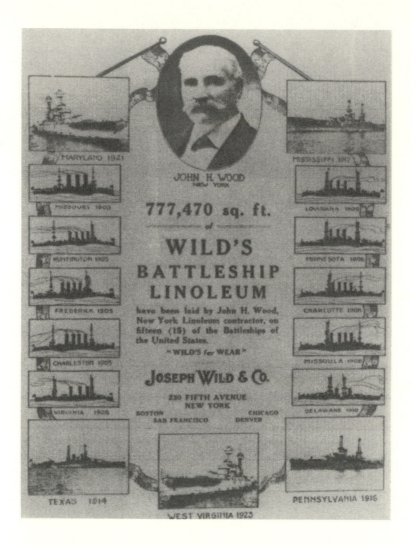

American War through World War I (fig. 54). The quarter-inch-thick linoleum specially produced for this use came to be known as "Battleship Linoleum," but its reputation for durability made it popular for schools, hospitals, and public buildings. Its plain color—Battleship gray or brown—was used everywhere, especially in government buildings.[62]

Surely the most grandiose claim for the durability of linoleum came from an exhibitor at the 1900 Paris Exposition. He had installed one-inch-thick linoleum in several driveways and courtyards to test it as a road covering, thinking it would muffle the sound of horses hooves and carriage wheels. The developer of this product was so confident of its success, he claimed he was negotiating with the French government for a contract to pave the entire Champs Élysées with linoleum.[63]

Obviously, roadcovering was not the future for linoleum, but it did become a ubiquitous part of ordinary middle-class homes, where it was prized as a comfortable, clean, durable, attractive floor covering. In 1919, a University of Missouri survey of farm families in the state found 374 homes with linoleum. In 1927, seventy-two of the eighty-seven applicants for the "Master Farm Homemaker" contest sponsored by the *Farmer's Wife* said they had linoleum in their kitchens. Even more revealing than the number who had linoleum is the fact that the question itself appeared on the application form. The implication was that having linoleum on one's floor was a mark of a good homemaker.[64]

LINOLEUM DESIGNS

One of linoleum's chief virtues was that it provided "art" at a reasonable price. This pitch was made again and again in the advertising literature: "Not so long ago linoleum was thought of only in terms of tile and mosaic designs, suitable for kitchen, pantry and bathroom. But now the Armstrong line alone comprises approximately 380 designs, including parquetries, jaspés, mattings, 'carpet' inlaids, granites and several new and beautiful plain colors. . . . From every point of view, linoleum . . . [is] a practical and attractive floor for any room in the house."[65]

Linoleum appeared in an amazing variety of patterns. The early solid colors of brown and gray were soon superseded by annual displays of new patterns. Companies such as Armstrong, Blabon, and Potter had in-house design departments. Blabon was even an industrial sponsor for the Philadelphia School of Art and hired several of their graduates to work for the firm. The companies also bought designs from free-lance designers, but that was more common in Europe than in America.

Nairn was one of the first to employ well-known designers. In 1867, Michael Nairn commissioned the British ornament specialist Owen Jones to create a floor oilcloth pattern for the firm.[66] Industrial design reformer Christopher Dresser included linoleum patterns in his *Modern Ornamentation* in 1886, offering them to any manufacturer who wanted to use them.[67] He also made designs specifically for Walton's Linoleum Manufacturing Company in 1874.[68]

Well-known German modernist designers Peter Behrens, Walter Fürst, Henry Van der Veld and Richard Riemerschmid produced linoleum patterns for the Deutscher Linoleum Werke Hansa. They were part of the German Werkbund, an association of manufacturers and artists who joined together in 1907 to promote the cause of German industrial art. The Werkbund's annual yearbooks, published from 1912 to 1930, presented the latest designs, most of which were abstract geometric patterns.[69]

In Austria, architect and decorative artist Joseph Hoffman and his Wiener Werkstätte colleagues also created linoleum designs. At the San Francisco Panama-Pacific Exposition in 1915, Hoffman's linoleum designs received awards and critical praise for their sophisticated geometries and color combinations.[70] American trade journals frequently commented on the artistry of such European designs.

An International Correspondence School publication in 1905 summarized the design situation in America: "There is virtually no limit to the kind of patterns that manufacturers of oilcloth and linoleum can successfully reproduce in printing. Sample books from the different factories show a great variety of styles from the simplest diaper pattern in two or three colors to elaborate floral scrolls in imitation of wallpaper and carpet designs printed in six or eight colors."[71] To encourage their correspondence school pupils, the writer of this text pointed out that while manufacturers might repeat a few best-selling designs, new patterns were also added every season. Created by either "public designers or designers for the trade, a large number of whom are women," the standard price for a new linoleum design for a free-lance designer was ten dollars.[72]

AESTHETIC DEBATES

In spite of its practical, durable, decorative, and inexpensive qualities, linoleum was not always universally admired. Its popularity and reputation as a cheap floor covering eventually brought it scorn. This is particularly true in the history of historic preservation. For years, linoleum was considered something to rip out to get down to the "real floor." Only very recently has linoleum received attention as a historic floor covering, something worthy of preservation and reproduction.[73]

Even in its heyday, linoleum sometimes faced criticism. In 1882, one writer referred to linoleum as a "makeshift" for "making bad floors tolerable."[74] That linoleum might serve as a temporary "makeshift" floor until one could afford something better was also indicated by the places it was used in the home. Advertisers said it was "suitable for every room in the house," but in practice, most consumers thought linoleum was perfect for kitchens, bathrooms, and entrance halls, but when they used it for other rooms such as bedrooms, dining rooms, or parlors, it was sometimes as a temporary expedient to be eventually replaced or covered with a rug. That was the case for Doreen Cross's family on Prince Edward Isle in the 1930s. When they built their modest house they put linoleum in the kitchen and bathroom, hardwood floors in the living-dining room area and linoleum over the subflooring in the upstairs bedrooms. As soon as they could afford it, however, they replaced the linoleum in the bedrooms with hardwood floors.[75]

Sometimes the objection was not to linoleum per se, but to the design patterns in which it appeared. The International Correspondence School's 1905 text book described three categories of design: (1) good, pleasing in form and harmonious in theory of design, "suited to educate the public," (2) floral devices, loud colors and contrast so "uneducated people can best get their money's worth in noise and brilliancy," and (3) design for the middle class that knows the second type is bad but is not sophisticated enough for the first, so they settle for "simple, inoffensive patterns."[76]

The hierarchical attitude reflected in this statement is often found in writing about industrial design of the period, but rarely is it quite so blatant. Most commentators simply argued for good design that would educate public taste. The International Correspondence School publication shows the actual practice of linoleum manufacturers who tried to meet the taste of their public. Of course, in their advertising, manufacturers always promoted their products as offering the best quality designs and never made distinctions between class and taste.

The question that bothered writers on aesthetic matters most was whether one material should imitate another. English art critic John Ruskin and his followers were clear that it should not, a point further discussed in chapter 7. But many of the newly manufactured products, including linoleum, did imitate natural materials. While most writers accepted flat, tilelike patterns as good design, imitations of wood, marble, and carpet were controversial. Charles Eastlake's *Hints on Household Taste* took up this issue in 1868: "A floorcloth

Armstrong's Linoleum
for Every Floor in the House

Armstrong's Molded Inlaid Linoleum, Pattern No. 5040, is the floor that was selected for this charming Breakfast Room.

Look for the CIRCLE "A" trade-mark on the burlap back

(A)

FLOOR BEAUTY LIKE THIS IS MODERN

A CHARMING room, a vivacious room. And not the least of its beauty proceeds from its floor—a quaint linoleum tile.

It is a far, far cry from such floor beauty to the early oilcloth patterns as known to Frederick Walton, the inventor of linoleum. He is eighty-eight years of age now; and it is more than sixty years since he commenced to search for a better floor material than the old-fashioned oilcloth of that day and, experimenting, noticed a paint can and the film that had formed on the surface of the paint, where the air touched it.

That rubbery film was oxidized linseed oil, and it gave Frederick Walton his great idea. He mixed it with powdered cork, then pressed the mixture onto burlap. Linoleum was invented, and from the moment of its invention found wide use. The mixture of cork, oxidized linseed oil, and burlap made a perfect floor material.

Linseed oil comes from flaxseed, and it binds the powdered cork together into a tough, durable, elastic material. The strong burlap back is woven from tough jute, and so linoleum is hard to tear. Cork is tough; so linoleum resists wear. Cork is springy; so linoleum is kind to feet. Cork deadens sound; so does linoleum. Cork is moisture-proof; so is linoleum. Cork does not easily stain; neither does linoleum. Cork does not splinter; neither does linoleum.

These qualities linoleum had from the start. But with time came the beauty element.

Men learned how to put color and design in linoleum, both printed and inlaid patterns. Today, you may select beautiful colorings and designs in Armstrong's Linoleum—plain and Jaspé linoleums for living-rooms, tile designs for breakfast rooms and sun porches, flowered designs for bedrooms—that interior decorators, architects, and thoughtful, intelligent women are making the basis of decorative schemes for every room in the house.

Go into good stores and see the development in modern designs and colors made in linoleum since Frederick Walton's day.

One point, however, is important to you. Inform your merchant that you are interested only in genuine linoleum—linoleum made of cork, linseed oil, and burlap. You can identify Armstrong's Linoleum and Armstrong's Linoleum Rugs by the Circle "A" trademark on the burlap back.

"FLOORS, FURNITURE AND COLOR"
by Agnes Foster Wright

You can get a copy of this book from us for only twenty-five cents. The author, Mrs. Wright, is an authority on this subject and was recently President of the Interior Decorators' League of New York. Her book tells how to use color in home decoration and furnishing and includes color plates that will help you plan different rooms. In addition, our Bureau of Interior Decoration will give you individual advice and suggestions without charge.

ARMSTRONG CORK COMPANY
Linoleum Division
1924 Mary Street, Lancaster, Pa.

like every other article of manufacture should seem what it really is, and not effect the appearance of a richer material. There are endless varieties of geometrical diaper which could be used for floorcloth without resorting to the foolish expedient of copying knots and veins of wood and marble."[77]

A similar criticism was leveled against the English by the *Deutsche Werkbund Jahrbuch* for 1912, but could have been equally applied to the Americans: "The English have not yet appreciated linoleum, they still today consider it a surrogate, which does not have a right to an appropriate decoration, but to something similar to the products that it must replace, that is wood parquet, tiles and carpets."[78]

Despite such admonitions, imitations of wood were immensely popular, especially for "linoleum surrounds"—a border into which a woven carpet could be inserted. The claims of verisimilitude sometimes seem a bit outrageous. In one Cook's ad a man holds up a square of linoleum parquet in one hand and wood parquet in the other and asks, "Which is Which?" It is improbable that anyone could have difficulty telling the difference between wood and linoleum, but that did not discourage the advertising claims.[79]

Linoleum's advocates offered a series of arguments as to why imitation was appropriate. Hazel Adler, a designer for Blabon, argued that linoleum was better than the materials it imitated: "Linoleum in tile, granite or marble patterns has all the advantages of tile, granite or marble, in giving a distinctive decorative atmosphere to the room, and yet, at the same time, does away with the disadvantages of a hard cold floor which is uncomfortable."[80] Margaret McElroy, writing for Congoleum-Nairn, suggested that linoleum's imitative qualities democratically extended ornamental effects: "Marble has always been associated with power, wealth and culture. Since the civilization's beginning, this imperial stone has adorned the world's palaces, cathedrals, castles and mansions." But, now, linoleum could "recreate the veinings, marking and coloring of nature's finest marbles in inexpensive resilient floor coverings" for everyone. She called it a "wonderful realism."[81]

Interior designer Frank A. Parsons, writing for Armstrong, said that it was a mistake to even call such designs imitation, since linoleum "is another material, recent in conception and suited to particular conditions because of properties that neither stone, clay nor wood have." It "stands on its own legs as a practical and attractive floor for any room in the house."[82]

The remarks of anyone writing for the linoleum industry might understandably be prejudiced. But when, as in these examples, they were interior designers of some reputation, their expertise lent credence to their comments. Their basic arguments were not only that imitation was appropriate since it could be done so convincingly, but that linoleum was a new and modern material that was better than the older materials it imitated (fig. 55). It was not cold like marble, would not splinter like wood, was not hard like clay tile. It was comfortable, resilient, easy to clean, durable, and attractive. Linoleum was something to be appreciated in its own right, and imitation was simply part of it.

There is plenty of evidence that the middle class agreed with them. British writer Paul Vaughan recalled the home his family built in 1934: "Of course there was lino throughout the house. Some of it was jaspé with a kind of imitation marble finish, but most of it was reproduction parquet." While professional layers installed most of the linoleum, "some of it, with much cursing and ill temper, my father laid himself. Then it was up to my mother to keep it polished, which she did with her O'Cedar mop, once a week."[83] Mrs. Vaughan was not alone. Linoleum was an international, multi-million-dollar business. In homes everywhere, housewives like Mrs. Vaughan blessed Frederick Walton's invention, even if they did not remember his name.

The development and mechanization of the production of oilcloth in the early nineteenth century serves as a background for the phenomenal growth of the linoleum industry in the latter half of the century. Invented by Frederick Walton in the 1860s, linoleum became a worldwide product by the turn of the century. It was eventually replaced by new hard-surface floor coverings in the mid-twentieth century, but for over ninety years it enjoyed an unparalleled popularity.

Advertised as comfortable, durable, and easy to clean, linoleum also provided a modern means of colorful decoration that had wide consumer appeal. The strong gender assumptions also inherent in the advertising will be further discussed in chapter 7. The next chapter, however, will consider an offshoot of linoleum, an embossed wallcovering called Lincrusta-Walton.

CHAPTER 5

Good Impressions:
Embossed Wall and Ceiling Coverings

In 1880, interior decorator Clarence Cook published a home advice book with the provocative title of *What Shall We Do with Our Walls?*[1] What most people were doing with their walls at the time, and had been doing for about fifty years, was covering them with wallpaper. Wallpaper originated in the sixteenth century and became an important luxury item for the wealthy in the eighteenth century. During the early nineteenth century, however, the steam-powered machines of the Industrial Revolution provided fast and inexpensive production. Prices fell so much that wallpaper became a standard decorative material for the middle class and, eventually, even the poor.[2]

By the 1880s, one answer to the question of what to do with the walls was to use a type of wallpaper called an embossed covering. This chapter is about that special category of wall and ceiling decoration. Architects and homeowners considered the embossed coverings, unlike wallpaper, to be a permanent form of architectural ornament. Highly imitative, they offered an inexpensive alternative to decorative plaster, wooden paneling, embossed leathers, and even ceramic tile. Their history, development, marketing, and design, as well as that troublesome question of the appropriateness of imitation, are all important aspects of the story considered here.

LINCRUSTA-WALTON

The first and most important of the Victorian wall and ceiling coverings was Lincrusta-Walton. Developed in 1877 by Frederick Walton, the same man who had earlier gained fame as the inventor of linoleum, Lincrusta-Walton was similar to linoleum, but its decorative patterns were in a raised relief. The formulae for the two materials was similar: oxidized linseed oil mixed with gum, resin, and a filler.[3] The major difference was that ground cork dust served as the filler for linoleum while wood pulp and paraffin wax were added to Lincrusta.

The production of Lincrusta was similar to that for linoleum as well. Both started with the fundamental but time-consuming process of oxidizing the linseed oil. Boiled oil was poured on linen scrims several times a day until a three-quarter-inch thickness of oxidized oil accumulated, a process that could take several months. One manufacturer claimed in 1905, "There are today several methods of arriving at this result or its equivalent, but the one adopted by Mr. Walton . . . yields by far the most satisfactory results in the permanence and quality of the production."[4] The oxidized oil next passed through rollers, which broke it into a curdlike substance. Melted and mixed with resin and gum, it became the "cement." A machine called a "kneader" combined wood pulp, paraffin wax, and pigments with the cement mixture. To this point, the process was nearly identical to that for linoleum, but since Lincrusta-Walton was meant for walls and ceilings, not floors, it could be thinner and more flexible. Instead of the further aging and mixing necessary for linoleum, the Lincrusta-Walton mixture was simply milled again and fed through rollers, one of which was molded to create the embossed patterns (fig. 56). If desired, a skilled worker using hand tools could undercut the design at this point to make it more three-dimensional.

At the same time as the embossing, the backing was applied. Originally, Walton had pressed Lincrusta onto canvas just as he had linoleum, but the result proved too stiff and cumbersome. In 1887, he substituted a waterproof paper backing which allowed greater flexibility.[5] At first, Walton assumed that Lincrusta would need curing time in heated stove rooms just as linoleum required, but by the late 1880s, he knew that was unnecessary: Lincrusta "could almost be taken off the machine and hung on the wall."[6] It did not have to be as hard as the floorcovering since it would receive far less wear on the ceiling or walls.

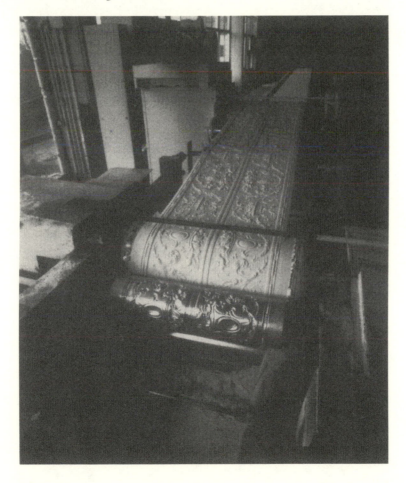

Fig. 56. Lincrusta-Walton in production. Reproduced by permission of Crown Decorative Products, Ltd., Darwen, England.

Walton told friends that he conceived his idea for the wall covering during the long voyage back to England from New York in 1874. After two years setting up the American Linoleum Company's plant on Staten Island, Walton was returning home to resume his duties as manager of the British Linoleum Manufacturing Company. But he soon found himself unhappy with several things done in his absence. C. F. Leake, who had been acting manager, had developed a form of molded, or stenciled inlaid linoleum (see chapter 4).[7] Walton thought this violated an earlier patent he owned as well as his contract with the company for developing it. In settlement, the Linoleum Manufacturing Company released Walton from his agreement to provide them with all patent rights to his future linoleum-related inventions. Thus freed, in 1877 Walton resigned as manager of the LMC, took out a patent on Lincrusta-Walton, and created a new firm, Frederick Walton and Company, to manufacture it.[8] The new plant, located at Sunbury-on-Thames, was in operation by 1878, financed by Walton's own capital.

At first Walton called the new material "Linoleum Muralis"—linoleum for walls. When the British courts ruled in 1878 that he could no longer have exclusive use of the name linoleum, Walton changed the wall-covering title to Lincrusta-Walton.[9] He was determined he would never again lose control over a trade name. Like linoleum, the new name came from Latin: *lin* or *linum* for "flax," and *crusta* for "relief." He added his own name to make sure that no competitor would appropriate his creation. To make it clear what the material was, he advertised it as "Lincrusta-Walton, the Sunbury Wall Decoration—A New Linoleum Product."[10]

Lincrusta-Walton was a huge and immediate success (fig. 57). Only five years after his patent, Walton wrote his father, "At the hotel we saw Lincrusta nicely fixed in the dining room—I also saw it the other day at the Queen's Hotel, Manchester, and in the new salon carriages of the London and North Western Railway Company—which are very handsome. We have received some large orders from America and business is very good on the whole."[11]

The reasons for Lincrusta-Walton's success, an 1880 pamphlet claimed, were that it was "warm and comfortable," "would not warp or be eaten by worms," "was not cold in winter

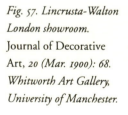

Fig. 57. Lincrusta-Walton London showroom. Journal of Decorative Art, *20 (Mar. 1900): 68. Whitworth Art Gallery, University of Manchester.*

or hot in summer like stone or terracotta," "did not absorb moisture and give it out like brick and plaster," and "was impenetrable and resistant to wet."[12] This latter quality drew particular attention. Linoleum already had a reputation as a nonabsorbent surface that was easy to clean; Lincrusta-Walton brought these admirable qualities from the floor to the wall. It was completely waterproof; soap and water or even diluted acids could be used to clean it. This point was made by the *Journal of Decorative Arts* in 1884: "Amongst the many contributors to these twin sisters, Hygeia and Art, the name of Mr. Walton is, and will long continue to be recognized as that of a man whose inventive powers have placed within the reach of the great bulk of the middle and upper classes, a material peerless as a sanitary agent and of a beauty that need fear no rival."[13] For its sanitary qualities, Lincrusta-Walton was awarded a Gold Medal at the 1884 International Health Exposition in London.

Besides its hygienic properties, Lincrusta-Walton was also noted for its durability. The company advertised it as "Solid in Color! Solid in Relief! Solid in Value!" It was so strong, it earned a reputation as the "indestructible wall covering."[14] The early literature even suggested Lincrusta might be used for exterior work, but this claim disappeared by the 1890s. Still, as an interior decoration, it was considered a permanent form of wall and ceiling covering, "tested and triumphant," capable of standing up to any sort of abuse.[15] British architect A. S. G. Butler humorously underscored this in a 1942 memoir recounting his work as a building inspector in bomb-damaged London. He wrote of "the triumph of Lincrusta," adding, "I do not mean aesthetically, but quite the opposite, in a military sense. No material, I think, has stood up to blast so stoutly. The bumpy, adhesive skin on wall and ceilings, aping rich plaster work has counteracted many blows from bombs, even sustaining whole surfaces by itself."[16] Butler's comments, even though humorously exaggerated, testify to Lincrusta-Walton's reputation for durability.

Besides being tough and long-lasting, Lincrusta-Walton's flexibility and elasticity made it easy to hang. All it took was a mixture of one-third glue and two-thirds paste brushed thickly on the back. Gimp pins held the Lincrusta panel in place as the installer gradually pressed it to the wall, using his hands and a roller. Working from the center outward, he was careful to make sure no air bubbles were trapped or they might appear as blisters after the adhesive had dried. If blisters did develop, the workman could prick them with a pin to let the air out, and then with the aid of a heated iron held near the Lincrusta, gently press the material to the wall. Unlike wallpaper, Lincrusta would not tear while being hung and any soiled spots could easily be cleaned with soap and water. The only problem was that in cold weather Lincrusta needed to be warmed before hanging to regain its flexibility. The assumption was that professional paperhangers would do all this.

Along with its reputation for cleanliness, durability and ease in hanging, Lincrusta-Walton was also noted for its ability to imitate other materials. The first products simulated carved plaster and wood, embossed leather and metal. In 1906 the company introduced a successful imitation of ceramic tile and, in 1912, an improvement to earlier efforts to simulate oak dado that proved to be wildly popular.

Its imitative qualities made Lincrusta-Walton ideal for friezes, wainscoting, borders for frames, mirrors and fire screens, splash screens, finger plates, and decorative panels for doors, mantels, or furniture. Lincrusta's chief uses, however, were for walls and ceilings. A popular late-nineteenth-century treatment was to divide the wall into three parts—a cornice frieze on top, wainscoting on the bottom, and a filler or field in between. Lincrusta could supply it all (fig. 58). The cornice could imitate plaster, the filler embossed leather and the wainscoting oak. Although Lincrusta came in a limited range of colors, usually a plaster white, a buff and a chocolate brown, the decorator could use paint, stain, gilding, or glazing to create any number of special effects.

In 1884, Elizabeth Le Prince, professor of "Tapestry and Lincrusta Painting" for the New York Society of Decorative Art, wrote a small booklet on practical instructions for decorating with Lincrusta. She gave detailed formulae for creating the appearance of Cordovan leathers, Florentine bronze, tapestry, Boule work, ceramic tile and "other beautiful and artistic styles of decoration."[17] Le Prince directed her remarks to professional decorators as well as to women amateurs who might wish to develop their skills at Lincrusta decoration just as they had china painting. The range of Lincrusta's appeal ran from sophisticated professional adornment of hotels and upper-class houses to do-it-yourself middle-class residences.

Lincrusta-Walton appeared in almost every conceivable setting from homes to hotels to government buildings, lodge halls, railroad carriages, yachts and ocean liners. In 1883, the *London Times* described the decoration of the new Cunard liner, the *Servia:* "The main staircase is the largest ever constructed in a passenger vessel. At the bottom . . . are panels executed in polished maple and Hungarian ash; but the rest of the staircase is done in embossed ornamentation. For this purpose a new material, called Lincrusta-Walton has been employed with singularly good effect."[18] Later Lincrusta would also be used in the *Titanic.*

Walton began to market Lincrusta in the United States in 1879, but it did not achieve wide popularity in America until Frederick Beck bought the patent rights and began manufacturing it at a plant in Stamford, Connecticut, in 1883. Beck used testimonials from such well-known architects as James Renwick and Richard Morris Hunt to promote

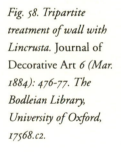

Fig. 58. Tripartite treatment of wall with Lincrusta. Journal of Decorative Art 6 (Mar. 1884): 476-77. The Bodleian Library, University of Oxford, 17568.c2.

Lincrusta-Walton. Renwick said it was "far superior to any wallpaper" and "the most valuable material for architectural and decorative purposes which has ever been invented." Hunt claimed, "Its many advantages, not the least of which is its comparative cheapness, will recommend it . . . to all interested in interior decoration."[19]

In the United States Lincrusta initially appealed to an upscale market. Examples include the John D. Rockefeller mansion in New York (fig. 59), the Pabst mansion in Milwaukee, and the California State Capitol in Sacramento. In 1886, the *Santa Fe Daily New Mexican* described the governor's rooms in the new territorial capitol building as being covered with Lincrusta-Walton of "various designs" which created "a most harmonious and really gorgeous effect." The Lincrusta decorated walls and ceiling of the senate chamber included a series of bronzed panels of cupids "engaged in all the industries known to modern times" and a frieze of thick foliage "in the shape of dates and palms." The reporter called it all a "novel" and "modern interior decoration."[20]

Besides mansions and state houses, Lincrusta-Walton also appeared in middle-class dwellings. In 1891, Philadelphia architect Frank Miles Day used decorative panels that convincingly imitated carved wood for the Harvey House in Radford, Virginia (fig. 60). In West Bountiful, Utah, Clarence and Effie Eldredge chose a Lincrusta imitation pressed leather for their parlor in 1904, while in Winston-Salem, North Carolina, the Ogden family selected an imitation oak Lincrusta wainscoting for their dining room and stairhall in 1912 (fig. 61).

Fig. 59. Lincrusta-Walton imitation leather hung in the dining room of the New York City home of John D. Rockefeller in the 1880s. Cooper-Hewett, National Design Museum, Smithsonian Institution/Art Resource, New York; gift of John Davidson Rockefeller, 1937-57-3.

By 1908, Sears, Roebuck and Company were advertising Lincrusta as a practical and "high class relief" decoration that would "last a lifetime." Far from the sophisticated glazing and decorative effects suggested by Elizabeth Le Prince's earlier booklet, however, the 1915 Sears catalogue suggested that a simple "coat or two of ordinary ready mixed house paint" might be applied to the Lincrusta if the consumer wanted to change the color. Sears also invited readers to compare prices, since its eighteen-inch-wide Lincrusta could be had for as little as thirteen cents a yard.[21]

In England, Walton also sold cheap versions of Lincrusta costing as little as a shilling a yard. In 1895, the company boasted that between January and July they had sold thirty tons of their new "ceiling designs in a cheap form."[22] But they also aimed at the higher end of the market by employing some well-known designers including Lewis F. Day, Christopher Dresser, and George Haité. Such famous names were necessary to win medals at the expositions and trade shows, and Lincrusta-Walton certainly won its share. The company claimed that although they employed "the leading designers of the day," they relied "upon the merit of the finished article for its sale rather than the names of the artists who designed them."[23] Still, the fame of these designers did not hurt. The *Journal of Decorative Art* recognized Walton's successful wide-market strategy in 1881: "Even the poorest households can have their walls made beautiful by Lincrusta-Walton, while those of unlimited wealth may indulge their taste and fancy to any extent." Lincrusta-Walton was a "beautiful, useful and permanent means of interior decoration."[24]

In France, Joseph Musnier had bought Walton's patents for Lincrusta-Walton in 1880 and set up a plant at Pierrefitte near Paris. In 1899, he worked with art nouveau architect-designer Hector Guimard to create special Lincrusta panels for Guimard's experimental

Castle Béranger (fig. 62). In 1903, Guimard again used Lincrusta panels for his *Style Guimard* pavilion at the international housing exposition in Paris. Besides this collaboration with avant-garde designers, the Compangie Lincrusta-Walton Française also supplied imitation wood paneling for numerous Parisian cafés and plasterlike panels for the interiors of French National Railroad cars. The company's products received a silver medal at the 1889 World's Fair and a gold at the 1900 exposition, both of which were in Paris.[25]

Lincrusta-Walton was probably the most widely used of all the embossed wall coverings and deserved its title of the "King of wall decoration." Its popularity, however, encouraged imitators, and other embossed materials soon appeared. The public appetite, at least in England, seemed to expand to consume whatever new versions manufacturers could supply.

ANAGLYPTA

Lincrusta-Walton's chief rival was Anaglypta, a paper pulp material developed by Thomas J. Palmer, the manager of Walton's London showroom. Palmer approached Walton in 1883 with the idea for a paper-based embossed covering that would be lighter, more flexible, and cheaper than Lincrusta. He thought it would be a complement to the older material. Walton, however, feared it would compete with Lincrusta and would have nothing to do with it. Later, Walton would regret his decision.[26] Palmer secured his own patent in 1886 and contracted with Storey Brothers of Lancaster to manufacture the new material. First shown in 1887 at the Manchester Royal Jubilee Exhibition, in the following year Anaglypta was available to the public. Palmer derived the name from two Greek words for relief carving.

To manufacture Anaglypta, cotton fiber pulp, about the consistency of thick cream, was spread on a traveling wire web where some of the moisture was removed. The pulp was then pressed between molded rollers which embossed the design. The material that emerged went by conveyer belt to the drying room and when thoroughly dry, was cut and rolled, ready for shipment. The process was quick compared to Lincrusta, taking only minutes to go from pulp stage to finished product.[27] For high-relief decoration, cast-iron plates die-pressed the pulpy material into decorative patterns. The panels were then taken to the drying chamber, dried and packed.

According to its manufacturer, Anaglypta differed from earlier embossed wallpapers "root and branch." First, high-quality cotton pulp rather than wood fiber was its base. Secondly, rather than embossing a sheet of paper, the cylinders and dies were used at the pulp stage. The paper thus had no "memory" of being flat and the resulting designs were crisper, firmer and did not lose clarity when pasted and pressed to the wall. The plasticity of the pulp also meant that Anaglypta could take on very deep relief. This was dramatically demonstrated in their popular imitation Jacobean ceilings with full pendant drops. Anaglypta was hollow so it was much lighter than Lincrusta and therefore more suitable for ceilings. When sized and painted, it was waterproof and could be gently cleaned, making it hygienic as well.[28]

In 1894, the Potter Company of Darwen, Lancashire, bought out the Storey Brothers to establish the Anaglypta Company, Ltd. at a new plant at Queen's Mill, Darwen. It named Thomas Palmer to its board of directors. The Potter Company was already one of the largest wallpaper manufacturers in England, so the acquisition boded well for Anaglypta's success. In 1897, just three years after the establishment of the new plant, *The Journal of Decorative Art* reported, "It is just a decade since the first public showing of Anaglypta. . . . So quickly did the new material 'catch on' that within two years of that time it had slipped into its place as one of the necessaries of a modern decorators establishment. It was as a ceiling decoration that Anaglypta in the early days made its great success. It seized the taste—and the pocket—of the public and literally jumped into vogue."[29]

Unlike Lincrusta, Anaglypta did not imitate a whole range of materials. It was primarily a substitute for plaster and an exceedingly effective one. The *Decorator* noted in 1904, "Anaglypta used intelligently for a ceiling has all the effect of a specially designed plaster ceiling which would, of course, cost a vast deal more besides causing the room to be closed and making a mess all over the house."[30] Anaglypta also came in patterns for friezes, dado and filler for walls.

Fig. 63. Christopher Dresser's Alahambra design for Anaglypta. Anaglypta and Salamander Decorations, 1909. Reproduced by permission of Crown Decorative Products, Ltd., Darwen, England.

Like Walton, Palmer also employed well-known designers. George Haité, Christopher Dresser, Owen Davis, Arthur Silver, and C. F. Voysey supplied patterns for Anaglypta (fig. 63). To catch the attention of decorators and win prizes at the exhibitions and trade fairs, the big name designers were a necessity. In actual practice, however, their work often did not sell as well as that of the company's own in-house designers.[31] Like Lincrusta-Walton, Anaglypta aimed at an upscale market where the big names would be important, but the company also produced designs for the whole market range and often advertised that they provided the "cheapest substantial relief decoration."[32]

There is little evidence of how Anaglypta fared in America. Unlike Lincrusta-Walton, no American manufacturer bought its patents. Import duties made it expensive, so surviving examples are usually found in the residences of the wealthy such as the Kearney Mansion in Fresno, California. Anaglypta never achieved the popularity in the United States that it had in Britain. In Great Britain, however, Anaglypta was so popular W. G. Sutherland quipped in 1893, that if Lincrusta-Walton was the "King of Wall Coverings," then Anaglypta was surely the "Prince Royal,"[33] but both had the competition of numerous pretenders to their throne.

TYNECASTLE TAPESTRY

Tynecastle tapestry was one of the competitors (fig. 64). William Scott Morton, an architect who set up a furniture and decorating firm in Edinburgh in 1870, created it. Morton became interested in fifteenth-century Spanish and Italian embossed leathers, and he sought a modern way to produce the same effects. Morton used a commission to complete the wall coverings for Lord Cadogan's library as an opportunity to experiment with leather facsimiles. He eventually developed a process to press paper pulp onto a canvas and emboss it with metal dies. Applied to panels, it was then painted and gilded. Tynecastle vellum was a related papier-mâché product embossed between metal rollers.

Several writers have given 1874 as the date for the invention of Tynecastle tapestry, suggesting it predates Lincrusta-Walton. The inventor's granddaughter, however, published several articles citing evidence that actual production was not well established until the 1880s, when Morton built a factory at the Albert Works in Edinburgh and took out his first patents. In 1882, he patented a "material for covering walls," and in 1885, an "Embossed Canvas for decorating walls." In 1892, he patented a method for fixing velvet to paper and embossing it and, in 1896, a method for achieving deeper relief for modeling canvas fabric.[34] While Morton's earliest experiments with embossing canvas began in the mid-1870s, they were done by hand and to special order. Not until the 1880s did he establish his factory and introduce mechanical production.

Morton sent his eldest son, William Stewart Morton, to the United States in 1889 to promote sales for Tynecastle tapestry. Equipped with samples and pattern books, he established an office showroom in New York, where he decorated the walls and ceiling with a variety of Tynecastle materials. His first sale was to the decorating firm of W. and J. Sloane for a client who bought twenty-two yards of a pomegranate design dado and frieze for $106.03, including a 25 percent import duty.

The younger Morton had arrived in America in July 1889. By December, he wrote his father recommending that they send out catalogues to the top architects and decorators

Fig. 64. Tynecastle
tapestry design for a
billiard room ceiling.
Tynecastle Canvas,
Vellum, Textures
catalogue, 1900, p. 137.
The Bodleian Library,
University of Oxford,
1784c17.

throughout the United States. He estimated they would need some twenty-three thousand
pattern books, and suggested British prices be converted at forty cents to a shilling, which
would include shipping and import duties.

The younger Morton had some success in America. He sold to such prestigious clients as
Cornelius Vanderbilt, J. P. Morgan, and Jay Gould. He could not, however, convince his father
to set up a plant for manufacturing Tynecastle in the United States. By 1890, when he embarked
on a two-month trip to secure clients and agents in other cities the import tariff had risen
to 50 percent. In Boston, Buffalo, Detroit, Chicago, St. Paul, Denver, Kansas City, St. Louis,
Cincinnati, Washington, D.C., Baltimore, and Philadelphia, Morton met with decorator firms,
left samples and pattern books, and arranged for agencies. When he returned to New York in
late December, he wrote his Boston agent, "We are about to close this office as it is evident that
our material can only be handled by the best decorators—especially as the duty is now 50% and
they can as easily deal direct with the Edinburgh house."[35] At the end of the month he returned
to Scotland.

The firm continued to deal with its American agents, and with others in Canada as
well, but the high cost of the material made it a luxury item solely for the wealthy. J. P.
Morgan chose Tynecastle tapestry for St. John's Church, Long Island, and Jay Gould ordered it for his villa in Paris. Tynecastle never had the breadth of appeal that Lincrusta-
Walton and Anaglypta enjoyed.

Other Embossed Wall Coverings

Besides Tynecastle tapestry, a host of other embossed wall coverings were also produced in the 1880s and 1890s. The Lincrusta-Walton Company itself developed a hollow-relief paper called Caméoid. D. M. Sutherland, the manager of the Sunbury factory, invented it in 1888, but production did not begin until 1896. Sutherland created Caméoid in the same year Palmer's Anaglypta reached the market. At first, Walton had no more interest in the former than he had in the later, but when Anaglypta captured a significant share of the market, Walton realized he needed a lightweight, cheaper, embossed paper to compete with it. A perceptive commentator observed that the Walton Company had always boasted that Lincrusta-Walton was "solid in all its expression, relief, colour, and value, so that their venturing on 'hollow' relief came as something of a shock to their friends."[36] But Walton had learned his lesson. Caméoid enjoyed a "large business" and a "wide circle of admirers."[37]

Cordelova, another embossed paper, started in Edinburgh in the 1890s. Subercorium, Calcorian, and Corticine wall coverings were rubber- and cork-based materials that made brief appearances in the 1880s and 1890s. Imitations of Lincrusta, they never achieved its success. Lignomur was the only American entry into the embossed-covering market. Based on a wood fiber pulp, it was first sold in 1880. The firm opened a London operation in 1886, but the Old Ford Company bought it out in 1896 and changed the formulae to a paper pulp base.[38] Old Ford also manufactured their own version of Lincrusta.

One of the last entries into the group was Salamander, which was introduced in 1896. Its advertisements declared it was made of "pure, natural asbestos" and promoted it for its fire proof qualities. One ad in the *Journal of Decorative Art* pictured a Dublin Hotel: the entire structure had burned but the Salamander ceiling was intact.[39]

In addition to these wood-, cotton-, and resin-based coverings, there were also embossed leather papers. The best-known were the Japanese. As W. G. Sutherland wrote in his 1893, *Modern Wall Decoration,* "Not the least remarkable of the developments which the opening up of Japan brought about was . . . the introduction of 'leathers.'"[40] Importers introduced them to Britain in the 1870s, but critics thought their designs "too Japanese." Alexander Rottmann set up a factory near Yokohama in 1884 to manufacture leather papers suited to European taste. The process entailed beating tinfoil into embossed mulberry paper to create the patterns. Coloring and several coats of lacquer made the metal look like gold and the background like leather. By the mid-1890s Rottmann, Strome and Company was sending "shiploads full" of the Japanese papers to Britain, North America, and Australia. The papers were convincing leather substitutes, but they were largely hand made and expensive compared to the other embossed materials. In the 1890s, a twelve-yard roll could cost between twenty and eighty shillings.[41]

The Wallpaper Manufacturing Company Combine

Market competition among these wall coverings was keen. In 1899, however, in a pattern common to big businesses in both Britain and America at the time, a combine called the Wallpaper Manufacturing Company (WPM) began buying up the independent manufacturers. In that year they acquired twenty-three wallpaper companies, including Anaglypta, Salamander,

Cordelova, and Lignomur. By 1901, production of the embossed materials was consolidated at the Queen's Mill plant in Darwen, Lancashire. In 1905, WPM acquired Frederick Walton and Company, but kept the Sunbury plant in operation until 1918, when they moved it to Darwen. At first, the individual companies were left some autonomy and published their own pattern books, but by 1920, Anaglypta, Lincrusta-Walton, and Caméoid were marketed together. In trade show booths and pattern books a combination of the materials was recommended: Lincrusta wainscoting with Caméoid filler and Anaglypta frieze and ceilings (fig. 65).

The WPM eventually owned thirty-one firms, 98 percent of the British wallpaper industry, including all the embossed coverings with the exception of Tynecastle.[42] WPM made trade agreements about prices and markets with the companies it had not been able to acquire, so competition was virtually eliminated. The firm, which became Crown Berger, and later, Akzo Nobel, continues to produce modern versions of both Lincrusta-Walton and Anaglypta at the Queen's Mill, Darwen plant.[43]

The Question of Imitation

Why were embossed wall coverings so popular in the late nineteenth and early twentieth centuries? Part of the answer is that they satisfied the public's desire for practical, durable, and economical interior ornament. The public also valued their hygienic qualities. Yet for all the praise that the trade press lavished on the embossed coverings, there is a recurrent defensiveness about their imitative qualities from both manufacturers and critics. Elizabeth Le Prince had noted in

Fig. 65. A combination of Lincrusta-Walton, Caméoid, and Anaglypta for a Jacobean design. Wallpaper Manufacturers Company Relief Decoration, c. 1920. Courtesy, the Winterthur Library: Printed Book and Periodical Collection.

her company-published booklet on Lincrusta-Walton that "it is urged by aesthetic writers that no imitative machine stamped ornament can be good. While we admit the theory and agree that no stamped Lincrusta can ever give to an art lover the keen pleasure to be found in the chasing of a 'Cellini' or a carving by 'Gibbons' or a 'Goujon;' we believe we are doing good work for art by making known that a material exists, within the reach of all, capable . . . of receiving an infinite variety of hand decoration."[44] A critic for the *Art Journal* defended Tynecastle tapestry in 1896 with the argument that "[it] is not a cheap and nasty material, it is like all good things, fairly high priced and extremely durable. . . . It is a worthy rival to the gilded leathers of the past."[45]

An obvious tone of apology and defensiveness about the materials pervades these comments—Lincrusta-Walton was not as real as a Gibbons carving, Tynecastle was not "cheap and nasty." The aesthetic writers Le Prince referred to were, of course, John Ruskin and his followers, who rejected machine-produced materials and condemned imitation. This theme had a long history in English aesthetic writing and carried over into the Arts and Crafts movement. William Morris once warned, "The real thing presently ceases to be made after the makeshift has been once foisted onto the market."[46] (See chapter 7 for further discussion of this point.)

The imitative nature of the embossed materials inspired not only apology, but sometimes out-and-out scorn. Lincrusta and Anaglypta were so popular in Britain and used so widely in middle-class dwellings, pubs, and public buildings, that ubiquity led to disparagement. A. S. G. Butler introduced his comments about Lincrusta standing up to German bombs by referring to it as "trashy decoration." He continued with mock regret: "It quite hurts me to think that something we have scoffed at for years has turned out to be an able ally in the fight. A pity it is so unattractive, especially when painted chocolate."[47]

Elite observers in the late nineteenth and early twentieth centuries obviously considered embossed coverings to be cheap substitutes for the real things. But the other side of the story is the materials' undoubted popularity. A closer examination of the arguments presented by their advocates reveals why the public so enthusiastically accepted them.

IN DEFENSE OF IMITATION

The claims made for embossed wall coverings are similar to those already encountered for concrete block, pressed metal, and linoleum. The chief argument was that they were better than the materials they replaced. They were, first of all, more durable. Lincrusta-Walton, for example, would not warp like wood, or be eaten by worms like paper; it was not cold like stone and would not absorb moisture like plaster or crack like leather. In other words, it was a new modern material that was superior to the things it imitated.

Advertisements and trade literature asserted over and over that the embossed coverings were better than plaster in particular. Plaster cracked, it produced dust, it was hard to clean. The 1904 advertisement for Anaglypta cited above pointed out that it not only had all the "effect of a specially designed plaster ceiling" but also would not require that the "room be closed" or that a "mess" be made all over the house when installing it.[48]

Cleanliness was another important feature of the embossed coverings. The late Victorian period sometimes seems obsessed with this issue. Products that could claim to be hygienic had a guaranteed market. All of the embossed materials made this claim, though Lincrusta-Walton was perhaps the most convincing. Lincrusta-Walton might have "many rivals when it came to aesthetics," said one observer in 1884, but it was "peerless when it came to the sanitary point of view."[49]

Embossed coverings were also promoted as being better than the materials they replaced because they were "modern." Rather than apologizing for them as products of industrialism instead of hand craft, promoters celebrated them for reflecting the modern age. They called Lincrusta-Walton the "new and beautiful development of industrial art."[50] They praised Cordelova for its imitation oak paneling that would enable the "decorator to undertake wood dadoes without calling in a cabinet maker."[51] In other words, machine production was better than hand production.

Another appeal of the embossed materials was that they offered ornament at a price consumers could afford. They were, therefore, "democratic." Lincrusta-Walton, for example, offered ornamental effects which "hitherto on account of their expense" had been "confined to a few grand buildings or to those of an age when loving and artistic labor could be obtained more easily and in greater quantities than now."[52] Lincrusta-Walton oak paneling and Anaglypta plaster effects provided the "look of oak and plaster but at a fraction of the cost."[53] An 1888 article touted Lincrusta-Walton and the other embossed wall coverings as "a modern idea, the products of a democratic age which seeks to chiefly ornament wall and ceilings in imitation of sculptures and reliefs of ancient times. Art in the past ministered to but a few who were lords of the earth. The temple and the palace were alone thought worthy of adornment. In the past it was the few only who were noble—in the future it will be the many and art is rapidly becoming democratic in the consequence."[54]

Embossed wall coverings emerged in the 1870s and 1880s as practical alternatives to other wall and ceiling decorative treatments. Lincrusta-Walton came first, patented in 1877 by Frederick Walton, but it was followed in 1886 by Anaglypta, a paper-pulp material that was much lighter and therefore better suited to ceiling ornament. Other embossed coverings, including the various Tynecastle products, as well as Caméoid, Cordelova, and Salamander, emerged in the 1880s and 1890s. The coverings gained wide acceptance, especially in Great Britain. In fact, it may be the popularity of these embossed wall and ceiling coverings that prevented pressed-metal ceilings from gaining the same acceptance in Britain that they enjoyed elsewhere.

Durable, clean, and modern, embossed wall coverings were the products of the industrial age. It is not surprising that the newly expanded middle class, largely created by the Industrial Revolution, would embrace the new products. Cheap, quick, and easy, these materials were also a practical and economical means to democratically expand the availability of ornamental effects.

CHAPTER 6

Grand Illusions:
Other Faux Materials

The materials discussed in the preceding four chapters were all mass produced with new technology between 1870 and 1930, but while they were the newest imitative architectural ornament, they were not the only forms available. Other faux materials, some of which dated from the eighteenth century or even earlier, were still being produced in the late nineteenth and early twentieth centuries. A few were factory made, but most still relied on hand craft. With one or two exceptions, these older ornamental forms did not achieve the same degree of widespread popularity as did concrete block, pressed metal, linoleum, and Lincrusta. But these other faux materials can offer further examples of substitute architectural ornament available in the 1870–1930 period. This chapter is about such lesser-known ornamental materials, their histories, methods of production, and the arguments used to promote and defend their imitative qualities.

COMPO

A material known as composition or, most commonly, as "compo," offered an inexpensive alternative to decorative wood carving. Although there were precedents for press-molded decoration in the Middle Ages and the Renaissance, the modern form of compo dates from the last quarter of the eighteenth century. Widely used for neoclassical ornament, it found its most famous proponent in British neoclassical architect, Robert Adam. Throughout the nineteenth century, compo remained popular for decorating mantels, columns, crown moldings, ceiling medallions, frames, and furniture. By the end of the century, large companies such as the Decorators Supply Corporation of Chicago sold it through trade catalogues.[1]

The formula for compo varied little from the eighteenth to the twentieth century. It was, as a 1914 decorator's book said, essentially "a putty like compound of whiting, glue, resin, and linseed oil." The author cautioned, "To make this material successfully requires considerable experience," but assured readers that picture frame manufacturers could supply it in bulk, an indication of one of its common uses.[2] To prepare compo, the worker mixed glue with resin and linseed oil to make a "batter." He then added whiting (a powdered chalk preparation) until he had a stiff paste, kneading the mixture with additional whiting to reach the desired doughlike consistency. By the turn of the century, kneading machines often did this last step.[3] Next, the manufacturer steamed the material to soften it before forcing it into hard wood or metal molds.

After drying, the compo ornament was softened again to give it greater flexibility and to reactivate the animal glue so the ornaments would stick to the substrate of a wooden mantelpiece or other piece of woodwork. Small brads sometimes reinforced the attachment. They could be punched down and concealed with more compo. After the final paint or stain, the compo ornament was a convincing imitation of carved wood or plaster.

In the eighteenth century and for most of the nineteenth century, compo ornamentation was entirely hand made. The most difficult part was the creation of the mold, which demanded a skilled artisan to cast or carve it. Once the mold negative was completed, any number of compo ornaments could be pressed from it. In spite of this reliance on skilled hand work, compo's widespread production in the eighteenth century and the repetitious nature of its design process foreshadowed the late nineteenth century's industrialized production of similar ornament, such as Lincrusta and Anaglypta. A few prolific early-nineteenth-century compo makers such as Robert Wellford in Philadelphia marketed their wares so widely that historians consider compo an early form of mass-produced ornament.[4]

Wellford, one of the best known of the American manufacturers of compo, emigrated from England in 1797 and established his Original American Manufactory of Composition Ornaments in Philadelphia in 1800. From 1800 to 1836, he supplied compo decoration for cities up and down the East Coast, including Charleston, South Carolina—a place historian Mark Reinberger says had "more compo per acre" than any other city in the United States.[5]

Wellford's advertising claimed, "A cheap substitute for wood carving has long been desirable for some situations, particularly enriched mouldings, etc. and various were the attempts to answer the purpose, the last and most successful is usually termed Composition Ornaments." Composition not only offered a "good embellishment at a moderate price" but also resembled "in some degree the art of printing and engraving."[6]

By the "art of printing and engraving," Wellford may have been referring to the production of inexpensive, multiple copies that imitated more expensive originals. Not everyone could afford an original painting, but "the art of printing and engraving" had made images such as John Trumbull's *Battle of Bunker Hill* or Gilbert Stuart's portraits of Washington widely available to a mass audience. So, too, compo decoration reproduced designs associated with sophisticated, elite, stylish ornament and made it available to a larger public.

Compo was extraordinarily popular for Federal-style ornaments in early-nineteenth-century America. And, when various eclectic styles became popular at mid-century, mold makers created ornament in the Rococo, Gothic, and Italianate styles. At the end of the century, Tudor, Jacobean, and Arts and Crafts interiors also included compo elements. In 1902, architects T. J. Collins and William G. McDowell included compo ornaments on the mantels of a Queen Anne–style house they designed in Lexington, Virginia (fig. 66). Many early-twentieth-century oak mantels or stair newel posts might have machine cut or pressed wooden details, but the delicate garland and its hanging ribbons were probably compo, grained and stained to convince everyone it was wood.

The Decorators Supply Company, founded in Chicago in 1893, was one of the largest manufacturers of such ornament. Their 1906 120-page catalogue of composition ornament claimed that 50 percent of the capitals, brackets, and ornaments shown were "kept in stock ready for immediate shipment." For special orders, they needed only ten days. The company had twenty branch offices in major United States and Canadian cities and claimed to

*Fig. 66. Compo
ornament on a 1902
mantelpiece in
Lexington, Virginia.*

be "equipped and have experience in handling contracts of the largest size in any portion of
the country."[7] They are still in business today.

In the twentieth century, compo ornaments were very popular for Depression-era movie
palaces and were used for the 1938 coffered ceiling in the National Archives library.[8] But
with the streamlined modernism of the post World War II era, compo use declined; by the
mid-twentieth century it was almost forgotten. The late 1960s and early 1970s preservation movement has renewed interest in composition and revived business for the few companies that still make it.

IMITATION PLASTERS: CARTON PIERRE, PAPIER-MÂCHÉ

With the popularity of the eclectic revival styles in the late nineteenth century, compo, plaster,
and other materials which imitated plaster were often sold by the same firms. In 1918, the
Lombard Company of New York advertised "plaster and compo ceiling centers, moldings
and capitals."[9] Jacobson and Company, also of New York, put out a catalogue in 1928 of
"Old English" ceiling designs imitating those in houses such as Audely End, Burton Agnes
and Hardwick in a "variety" of materials.[10] In a catalogue that probably dates to about 1900,
the famed English firm of George Jackson and Sons advertised ceilings made of "carton-
pierre, papier-mâché, and patent fibrous plaster."[11]

The Jackson firm, by tradition, traces its founding to George Jackson, one of Robert Adam's
carvers. They originally specialized in composition ornament. By the early nineteenth century
they had added carton pierre and papier-mâché to their line. Papier-mâché is the general term

for any three-dimensional object made from paper or paper pulp.[12] Its history can be traced to the origins of paper itself, but it first appeared as an architectural feature in the seventeenth century. Builders and decorators used it extensively in the eighteenth century, as in the famous example of Horace Walpole's Strawberry Hill, where many of the "Gothick" quatrefoil vaults and their star and rose bosses were in papier-mâché. Across the Channel, a French publication in 1788 stated, "The English cast in cardboard (*'carton'*) the ceiling ornaments that we make in plaster: they are more durable; break off with difficulty or if they do break off the danger is nil and the repair cheap."[13] In the New World, George Washington asked his London agent about papier-mâché ceilings in 1771, and papier-mâché ornaments adorned the Miles Brewton House in Charleston in the 1760s.[14]

Curiously, although papier-mâché is composed of two French words meaning "paper" and "chew," the term itself may not have originated in France. When it appeared in a French publication for the first time in 1778, it was cited as coming from an English source. Modern scholars think the name probably originated among French émigrés working in English papier-mâché factories in the eighteenth century.[15]

A passage in an 1828 biography of the sculptor Joseph Nollekens supports this theory. The biographer reported a conversation between a Mr. Twigg, a fruit seller in Covent Garden, and Mrs. Nollekens. Mr. Twigg remarked that a certain London house had been the home of two old French women who had come to England to chew paper for the manufacturers of papier-mâché. Mrs. Nollekens replied, "Ridiculous!" since "the elder Mr. Wilton . . . was the person who employed people from France to work in the *papier-mâché* manufactory, which he established in Edward-street, Cavendish Square." But Mr. Twigg insisted that these two women had chewed paper, buying cuttings from stationers and bookbinders and "produced it in that way, in order to keep it a secret, before they used our machine for mashing it."[16]

While Twigg's claim that old French women actually chewed paper for papier-mâché is suspect, the factory in Cavendish Square referred to by Mrs. Nollekens was one established in the 1720s by William Wilton, father of the noted English sculptor Joseph Wilton. Twigg's comments suggest that while the technique of using paper for ornament came to England from France, the English had developed the production process. Charles Bielefeld, an important early-nineteenth-century papier-mâché manufacturer, would later assert that while the French may have used papier-mâché for snuffboxes and small articles, it was in England that the material was first used for architectural purposes.[17]

Papier-mâché was usually made of recycled paper which was either pulped or layered with a binder of glue or gum arabic. Sometimes flour, sawdust, plaster, or resin was added to the mix. By the early nineteenth century this was done by steam-powered machines. The material was then pressed into molds, and the excess water drained. The finished product was waterproofed and hardened with linseed oil and then dried. Pulp could also be made into pasteboard slabs with the aid of machines which kneaded the pulp and then pressed it through rollers to achieve a uniform thickness. Laminated layers of paper were also used to make pasteboard.[18]

Carton pierre was one version of papier-mâché which depended on a fully pulped paper fiber. Hardened with glue, whiting and gypsum plaster as well as alum and flour, it was lighter than plaster but heavier than papier-mâché.[19] It could be cast in molds into ornamental forms. One writer described it in 1879 as having "been used very largely in France for many years . . . but not so long in England." He also claimed that in Berlin, carton pierre had been used for "statuettes and other sculpture."[20]

In Dublin in 1754, Augustin Berville advertised his version of papier-mâché, which he called a "Pasteboard Stuccoe." He claimed it had "as much Boldness, Relief and Beauty, as that of any other Stuccoe [ornament]" and could be used for ceilings "without sullying or hurting the Furniture or lumbering the Room." It was also "by much the cheapest and not subject to split or crack, or fall."[21] Though this eighteenth-century product was made largely by hand processes, the arguments as to its advantages as an imitative substitute for plaster are much the same as those that would later be made for Anaglypta, Lincrusta-Walton and even metal ceilings.

Inventor and manufacturer Charles Bielefeld marketed an "improved papier-mâché" in the 1840s, which he said was vastly superior to the eighteenth-century product. He did not reveal the details of manufacture or his exact ingredients but claimed that with the aid of steam power, his new papier-mâché was distinguished by its "hard compactness, its strength, its imperishable nature, its tractability" as well as "lightness" and "finally its cheapness."[22]

Bielefeld first developed his papier-mâché for cornice decorations at St. James's Palace "on the accession of his late Majesty," William IV in 1830. Bielefeld wrote that while his new papier-mâché had been used in such impressive buildings as the Carlton, the Oxford and Cambridge Club houses, and the British Museum, it was also popular for ceiling centerpieces and interior cornices in "the smaller class of private dwellings, the erection of which the increasing population of the country is requiring in almost every town in the kingdom."[23] Besides furniture and ceiling ornament, his papier-mâché was also used for theatrical decoration.[24]

Papier-mâché was produced and distributed by firms such as Bielefeld and George Jackson and Sons throughout the nineteenth century. Like the embossed coverings of the 1880s and 1890s discussed in chapter 4, papier-mâché could be colored and stained to imitate plaster, wood or leather.

Many of the late-nineteenth-century paper-pulp embossed coverings were essentially modern versions of papier-mâché. Their formula and manufacturing processes varied, but the basic material and concept were the same. Recounting the history of such decorations in 1904, one observer made the connection between eighteenth- and early-nineteenth-century versions of the ornament and its modern forms when he offered brief descriptions of carton pierre, papier-mâché, and compo, and then went on to say, "Today the sale of decorative relief wall hangings is enormous" and "words have been added to our vocabulary that our fathers dreamt not of—Anaglypta, Lignomur, Tynecastle Tapestry and Cordelova" (see chapter 4).[25] Today, Anaglypta, the modern descendent of papier-mâché, is the only paper pulp-based architectural ornament still on the market.

ARTIFICIAL MARBLES

Besides compo and papier-mâché, another material with a long history as imitative architectural ornament is artificial marble. Although there were precedents in antiquity for using pigmented plaster to imitate marble, it was in the late sixteenth and early seventeenth century that scagliola, the best-known form of architectural artificial marble was invented. Although historians differ on the details, David Hayles attributes scagliola's origins to the Fistador family in Munich.[26] The process was known in both Italy and Germany, though it was largely kept secret until the eighteenth century. The architects and decorators of the Bavarian Baroque were particularly exuberant in their exploitation of scagliola for spectacular color effects in columns, altar pieces, and ceiling ornament. By the early nineteenth century, the process was known throughout northern Europe, and English craftsmen were equally as adept as the Austrians, Germans, and Italians in creating scagliola.[27]

Architect James Wyatt is usually given credit for one of the earliest uses of scagliola in England for his columns in the 1772 Oxford Street Pantheon. They were reported to be of "a newly invented composition which rivals the finest marbles in colour and hardness."[28] Robert Adam used scagliola for the anteroom floor of Syon House, 1762–65, because the slow-setting nature of the material made it ideal for inlaying patterns.[29]

In the United States, scagliola appeared in important public buildings such as the Capitol and the old Baltimore City Hall, but a variation on the technique, called "marezzo," was even more popular since it was less elaborate and cheaper. Examples of marezzo include the state capitol buildings of New Jersey, Kentucky, Pennsylvania, Mississippi, and Montana. Marezzo was so widely used in the United States that it was sometimes called "American Scag."[30]

The traditional techniques for making scagliola and marezzo are complicated. The work was done entirely by hand by skilled artisans who were often secretive about their methods. The basic formula for scagliola called for plaster of Paris, animal glue and natural pigments. The craftsman prepared differently colored batches and mixed them to the consistency of bread dough. He then pressed together the "loaves" and sliced them to reveal variations in color and texture. He next brushed on dry pigmented plaster to create darker veins between the color sections. The sections, called "breche," he then placed in a softer plaster mixture, which served as the matrix for holding it all together. Chips of hard plaster and alabaster were also sometimes added. The worker then cut the conglomerate of breche, plaster, and stone to a uniform thickness, usually about one-half inch, and applied it to a prepared plaster backing. If the material was to be molded, it would be pressed into the molds at this point. The key to the process was that the material dried slowly, since the animal glue retarded the hardening of the plaster of Paris. That gave the craftsman several hours to manipulate it. Eventually, however, it dried into a very hard, stonelike finish which was planed and polished.[31]

While scagliola was made face up, marezzo was made face down. Composed of similar materials, the initial plaster mixture for marezzo was more like the consistency of heavy cream than bread dough. The veining was produced by placing pigmented skeins of silk into a mold. Background colors were applied by dripping, pouring, splattering, and so on, to imitate marble. When the right thickness was achieved, the silk skeins were pulled through the mixture leaving a pigmented trace that imitated marble veins. The mixture was then dried, a plaster and scrim backing was added, and it was removed from the mold. Any gaps were filled and the surface was honed and polished just as in scagliola.[32]

Different artisans had their own subtle variations on these techniques, but all were dependent on the slow setting of the plaster, a factor sometimes difficult to control. One of the most important nineteenth-century developments in the making of artificial marble was the introduction of Keene's cement. Patented in England in 1838, this fine, hard-drying plaster was very slow in setting, giving the craftsman more time to manipulate the material. Most American scagliola and marezzo was made with Keene's cement or a similar "patent plaster."

The American Art Marble Company of Philadelphia advertised in 1906 that "Artificial

Marble is well known to Architects and to the general Building Trade, as a scientific reproduction of fine natural marbles in colored Keene's Cement," and it warned that its customers should not confuse it with the "old-fashioned scagliola," which was fragile. They claimed their material could not "be distinguished from the original marble" and their reproductions were better because they were of "moderate cost," came in "sizes larger than can be obtained in natural stone," and were "stronger and more homogeneous than most real marble." The company offered experienced craftsmen to erect and finish the work, boasting that their factory was "the largest and most complete," and their staff and equipment the "most modern and efficient in the country." Among the buildings their artificial marble adorned were Wanamaker's Department Store in Philadelphia, The Hotel Jefferson in Richmond, Virginia, and the Senate Chamber in Trenton, New Jersey.[33]

Besides the Philadelphia American Art Marble Company, there were many other American manufacturers, including the Artificial Marble Company and the Mycenean Marble Company, both of New York, as well as the Pamelston Company of Chicago. Employing a familiar rhetoric, they all claimed to have the "best equipped plants" and the "most skilled workmen." They also said their marble was indistinguishable from the real thing and better than natural stone since it was cheaper, easier to use, and more adaptable to the architect's needs.[34] These are the same arguments used for other imitative materials in the period. Unlike concrete block, metal ceilings, linoleum, and Lincrusta, however, few aspects of artificial marble making had been mechanized by the end of the nineteenth century. It was still labor intensive and largely dependent on skilled hand work. Moreover, it was not mass produced. Most of the manufacturers did not keep marble ornaments in stock but instead made them by special order for each project.

Besides scagliola and marezzo, other artificial marbles also made brief appearances in the 1870–1930 period. In 1902, a British Company advertised "Moreau Marble," which they claimed was "not a composition" but a "natural, soft, white limestone" quarried in blocks and hardened and "converted into marble by a patented process." In its soft state, the limestone was carved into the desired shape, then colored and baked before being put into an "indurating bath." The company claimed that the process was a "skillful and up-to-date abbreviation of nature's own method, reducing the time required for making marble from many centuries to a few days." The marble produced was "equal to Nature's own," hard, durable and capable of taking a high polish.[35] It may have been, but aside from a few advertisements, very little is known of its production, manufacture or use.

"Sani Onyx" was another artificial marble advertised in the 1920s by the Marietta Manufacturing Company of Indianapolis (fig. 67). Described as a "modern vitreous building material of far greater strength than either marble or tile," it was "fused from rock ingredients at 2600 degrees Fahrenheit." Its makers recommended it as a covering for walls, floors, ceilings and wainscoting, and added, "We cannot too strongly emphasize the fact that Sani Onyx isn't an inferior makeshift material. It is a superior substance with distinct advantages not shared by any other product. Sani Onyx has come to *supplant* not to substitute."[36]

Other advertisements boasted that Sani Onyx would not crack, chip, check, or discolor, was easy to clean, and would outlast the building it was installed in. "Don't confuse Sani Onyx with commonplace marble, plaster or tile. It's a brand new revolutionary material,

Fig. 67. Sani Onyx advertisement. The Building Age and National Builder *49 (Apr. 1927): 40. Hagley Museum and Library.*

bringing colors, surface textures and effects never before possible with any material."[37] Although advertised in the 1920s and pictured as a ceramic-like material, Sani Onyx disappeared from the building journals in the following decades.

Another type of artificial marble was terrazzo flooring. Made with small pieces of marble or other stones embedded in a Portland cement matrix, it was often laid in decorative, colorful patterns with metal strips separating the sections. When hardened, the floor was ground and polished to a smooth, stonelike finish.[38] Terrazzo manufacturers claimed a lineage from antique mosaic floors, but the modern version probably owes more to the eighteenth-century Venetian technique called *paviemento alla Veneziana,* in which marble fragments were laid in a cement base. Introduced to the United States in the late 1890s, terrazzo was sometimes called "concrete mosaic." The L. Del Turco and Brother Company of Harrison, New Jersey, was the first to subdivide the surface with brass divider strips. Before that, the floors were laid as monolithic slabs and consequently were vulnerable to cracking. The metal strips served to form decorative patterns as well as to relieve stress. The introduction of electric grinders in the late 1910s was a boon for the industry, which had previously relied on hand polishing.[39]

Terrazzo was very popular for 1920s and 1930s Art Deco– and Moderne-style floors, since curvilinear patterns could be produced by the metal strips and colored stones. "Terrazzo, the flooring of the centuries" a 1923 advertisement claimed, was "equal in beauty and durability to any flooring," low in cost, sanitary and capable of "endless variety of architectural treatment."[40]

Marbleized slate was another type of artificial marble. Popular from the mid-nineteenth century to the early twentieth, especially for Eastlake-style interiors, it was made by using paint to create marble designs on pieces of slate. One guidebook described the process as a "transferring" method in which colors and "Japanese gold-size" were mixed in turpentine and floated in a tank of water. Workmen used a feather to agitate the surface and create the mottled, marbleizing patterns. They then lowered pieces of slate, precut to form the parts of the mantel, to the surface. The marbleized pattern transferred from the water to the stone. The slate pieces were then "stoved" to bake the colors to the surface and "drive away moisture." The guidebook writer concluded, "This, of course, is essentially a process for manufacturers, and is quite outside the scope of the painter who aims at truer effects."[41]

An 1880 catalogue from one such manufacturer, the Keystone Slate and Soapstone Works of Philadelphia, claimed, "Marbleized Slate has established its claim as an object of beauty and utility and is now fully acknowledged to be superior to marble." Its chief advantages were that it would not stain like marble, was easier to keep clean and "was more enduring." But most of all it was cheaper. The Enterprise Slate and Soapstone Works, also of Philadelphia, made this point in an 1886 catalogue: "Having gained public esteem through its intrinsic merits," marbleized slate mantels made it possible for "persons in moderate circumstances" to "indulge aesthetic taste, or embellish their homes with a lavish display in faithful imitation of costly marble" which, if done in natural stone, would "exhaust the coffers of a millionaire."[42]

Expense may have been a consideration for post–Civil War Washington College when marbleized slate mantels were chosen for the house built for the new president, Robert E. Lee, in 1868 (fig. 68). The Lexington, Virginia, college tried to economize in the project, but it was not "cheapness," but stylish modernity that the local newspaper editor noted when he toured the completed home: "We are particularly pleased with the mantels. They are made of slate and beautifully designed in the manner which has lately come into vogue."[43] He also reported that the mantels had been made in the larger nearby city of Lynchburg and supplied to the building contractor by a local hardware and general merchandising firm. The mantels remain in fine condition today.

ARTIFICIAL STONE

Chapter 1 focused on the history of concrete block, a material that especially in its rockface form could be considered an artificial stone. A more specialized version, however, often called "cast stone" also appeared in the late nineteenth and early twentieth centuries. The basic idea was the same: a mixture of cement, water, sand, and aggregates was shoveled or poured in molds and cast into ornamental forms. The difference was that "cast" or "artificial stone" required a refined mix of Portland cement and a much higher quality of stone, often granite or marble, for the aggregate. It was popular for exterior wall veneer, sculptural, and ornamental features. In fact, almost any type of architectural feature from consoles to capitols, or building blocks to whole columns, could be made with artificial stone.[44]

In 1868, Chicagoan George Frear received one of the first U.S. patents for a cast stone.

Fig. 68. Marbled slate mantel in the Lee House, Washington and Lee University, Lexington, Virginia. Photograph by Sally Mann for The Architecture of Historic Lexington, Historic Lexington Foundation.

The Pacific Stone and Concrete Company of San Francisco, also active in the late 1860s, operated under a patent from Frederick Ransome. With the development of American brands of Portland cement in the last three decades of the nineteenth century, the number of U.S. patents for cast stone multiplied. An important early-twentieth-century firm was the Benedict Stone Company founded by James Benedict in 1919. He had an office in New York and a plant in West Chester County, but moved the operation to Chicago in the 1920s, when his firm received the commission to build Soldier Field. They also had an office in Montreal. In 1930, Benedict formed a partnership with the Dextone Company for making decorative cast-stone work.[45]

Also called art stone, *béton,* and composite stone, the process used to manufacture cast stone was similar to that of concrete block. The cement, aggregates, sand, and water were mixed and poured into a mold in either a dry or wet mixture. Sometimes a decorative outer layer with pigment and special aggregates such as granite or marble chips was cast around an inner core. The piece was then removed from the mold and "cured" to harden.

To create the illusion of marble veining, dye-soaked strings were sometimes placed in the mold and then removed before casting, leaving the pigment markings in the mold to be absorbed by the cement. Marble veins could also be simulated by painting directly on the newly cast stone, or by not thoroughly stirring the concrete mix after adding pigment.

The cast stone could also be cut after casting to add sculptural detail (fig. 69).[46] That was probably what a 1901 Cretan Art Stone advertisement referred to in calling its cast-stone

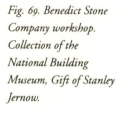

Fig. 69. Benedict Stone Company workshop. Collection of the National Building Museum, Gift of Stanley Jernow.

mantels "hand-carved": "Modeled after masterpieces with the color, texture and serviceable characteristics of any natural stone, Hand-Carved Cretan Stone Mantels lend a substantial elegance unattainable in wood, tile, or brick, yet the cost is little greater."[47] In general, cast stone was laid up with mortar exactly as if it were natural stone.

In the building slowdown of the 1930s Great Depression, many cast stone companies turned to precast concrete products such as burial vaults and manhole covers in order to stay in business. Their specialized, handmade ornament could not compete with the increasing mechanization of the concrete block and precast concrete industry. The companies either adapted or disappeared.[48]

TERRA COTTA

Since antiquity, builders have used fired clay for architectural features, but the term "terra cotta" (baked earth) dates from the eighteenth-century revival of the medium. The most famous eighteenth-century example was "Coade Stone." While Mrs. Coade called the gray or buff-colored substance she produced an "artificial stone" and kept the formula for it secret, modern analysis has shown it to be a form of terra cotta.[49]

Eleanore Coade and her mother (who was also named Eleanore) established their business in Lambeth, England, in 1769. Earlier historians assumed that the mother ran the business, but Allison Kelly has recently proved that the daughter Eleanore was in charge. Although Eleanore never married, she used "Mrs." as a courtesy title for a woman in trade.[50] In 1771 when a former manager misrepresented himself as her partner, Eleanore Coade advertised that she was the sole proprietor. Her 1821 obituary recorded that she was both the proprietor of the company, and the inventor of Coade Stone.

Mrs. Coade's stone differed from other artificial stones because it contained no cement. A specially created ceramic mix, it was cast in molds and then fired in a kiln. Ingredients included clay from Dorset, grog, flint, crushed stoneware, sand, and soda-lime-silica glass. The resulting highly vitrified product was extremely weather-resistant. In appearance Coade Stone was almost indistinguishable from fine-grained limestone.[51]

Eleanore Coade's 1784 catalogue advertised 778 different Coade Stone items ranging from figures, busts, capitals, vases, and urns to chimney pieces. In her London showroom, called Coade's Gallery, opened in 1799, the public could view samples and pattern books. Among her well-known English customers were architects Robert Adam, Sir William Chambers, Sir John Soane, and John Nash. In America, Charles Bulfinch and Benjamin H. Latrobe, among others, used Coade Stone. When Eleanore Coade died in 1821, her business went to a cousin. He and his successors operated it until 1843 when they sold all the molds and stock. The secret formula was lost from 1843 until modern scholars reconstructed it.[52]

In spite of its adoption by well-known architects, Coade Stone sometimes met the same objections that would later greet other imitative materials. Coade's wayward former manager, a man named Picot, published a booklet in 1770 in which he tried to establish his claims to the material. In discussing the difficulties of getting workmen to accept artificial stone, he noted that the masons were "decrying the material," claiming that "'Nature must be better than art; it [artificial stone] is but an imitation, a meer [sic] makeshift. Is it not more to your credit to have real stone than to stick up earthenware?'"[53]

Michael Stratton's recent study of terra cotta shows that by the 1880s critics were of two opinions about the material. From one point of view, terra cotta was a development of brick and ceramic modeling, while from the other it was a substitute for stone. If the former, it was generally acceptable; if the latter, it was often considered a "deception." In 1870, the *Building News* referred to the terra cotta decorations of the new Victoria and Albert Museum (Fowke and Sykes, 1864–67) as "sham columns in a casing of crockery."[54] The editors thought terra cotta another example of High Victorian makeshift materials. Others, however, claimed terra cotta was better than stone since it resisted the corrosive and dirtying effects of smog, was more fireproof, and offered more stylistic possibilities. It was also cheaper than carved stone.

James Doulton, the pottery manufacturer, described terra cotta as "that class of ware used in the construction of buildings which is more or less ornamental and of a higher class than ordinary bricks, demanding more care in the choice and manipulation of the clay and much harder firing, and being, consequently, more durable and better fitted for moulded and modeled work."[55] Prominent examples of its use in London besides the Victoria and Albert Museum include Alfred Waterhouse's Natural History Museum, 1871–81, and the Savoy Hotel extensions by T. E. Collcutt, 1904–5. In the later example, Doulton's Carraraware, a white-glazed ceramic block, imitated the elegance of marble, but supplied a hard-surfaced, more durable covering for the steel-framed building. In its reddish tones, terra cotta was also extremely popular for more modest houses and churches.

America was home to some early experiments with terra cotta architectural features in the 1840s and 1850s. Architect James Renwick collaborated with a sewer-pipe manufacturer to develop terra cotta for several architectural projects, but the enterprise proved unprofitable. Despite other attempts at manufacture and the use of imported British terra cotta by some architects, the material was not widely accepted in America until the 1870s.

Chicago became the center for the growing industry in that decade, in part because of the Great Fire of 1871. Terra cotta proved itself a fireproof material and was in great demand for rebuilding of the city. The Chicago Terra Cotta Company was established in 1861. In the 1870s, its head, Sanford Loring, invited British manufacturer James Taylor to help him develop the company. Taylor dismissed the firm's earlier products as "a clay imitation of an iron imitation of a cut stone."[56] He thought they should make whole building facades, not just vases and window hoods. Loring and Taylor advertised terra cotta details and completed buildings in their catalogues. They developed a successful business supplying terra cotta for such notable architects as William LeBaron Jenny. As successful as the firm was initially, financial problems resulted in liquidation in 1879. Its employees, however, immediately organized another company that eventually became Northwest Terra Cotta. They worked for many of the Chicago School architects and by 1900 were the largest manufacturer of terra cotta in the United States.[57]

By one 1880 estimate, 95 percent of all American terra cotta came from Chicago companies. In the next two decades, however, important firms opened in Boston, New York, and New Jersey, several of them with the technical expertise of James Taylor, who became known as the "Father of Terracotta in America."[58]

The National Terra Cotta Society published a set of standards for construction and installation in 1914. Paralleling the development of concrete, the industry organized,

Fig. 70. Eberhart Garage,
Gettysburg,
Pennsylvania. National
Terra Cotta Society,
brochure series, The
Garage, vol. 5, 1915, p.
29. Hagley Museum and
Library.

professionalized, and increasingly mechanized in the early twentieth century. By the 1910s, many companies advertised stock terra cotta as well as special orders made to individual architect design. Particularly in its glazed form, sometimes called faience, terra cotta was popular for modest commercial buildings such as garages (fig. 70) as well as major structures such as Cass Gilbert's 1913 Woolworth Building.[59]

Stratton claims that Americans were far less critical of terra cotta's aesthetic qualities than the British. The American press seldom referred to "shams." Perhaps by the time terra cotta was widely used here, it was an accepted material with such a distinguished reputation, that it was not considered imitative. When there were criticisms, however, it was usually over the gray-colored terra cotta that seemed closest to stone. American critics thought it too British, preferring the redder hues, and later, the glazed surfaces.

Marbling and Graining

Most of the materials discussed thus far in this chapter were manufactured. Though many required individual, skilled handicraft, by the late nineteenth century, most were factory- or workshop-produced and marketed with catalogues and national advertising. There is another form of imitative ornament to consider that is not so much a material as a treatment—the imitation of marble and wood by illusionistic painting. Individual craftsmen usually created these effects for special order on site. Although some industrial techniques were applied to this art form in the late nineteenth century, by and large, it remained a hand craft.

Marbling was the more ancient of the two techniques. It appeared on Mycenean pottery, and in Egyptian and Roman architecture. Descriptions of marbled pillars and arches were also recorded in thirteenth-century England. But the heyday for painted imitations of marble was in the Renaissance and Baroque periods when illusionistic painters lavishly marbled churches and palaces all over Europe. For his Sheldonian Theater in Oxford (1669), for example, Sir Christopher Wren used elegantly painted marbled wooden columns.[60]

In America, the Virginia House of Burgess adopted a resolution in 1707 requiring the woodwork and wainscoting in the General Court to be "painted like marble."[61] Nina Fletcher Little found painted imitations of wood, marble and stone in "all manner of buildings" in New England in her important study of the eighteenth- and early-nineteenth-century versions of the art form.[62] Laura Philips has documented an extraordinary group of nineteenth-century marbled houses in North Carolina.[63] Ann McCleary found surviving work of one particular late nineteenth decorative painter in the Valley of Virginia.[64] Virtually every state architectural survey offers abundant examples of surviving nineteenth-century marbling on mantels, stair risers, baseboards, and wainscoting.

Nineteenth-century house decorators' guides often claimed that while marbling was an ancient craft, the art of imitating wood graining was much younger. Historian Ian Bristow traces its origins in England to the sixteenth century. Much practiced in the seventeenth century, graining as well as marbling fell out of favor in early-eighteenth-century England, but returned to favor by the mid-eighteenth century.[65]

In America, graining seems to have been practiced throughout the eighteenth century, but was particularly popular in the early nineteenth. Guidebook author Peter Nicholson listed marbling and graining as one of the four branches of the house painter's art in his 1823–25 volume.[66] There is ample documentation for graining in America. Thomas Jefferson hired Richard Barry to grain the woodwork at Monticello in 1805, paying him thirty dollars a month for a year and a half's work.[67] In 1815, E. W. Hudnall, a New Canton, Virginia, decorative painter, offered his services to a client claiming to be "a first rate house-painter, and most faithfully promise you to execute your painting in the most elegant state." He proposed that the "Chimney pieces shall be of various marbles, wainscuting [sic] of marble, stone-colours, and mahogany, with elegant borders, the Doors Mahogany. The whole of the painting to be varnished and pollished [sic], I will also guild [sic], and paper." Hudnall promised that his "colours shall never fade, and may be washed and always kept clean."[68]

In 1846, a writer in *Scientific American* claimed that the art of decorative painting "has probably never been so much in vogue as at present. Imitations or pretended imitations of oak, maple, mahogany or marble, may be seen on three-fourths of the doors of houses in the cities, besides wainscoting, chimney pieces and furniture."[69]

Andrew Jackson Downing recommended graining in his 1850 *Architecture of Country Houses,* saying that while the "most satisfactory wood-work or wainscot" was that "composed of native wood of the district where the house is built. . . . As a substitute, however, we would strongly recommend that the wood-work be either grained in imitation of these woods, or, in the cheapest cottages, stained to have the same effect."[70]

As late as 1915, one guidebook proclaimed, "A painter takes pride and pleasure in executing a good specimen of graining; and the imitation of the graining of expensive and high-class woods is still a favorite method of embellishing woodwork that is subjected to hard wear."[71]

The widespread popularity of marbling and graining in the nineteenth century may have been one factor in John Ruskin's furious attack on the art form. In the *Seven Lamps of*

Architecture, he said, "Touching the false representation of material, the question is infinitely more simple, and the law more sweeping; all such imitations are utterly base and inadmissible. It is melancholy to think of the time and expense lost in marbling the shop fronts of London alone."[72] Later, in the *Stones of Venice,* Ruskin added, "There is no meaner occupation for the human mind that the imitation of the stains and striae of wood and marble."[73] Ruskin was, of course, one of the most important art critics of his day. (See chapter 7 for a fuller discussion of his ideas.) He abhorred machine-made ornament and rejected "shams" and deceptive imitations as dishonest. His condemnation of graining and marbling was something craftsmen could not ignore.

The British journal *Carpentry and Building* offered a "dissent from Ruskin's views" by publishing a letter in 1878 from a man from Manchester. The journal described the letter writer as "a practical man who has many supporters," while Ruskin was "the most eminent art theorist whom many also believe in, even to the extent of blindly following any canon he may promulgate without a too critical examination of its value."[74] Having thus sided with the practical man, against the eminent art theorist, the editors published the letter.

The practical man from Manchester first defended the art of graining and marbling as honest work, not pretense: "Neither pillar nor door of themselves ever pretended anything, and no grainer ever gave himself out as a marble mason or a cabinet maker. He uses real paint, colour and varnish." He then asked, If such painting is a deception, who is being fooled? "Neither the employer or the owner of the property is imposed on. They simply pay for painting, not real wood." He wondered why craftsmen should be condemned for supplying what their employers ask for: "When a gentleman furnishes himself with a wig, a set of artificial teeth, a glass eye, or a wooden leg, no one thinks of calling the useful artisans who furnish them liars or impostors."[75] Why should Mr. Ruskin do so to the honest craftsman who practiced their trade?

Other English writers on aesthetic matters like Owen Jones and Digby Wyatt defended the art of graining and marbling but recommended it only for certain treatments. The basic rule was: use it only where the imitated original materials would logically appear. Thus iron railings and rainwater spouts should not be marbleized because marble would never be used for such purposes. But in the appropriate places, especially when making an inexpensive wood like pine appear like a more expensive mahogany, decorative painting could be useful and attractive.[76]

The argument that imitative painting was not really meant to fool anyone appeared as early as 1833: "Recommended that all woodwork if possible be grained in some natural wood, not with a view of having the imitation mistaken for the original, but rather to create an allusion to it, and by a diversity of lines to produce a kind of variety and intricacy which affects more pleasure to the eye than a flat shade of color."[77] If graining was not an imitation, then it could not be condemned as a deception. Just as a landscape painter might create a mountain sunset, and everyone would accept it as art rather than imitation, so too the grainer who had raised his craft to the level of an art form could confidently say his work might be even better than the wood it imitated.

The author of a 1915 guidebook took this argument a step further in discussing examples of modern transfer papers with photographically reproduced wood grain (fig. 71). The craftsman was supposed to wet the paper, apply it to the wood, and rub off the graining pattern with a special roller. He thus had a design to follow in creating his wood effects. Was this better than the older tradition of hand work? That depended on the skill of the grainer. For small jobs where the worker was fairly unskilled, the writer thought it fine, but cautioned that the printed graining papers were "slavish copies, mere duplication of the originals and not evidence of the grainers' art."[78] The argument was that the true grainers' art was something more than imitation. It might allude to a familiar or costly wood, but exact duplication was not the goal, nor was deception. By extension, the author was also calling into question the role of mechanical reproduction and championing the hand work of the artisan over the "mere duplication" of the camera.

THE ART OF IMITATION

The art of imitation has a long and distinguished history as this brief survey has shown. Many of the materials discussed here originated in antiquity; most of them made their modern appearance in the eighteenth century. Unlike concrete block, sheet metal, and linoleum (but with the exception of terra cotta and compo), these were not, in general, mass-produced items. Most remained primarily hand crafts practiced by trained artisans for special order. Yet some form of factory production and popularized marketing affected nearly all of them by the end of the nineteenth and beginning of the twentieth centuries.

Interestingly, the arguments used to attack and defend the imitative qualities of these faux materials in the eighteenth and early nineteenth centuries were strikingly similar to those used later for modern products. "Cheapness" was a recurring theme. Imitative materials were good because they cost less, and economy was the primary motive for production. Robert Wellford, for example, argued that compo supplied a long-felt need for a cheap substitute for wood

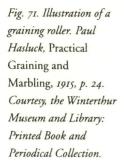

Fig. 71. Illustration of a graining roller. Paul Hasluck, Practical Graining and Marbling, *1915, p. 24. Courtesy, the Winterthur Museum and Library: Printed Book and Periodical Collection.*

carving. When Berville boasted of the quality of his papier-mâché ceiling ornament in 1754, he claimed it was an obvious choice because it was cheaper than plaster. Artificial stone, marbleized slate, and terra cotta were cheaper than natural stone. Though other qualities might be championed, the material's cheapness was always a primary factor to recommend it.

Arguments about durability were almost as frequent as those about expense. Like the claims made for concrete block, pressed metal, linoleum, and Lincrusta, all of the faux materials discussed here were purported to be better than what they imitated, not only because they cost less, but also because they held up better. The American Art Marble Company claimed its artificial marble could be produced in larger sizes and was stronger and more homogeneous than the natural stone. Terra cotta was better because it resisted the corrosive coal-smog of London and was fireproof. Sani Onyx would not crack, chip, check or discolor, was easy to clean, and would "outlast the building."

The heart and soul of all the debates over imitation, however, whether they took place in the eighteenth, nineteenth, or twentieth centuries, dealt not with expense or durability, but with the propriety of imitation itself. It is fascinating to find that as early as 1833, defenders of illusionistic graining could argue it was not "pretense" because it fooled no one. This cannot be extended to all these materials; many made a point that their imitation was so good no one could tell the difference. But the statement that graining could be an "allusion" rather than an "illusion" echoes arguments later made in defense of concrete-block and sheet-metal ornament.

Whether or not it was proper for art to attempt to imitate nature was an issue raised in 1770 in Picot's report of masons' objections to Coade Stone. "Nature must be better than art" they claimed. Any mechanical imitation of nature produced mere "makeshifts." Ruskin would later agree with them. But this idea was not always shared in the nineteenth century. The makers of Moreau Marble claimed they had simply used science to "speed up" nature's natural process, a reflection of a fundamental tenet of nineteenth-century ideology—the idea of human progress. People could make things better. They could even improve on nature by the application of science to industry. To make a new material was to demonstrate the power of human ingenuity. That is why Sani Onyx claimed it had come to "supplant" not "substitute." It was a "revolutionary" new material that could do things natural stone could not. It was better because it was "modern."

All of these arguments deserve a fuller discussion, not only within the context of the faux materials considered here, but also within the context of the industrialized, mass-produced materials that form the core of this study. The aesthetic issues and the social implications of the debate over the appropriateness of imitation are the subject of the concluding chapter.

CHAPTER 7

Substitute Gimcrackery:
Aesthetic Debates and Social Implications

> [A tasteless] new middle class society . . . accepted substitute gim-
> crackery for traditional materials and ideas.
>
> —ADA LOUISE HUXTABLE, 1960

As the previous chapter revealed, the debate over the appropriateness of "substitute gimcrackery" began in the late eighteenth century, though its fullest and most vociferous expression appeared in the mid- to late nineteenth century.[1] While faux materials have a long
history, the Industrial Revolution's creation of a virtual flood of machine-made ornament
spurred the calls for "honesty" in architectural forms and the condemnation of "deceptions."
Anti-industrial critics such as A. W. N. Pugin, John Ruskin, and William Morris were the
most articulate in rejecting "sham materials," but others in England and America joined
them. The rejection of the machine and the call for a return to hand craft were also part of
the Arts and Crafts movement of the late nineteenth century.

While some critics rejected the machine, others foresaw the possibility that art and industry might work together. British industrial designer Christopher Dresser, writing in the
1870s, thought educational reform would create artists who could accommodate the nature
of the machine and improve the quality of industrial products. Later, American architect
Frank Lloyd Wright also called for a new design mentality that accepted and exploited
machine potential.

Against this vocal, public debate by critics, designers, and architects, ordinary people
simply went on buying the "substitute gimcrackery" and delighting in its cheap, quick, and
easy properties. Advertising literature suggests some of the reasons for the popular acceptance of the new ornamental materials. It promoted them as cheaper, more durable, cleaner,
and easier to use than traditional decorative forms. But promoters also championed the new
materials as expressions of modernism, democracy, and progress—values with deep cultural
meaning in the late nineteenth and early twentieth centuries.

Imitative architectural materials were the products of the vast industrial and social
changes that occurred between 1870 and 1930, and they were also expressions of that change.
The debates over their aesthetic propriety and the social implications of their manufacture

and use are the subjects of this concluding chapter. To understand why these materials were so popular and what they represented to the people who made and used them, it is necessary to consider the ideological context of the period.

AESTHETIC DEBATES: AUGUSTUS WELBY NORTH PUGIN

The 1770 comments of the stonemasons who condemned Mrs. Coade's stone as "meer [*sic*] makeshifts" suggest that even in the late eighteenth century there was some rejection of imitative architectural materials. But only in the early nineteenth century, in the face of the expanded use of manufactured ornament, did the debate gain full force. No longer merely the grumblings of workmen who feared for their jobs, criticism of imitative decoration was taken up by nineteenth-century critics and architects who called for "honesty" in architecture and did so in influential publications.

One of the earliest and most important writers to question machine-made ornament was the noted Gothic revival architect, Augustus Welby North Pugin (1812–52). In 1841, in *True Principles of Pointed or Christian Architecture,* Pugin condemned modern Gothicizing achieved by the shortcut of allowing cast iron to imitate stone. "Cast-iron is a deception," he wrote. "It is seldom or never left as iron. It is disguised by paint, either as stone, wood, or marble. This is a mere trick, and the severity of Christian or Pointed Architecture is utterly opposed to all deception: better is it to do a little substantially and consistently with truth than to produce a great but false show."[2] The "true principles" of the Gothic demanded honest workmanship, authenticity in materials, and appropriate purpose. For Pugin, any disguise was dishonest.

Besides iron, Pugin also objected to plaster and composition ornament. "Painted like stone or oak," they were "mere impositions" and "utterly unworthy of a sacred edifice." He declared, "We should never make a building erected to God appear better than it really is by artificial means." Those "showy worldly expedients" were only suitable for "theatricals, mountebanks, quacks, and the like."[3] He also objected to marbling and graining, condemning them as "vile imitation."[4]

Pugin's warning that "trick and falsehood" might appear "rich and beautiful in the eyes of men" but would never escape "the all-searching eye of God" was repeated by the *New York Ecclesiologist* in 1848, when they criticized the painted marbling and graining effects used in the Chapel of the Cross in Chapel Hill, North Carolina. The decorative painting on the altar was condemned as "childish folly." Paraphrasing Pugin, the editors declared, "By painting wood like marble, or imitating stone in plaster, we cannot, it is needless to say, deceive God, however we may expect to impose upon our fellow men."[5]

In his monumental account of the use of color in British interiors between 1615 and 1840, Ian Bristow argues that marbling and graining were revived with such enthusiasm in the late eighteenth and early nineteenth centuries in both Britain and America, that part of Pugin's and others objections to them stemmed from the sheer excess of the practice.

Pugin, like all reformers, was railing against what was commonplace. If the practice was not common, there would be no imperative to rail against it. Pugin also suggested that imitative ornament represented inappropriate social overreaching: "Cheap deceptions of magnificence encourage persons to assume a semblance of decoration far beyond either their means or their station, and it is to this cause we may assign all that mockery of splendor which pervades even the dwellings of the lower classes of the society. Glaring, showy . . . ornament was never so much in vogue as at the present; it disgraces every branch of our art and manufactures, and the correction of it should be an earnest consideration with every person who desires to see the real principles of art restored"[6]

As many critics have pointed out, one result of the widespread availability of cheap ornament was the democratization of decorative forms. Anyone could afford it, all could have it.[7] Pugin and others complained that the cheap, gaudy ornament was in bad taste and its proliferation threatened to corrupt the public's standards for good art. The implication was that it also threatened existing class and social structures. In a society sensitive to nuances of rank and privilege, the embrace of cheap, showy, imitative ornament seemed a temptation not only for the lower classes but also for the upwardly mobile middle class and the nouveau riche.

Pugin complained that Britain's new industrial wealth had spawned a profusion of ugly modern buildings in which imitative decoration abounded: "England is rapidly losing its venerable garb; all places are becoming alike; every good old gabled inn is turned into an ugly hotel with a stuccoed portico, and a vulgar coffee-room lined with staring paper, with imitation scagliola columns, composition glass frames. . . . Timbered fronts of curious and ingenious design are swept away before the resistless torrent of Roman-cement men, who buy their ornaments by the yard, and their capitals by the ton. . . . Mock stone columns are fixed over a front of plate glass."[8]

The list of imitative materials that Pugin condemned in 1841 was already impressively long. It included cast iron, plaster, composition, scagliola, painted marbling and graining, and artificial stone. By the latter half of the century, there would be many more machine-made decorative forms, and Pugin's essential arguments would be repeated by others as the aesthetic debate continued. Probably his most important contribution to the ensuing discussion was the moral fervor of his call for honesty of materials and for a return to craftsmanship. His claim that machine-made ornament was inherently inferior because it was false and because it was common would be echoed by other reformers, in particular by the man who was considered the most important art critic of his day, John Ruskin.

JOHN RUSKIN

Unlike Pugin, John Ruskin (1819–1900) was not a practicing architect but an art critic. Son of a prosperous sherry merchant, he had inherited a substantial fortune that allowed him to pursue his interest in the arts. Educated at Oxford, he returned there in 1869 as the first Slade Professor of Fine Art. Ruskin's writing on art and architecture was so prolific and so influential that he became what some have called the "aesthetic czar of the Anglo-American world."[9]

Ruskin's most important architectural criticism is contained in two books: *The Seven Lamps of Architecture,* 1849, and *The Stones of Venice,* first published in 1851 and expanded in 1853. Although he scarcely acknowledged his debt to Pugin, Ruskin made a similar call for moral honesty in architecture. Like Pugin, he championed the Gothic over the Classical and believed that architecture reflected the age that produced it. But Ruskin went further, asserting that art and architecture could actually improve society. In a kind of "moral environmentalism" he held that art not only reflected but caused the moral temper of the time.[10] An honest worker would make honest ornament, but an honest, moral, Christian style of architecture would also help make happy, honest workers.

One of the keys to Ruskin's rejection of machine-made ornament was his belief that workers must have pleasure in their work. That was not possible when machines made "slaves" of people, divided their tasks into small, repetitive parts, and denied them the joy of creation. True art was hand made, with the skill, talent, and intelligence of the artisan shaping its free, natural form. Machine-made ornament, on the other hand, was inherently false.

Ruskin argued further that any architectural form that set out to deceive was morally reprehensible, including such hand-produced decorative techniques as marbling and graining. "Touching the false representation of material . . . all such imitations are utterly base and inadmissible," he proclaimed. "It is melancholy to think of the time and expense lost in marbling the shop fronts of London alone, and of the waste of our resources in absolute vanities, . . . which do not add one whit to comfort, or cleanliness, or even to that great object of commercial art—conspicuousness."[11]

So much for marbling. As to the "wretched labors of the 'Grainer,'" Ruskin declared, "There is not a meaner occupation for the human mind than the imitation of the stains and striae of marble and wood. . . . I know not anything so humiliating as to see a human being, with arms and limbs complete, and apparently a head, and assuredly a soul, yet into the hands of which when you have put a brush and pallet, it cannot do anything with them but imitate a piece of wood."[12]

For Ruskin, art had to combine the skill of the hand and the labor of the mind. To simply imitate a piece of wood or marble was not only useless, mindless labor, it was morally wrong because the intent was to deceive. "Intent" was the key. Ruskin defined two types of deception. One was "surface deceit," as when someone induced the appearance of "some form or material which does not actually exist; as commonly in the painting of wood to represent marble, or in the painting of ornaments in deceptive relief, etc."[13] The other was "operative deceit," that was, the "substitution of cast or machine work for that of the hand":[14]

> One thing we have in our power—the doing without machine ornament and cast-iron work. All the stamped metals, and artificial stones, and imitation woods and bronzes, over the invention of which we hear daily exultation—all the short, and cheap, and easy ways of doing that whose difficulty is its honor—are just so many new obstacles in our already encumbered road. They will not make one of us happier or wiser—they will extend neither the pride of judgment nor the privilege of enjoyment. They will only make us shallower in our understandings, colder in our hearts, and feebler in our wits.[15]

Ruskin felt that machine-made ornament was both inherently bad work and dishonest. The beauty in ornament came from the human labor and care spent on it: "Its true delightfulness depends on our discovery in it the record of thoughts, and intents, and trials, and heart-breakings—of recoveries and joyfulness of success."[16] Even if one could not see all this at a glance—and Ruskin conceded that a paste imitation might seem as bright as a real diamond to the untrained eye—still, "a woman of feeling would not wear false jewels." So too, a "builder of honor" should "disdain false ornaments." To use them would be "an inexcusable lie" as well as a "vulgarity, an impertinence, and a sin."[17]

As these last comments make clear, Ruskin was writing for his own class. He felt it was the responsibility of people with wealth and power to be good consumers, to demand honest work, and to take the responsibility for creating working environments in which good work could be done.

In an 1859 lecture on "Manufacture and Design," Ruskin addressed himself to the manufacturers, telling them it was their business to "form the market, as much as to supply it." He warned that if they were "short-sighted and reckless" for wealth and tried to "attract attention by singularities, novelties, and gaudinesses" they would never produce good design. They might "by accident snatch the market; or, by energy command it," but the whole of their lives would have been spent "corrupting the public taste and encouraging public extravagance." They would have succeeded only in "retarding the arts, tarnishing the virtues, and confusing the manners" of the country.[18]

Ruskin's contributions to the anti-imitation debate were twofold. He intensified the moral argument about the deceitful nature of imitative ornament, and he placed the antimachine argument in the context of social reform of industrial practice. Ruskin's emphasis on the worker's happiness, on an environment in which labor would not be degrading, and on the responsibility of manufacturers to bring this about, would all be influential for his successors, in particular for William Morris.

But Ruskin was first concerned with art. The virulence of his critique of the taste of his contemporaries and of their embrace of gaudy abundance arose from his fear that art itself would be cheapened. At heart, it was an elitist argument that the rapid expansion of the middle class would bring not only confusion in the social ranks but also a loss of elite standards, perhaps even the loss of the ability to judge what was good in art.

These fears would be taken up by Ruskin's contemporaries and followers. Among the most influential were Sir George Gilbert Scott and Charles L. Eastlake.

Scott and Eastlake

Many consider the architect Sir George Gilbert Scott (1811–78) as Pugin's successor in extending the Gothic revival style into the High Victorian period. Scott published *Remarks on Secular and Domestic Architecture, Present and Future* (1858) in part as a plea for the pointed Gothic in domestic building. He argued that architects should think of the Gothic not as an antiquarian style, but as one adaptable to "every change in the habits of society" including new materials and systems of construction. Every "invention or improvement, whether artistic, constructional, or directed to the increase of comfort and convenience" could be accommodated by the style.[19]

As open to new materials as this might sound, however, Scott had no use for imitative ornament. He condemned the use of plaster as the "grand vehicle for the abominable and contemptible shamming which has degraded the architecture of our age." He found both wood and plaster imitations of stone "monstrosities" that were "beneath contempt." He feared that the practice of "shamming" had become so common that architects accepted it as if it were a part of the Gothic style.[20]

Scott declared that "as in morals nothing is so certainly indicative of a degraded state of society as the decline of truthfulness and the prevalence of deceit." So also in art, "the surest signs of degradation" were the "general adoption of systems of deception or sham." This was particularly so in domestic architecture where the "taste for counterfeits" was "so deeply rooted."[21]

Scott complained that rather than being mortified by this, many people had found "the perfection to which we have brought the art of shamming" a "thing to be proud of,—one of the great results of England's freedom,—and that the liberty of shamming is as much one of our national bulwarks, as liberty of the conscience or of the press."[22] Stucco that made brick houses look like stone, "plaster, wood or paper painted to look like marble and granite," metal made to look like wood, and wood that looked like metal—all were objectionable to Scott. Whatever potential new materials might have, they were, nonetheless, degraded by "being made to pander to the universal preference for falsehood over truth."[23]

Scott's arguments are interesting for several reasons. First, they extend Ruskin's critique of imitative forms by speaking of specific practices. Second, they make clear how common, even universal, those practices were. For all the supposed power and authority of nearly twenty years of first Pugin's and then Ruskin's condemnation, imitative materials had become so commonplace that champions of England's industrial progress claimed them as a source of national pride. Scott found himself a minority voice decrying this development. His attacks against a "system so inveterate" in English culture, he complained, had brought not reform but only "low and silly sarcasm" and vilification in response.[24]

In letters to popular architectural journals, contemporary mid-nineteenth century defenders of faux ornament had argued that if imitation was acceptable in one instance then it would be hypocrisy to condemn it in another. Thus, if critics like Scott and Ruskin accepted gilding, allowing wood to look like gold, then why object to making a cheap wood look like a more expensive wood, or plaster like stone?[25] The letter writers also cited ancient practices such as stucco or marble veneering as precedents that allowed for modern imitation. Painting itself was offered as a form of imitation, "representations of foliage or flowers" being as "much an imitation as grained wainscot." The gist of the defenders' arguments was that Scott's objections to shams were "a mere piece of idle purism reducible *ad absurdum.*"[26]

Ruskin had condemned imitation on the basis of a Christian critique of honesty, but Scott answered his opponents with a more abstract principle of morality. One might start a letter "Dear Sir," he argued, without any feeling of friendship, but that did not mean that the exact line between truthfulness and deception had become so difficult to discern that truth had ceased to exist. "The fact, however, is" he declared, that the difference between truth and falsehood is usually "distinct and patent to the most ordinary apprehension." As in personal ethics and morality, so too in art, the boundary between right and wrong was clear; anyone who had the "desire" to discern it could. The great demarcation was the *"intention to deceive."*[27]

Scott conceded that the homeowner with imitation stone walls and grained doorways might not actually mistake the material for real stone or high-class wood, or think that anyone else would be fooled by the imitation either. Still, the homeowner had chosen to participate in a system that had deception as its purpose. He was, Scott claimed, like a man who had "become so inured to lying, that his most frivolous remarks" were "garnished with petty falsehoods" from mere habit. "The whole system of marble-papers in halls, marble and granite-painting on shop-fronts etc., etc. is of the latter class,—a sort of petty lying without wishing to be believed." If "the principle of truth and reality" were acknowledged, then all such falsehood would be inexorably rejected.[28]

Moral principles, then, should guide architects and builders as well as consumers as they made their choices. "All ages have had their gimcracks," Scott declared, but if one wanted to be ranked with "rational beings," then "for goodness sake let us . . . not enshrine ourselves and our children in temples of falsehood."[29]

Another formidable taste-maker of the mid-century who rejected imitative, machine-made ornament was Charles L. Eastlake, author of the popular home decorating advice book, *Hints on Household Taste* (1878). Eastlake followed Ruskin's principles of condemning deception, but put them in easy-to-read, straightforward, practical terms. Why, he asked, paint a cheap wood to imitate oak? "Everybody can see at a glance that it is not oak, and as far as appearance is concerned, there are many modes of treatment which would be far more effective." He went on to suggest staining and varnish for doors which would reveal the natural veins of the wood, or painting with a solid color. Both would protect the wood and both would be "more honest and artistic" as well as "a less expensive style of decoration."[30]

Eastlake pointed out that when floorcloth was first introduced to the country it was often made to imitate marble and parquetry. He had even seen "a pattern which was intended to represent the spots on a leopard's skin." These were absurd conceits. Floorcloth, "like every article of manufacture to which design can be implied, should seem to be what it really is, and not affect the appearance of a richer material." What was acceptable for floorcloth design? Any variety of "geometrical diaper" would do better than the "foolish expedient of copying the knots and veins of wood and marble." Floor-covering patterns should, in all cases be flat and not imitate relief. He also cautioned that even in geometric patterns care should be taken to avoid too many bright colors. They might look good in the shop, but ought to be avoided for the private home.[31]

As for hallways, Eastlake noted that in "former days when wood was cheaper than it is now, oak panels were commonly used." But now "when both marble and oak are beyond the reach of ordinary incomes, the usual practice is to cover the walls with a paper stained and varnished in imitation of marble." This was, he thought, a more "excusable sham than others to which I have alluded; but still it *is* a sham, and ought therefore to be condemned." He suggested modern encaustic tile as an affordable and attractive substitute for marble flooring and oak wainscoting.

Eastlake's comments about marble and oak being cheaper and more commonly used in former days but now being "beyond the reach of ordinary incomes" is an interesting case of class confusion. Even in "former days," people with "ordinary incomes" rarely had marble floors and oak wainscoting; only the wealthy did. Mid-nineteenth-century middle-class homeowners used paper marbling and graining not because they could no longer afford the real thing, but because they now had the means and the ambition to try to imitate their betters.

Why did Eastlake present his admonition in such a light? Earlier, Pugin and Ruskin knew they were writing for their peers, the educated bourgeois elite, and did not hesitate to condemn both materials and people who pretended to be something they were not. Eastlake, however, was writing directly to a new middle class that was not always sure of its taste. He did not want to alienate his audience. He wanted to convince them, to better their taste and to improve the appearance of their homes. Thus he subtly created a flattering fiction that at one time his readers might have afforded real marble and wood. Since no one of "ordinary income" any longer could afford such things, the practical solution was not to imitate marble and wood with cheaper materials, but to choose modern alternatives like encaustic tile.

Both Scott and Eastlake extended Pugin's and Ruskin's arguments about the rejection of imitative materials. Scott applied the abstract idea of morality to the problem while Eastlake presented practical advice and alternatives. As important as both of them were, however, their influence seems dwarfed by the impact of the writing and artwork of William Morris.

WILLIAM MORRIS

As William Morris lay on his deathbed in 1896, it is said, someone inquired of his doctor what the great man was dying of and the doctor replied, "Of being William Morris." Architect, artist, designer, business man, preservationist, poet, translator, publisher, socialist, reformer—Morris was all this and more. Born in 1834, the son of a stockbroker, he inherited wealth enough to pursue his wide-ranging interests. At Oxford in the 1850s he met many of the people who would be involved with the Pre-Raphaelite brotherhood and his later Morris and Company enterprises. Trained as an architect, Morris soon abandoned that profession for the more general pursuits of artist and designer. In 1861 he set up Morris, Marshall, Faulkner and Company, Fine Art Workmen in Painting, Carving, Furniture, and Metals. Morris bought out his partners in 1875, and as sole owner made Morris and Company one of the leading decorating firms of the period.

Deeply influenced by Ruskin's writing, Morris extended the older man's ideas by applying them to a secularized vision of society. "The essence of what Ruskin taught us," Morris wrote, was "that the art of any epoch must of necessity be the expression of its social life, and that the social life of the Middle Ages allowed the workman freedom of individual expression, which on the other hand our social life forbids him."[32] Morris was taken with Ruskin's idea of art being "man's expression of his joy in labour."[33] Crucially, Morris democratized Ruskin's concept. All people had the right to work "which shall be worth doing under such conditions as would make it neither over-wearisome nor over-anxious."[34] Workers should have decent surroundings, ample space, good lodging, and some measure of control over their production. Like Ruskin, Morris felt that modern industry had removed the soul from labor by making machines of the workers. His critique was of industrial capitalism itself as the source of the problem; his solution was socialism.

In his own workshops, Morris involved his workers fully in the craft process. He did not abandon machines, however. Morris believed they could be useful, even necessary, to relieve drudgery. Recent historians have shown that earlier characterizations of Morris as a machine-hating Luddite were mistaken. Morris and Company contracted out some of their carpet and wallpaper designs to manufacturers who used power equipment to produce more affordable versions of the firm's products.[35]

In 1871, Morris even produced a design for a "Corticine Floorcloth." Corticine was a cork-based, linoleum-like floor covering which relied on polymerized linseed oil rather than Walton's oxidized version. While we do not know which company made the Corticine, there is no doubt that Morris contracted it out to a floor-covering manufacturer since the process depended on mechanization. In fact, the change from the labor-intensive production of floorcloth to the industrialized system used for linoleum or Corticine is a perfect example of what Morris meant when he said machines could relieve the drudgery of labor.

Still Morris was voluble in criticizing machine-made, cheap ornament that imitated handmade materials. He condemned it as "a ghastly pretense of ornament which is nothing but a commercial imposture."[36] Defending the art of weaving, for example, he dismissed modern mechanically made carpets as "makeshifts for cheapness' sake" and floorcloth as a degrading of the craft.[37] But he did not often single out individual architectural materials. Instead, he usually lumped them all together as part of the problem, finding modern building "hopelessly hideous and vulgar" with "feeble and trumpery attempts at ornament."[38]

To Morris the issue was not cast iron, plaster, or marbled papers; it was a problem with the system. He berated his countrymen for their willing acceptance of "makeshifts." In an 1894 essay, he declared that future generations would probably call this period the "Age of Makeshifts" and went on to illustrate why with examples such as modern bread made with wheat that had been reduced to a "white powder like chalk" produced by methods "imported from America," that "special land of makeshift." Along with the loss of hearty, grain-filled brown bread, Morris also lamented the substitution of margarine for butter; of drab, uniform, machine-made garments for more colorful, handmade clothing; and of standardized machine-made shoes for handmade ones that fit.[39] The point was that once the "makeshift" was "forced on the whole population" the "original and genuine article" ceased to exist.[40]

Morris devoted himself to making sure the "original" continued to exist by calling for the revival of hand craft. He became a powerful influence on the Arts and Crafts Movement. In 1888, he acknowledged that the revival of hand craft might seem an impossible task when measured again the "gigantic fabric of commercialism," but "taken in conjunction with the general movement towards freedom of life for all . . . and a token of the change which is transforming civilization into socialism, it is both noteworthy and encouraging."[41]

Morris thus extended the anti-imitative, antimachine argument with a critique of capitalism as the core of contemporary social evils. His own individual designs and the products of his company offered an alternative to machine-made ornament, even though his products were often so expensive that only the wealthy could afford them. Still, as extensive as his influence was, not everyone who took up Morris's design ideas was also ready to embrace his socialism. Many simply ignored it, especially in America. Nor were all design reformers quite as antimachine as Ruskin and Morris (at least in his writing) had seemed. The aesthetic debate would take another direction in the second half of the nineteenth century to a middle ground where art and the machine might be reconciled.

INDUSTRIAL DESIGN IN ENGLAND

A few critics thought the best response to the flood of machine-made, cheap ornament was not to reject the products but to reform their design. If manufacturers could be helped to create objects that would be not only cheap, practical, and durable but also beautiful, then the prestige of industry itself would be improved.

Parliament initiated one of the first efforts to do this in Britain by appointing a select committee in 1835 to investigate industrial design education. The committee concluded that Britain was "very much superior to foreign countries in respect of the general manufacture, but greatly inferior in the art of design."[42] Consequently, the government established the first national School of Design at Somerset House in 1837 and funded several regional schools as well. As promising as the idea seemed, critics later complained that the schools did not teach industrial design, but simply gave instruction in traditional fine art drawing. In fact, few of the instructors had any training in practical design at all.

The direction of industrial design education began to change in 1851, after what many thought was a poor showing of British design in the Crystal Palace Exhibition. Government reform of the schools of design was led by critic Henry Cole. He helped establish the Department of Practical Art under the Board of Trade and hired Richard Redgrave as the art adviser. Cole and Redgrave intended to provide commercial training for designers with a curriculum that included "Artistic Anatomy, Practical Construction, Wood engraving for ladies, Porcelain Painting, decoration of Woven Fabrics and Flat surfaces, and ornamental treatment of Metals." They also offered classes in "Practical Geometry, Carpentry, Masons' Work, Plastering and various branches of Constructive Architecture, Upholstery and Interior Decoration." Lectures on "History and style of Ornament" complemented all this.[43]

The practical training elements of the curriculum proved to be short lived. The apprenticeship system was still strong, and trade and manufacturers groups objected to what they saw as undue government interference in their business. A carpenter, plasterer, or upholsterer still had to learn the trade on the job, but the art student could learn how to create good designs for them for use.

The school moved from Somerset House to Marlborough House in 1852, and in 1857 to South Kensington. Funds provided for the purchase of decorative arts from the Great Exhibition helped to form the South Kensington Museum, the nucleus of what is today the Victoria and Albert Museum collection.[44] Cole and Redgrave considered the museum a means of educating both artists and the public about the importance of ornamental art. The educational program of the South Kensington Museum School also included annual exhibits and competitions where students from the regional schools could display their efforts.

Among the many well-known designers associated with the school and its reform ideas were Matthew Digby Wyatt, Owen Jones, Lewis F. Day, and Christopher Dresser. Dresser (1834–1904), perhaps the most important for this discussion, wrote extensively about his ideas for design reform. Born in Glasgow, the son of an excise officer, Dresser attended the School of Design at Somerset House. He gained early fame as a botanist, for which the University of Jena conferred upon him a Doctor of Philosophy degree in 1860.

Dresser wrote a series of articles in 1857–58 for the *Art Journal* on "Botany as adapted to the Arts and Art Manufacturers" in which he based his designs on principles he found in natural plant forms. He followed this original work with four books on ornament: *The Art of Decorative Design* (1862), *Principles of Decorative Design* (1873), *Studies in Design* (1876), and *Modern Ornament* (1886).

Unlike Morris, Dresser designed explicitly for machine manufacture. The leading industrial designer of his day, he provided both product and ornamental designs to over thirty British manufacturers. In 1899, a writer in the *Studio* called Dresser "perhaps the greatest of commercial designers" and a man who had "imposed his fantasy and invention upon the ordinary output of British industry."[45]

Dresser expressed his views on the importance of industrial design in an address he delivered to the Society of Arts in London in 1872. He began with a declaration that art had great commercial value. In fact, he claimed, decorative patterns on manufactured products were of greater importance than the objects themselves: "Bad note paper in a handsome wrapper sells; bad carpet, if it has a graceful pattern sells." In other words, no matter how good or bad the product might be, the artistic quality of its design sold it to the public. Manufacturers had to ensure the quality of the design of their products. Their economic interest required it.[46]

But Dresser's focus that night was not the importance of good design to manufacturers, it was the importance of educating designers to produce quality products. Striking a nationalist note, he declared, "Whatever hinders the progress of applied art stands in the way of our commercial success and militates against national progress."[47]

Dresser felt it was necessary to educate the public as well as the designer. He complained about consumers who were "utterly ignorant, having no art knowledge" and who were "pleased with whatever is 'loud' and showy." Their lack of taste encouraged manufacturers to "cater for the patronage of the most vulgar." But as a typical nineteenth-century believer in progress, Dresser thought that with public education, "this hindrance will disappear with the increase of art knowledge."[48]

Elsewhere Dresser made clear his strong objections to "the imitation of one material with another."[49] Echoing Pugin and Ruskin, Dresser decried sham materials. "Falsity and the untrue" were "natural adjuncts of immorality and vice."[50] He condemned graining, marbling, false marble pillars, fictive architectural details, even floorcloth when its patterns imitated carpet or matting. "These are all untruths in expression, and are, besides, vulgar absurdities."[51] One might find "imitation pillars, recesses, and arches" in "low music halls," where one would not expect "truth or any manifestation of delicacy of feeling." But in the "abodes of those who pretend to purity and truth" and in the "buildings which they frequent," such false decoration could not be tolerated.[52]

Dresser did not object to new machine-made materials, only to imitation. As earlier noted, Dresser supplied designs for linoleum, Lincrusta-Walton, and Anaglypta. So long as the patterns suited the nature of the material and followed natural principles of order, repetition, and proportion, good industrial designs could be produced. But artists must not simply imitate nature; they had to employ their creative imaginations. "A monkey can imitate, man can create."[53]

Dresser, perhaps, more than any other individual of his generation, elevated the status of ornamental design and adapted it for the machine. Decoration, "if properly understood," he wrote, "would at once be seen to be a high art in the truest sense of the word, as it can teach, elevate, refine."[54]

The *Art Journal* noted in 1883 that thanks to the influence of Dresser as well as Digby Wyatt, Owen Jones, and others, art critics no longer "scorned" the manufactured decorative arts.[55] Lewis F. Day, another prominent British designer of the period could also have been added to their list. In 1885, Day explained the difference between those who accepted the machine and those who didn't. The former, the more "modern" and "scientific" thinkers, looked "upon machinery as the key to everything that is hopeful for the future," while the latter feared that "the arts must eventually be crushed out of existence."[56]

Day did not think the two schools could be reconciled and staked out a position somewhere between them. He acknowledged that the "great mass of existing manufactured ornament is absolutely intolerable"; still, "it is not all bad, any more than it can be said all hand work is good." Dismissing Ruskin's and Morris's anti-industrial bias that good work came only from happy craftsmen content in their control over production, Day found no inherent reason to consider machine-made art "false in taste or unsatisfactory in effect."[57]

The ease of manufacturing ornament had sometimes meant excesses that led to the "association of the mechanical reproduction with cheapness, and to a corresponding nastiness." The "deepest wrong" that machinery had done to art was to make ornament "so easy to get that uncultivated persons" had unrestrained use of it. Like Dresser, Day believed that educational reform could create greater discrimination among manufacturers, designers and the consuming public. He quoted Morris's call for an art "*for* the people" and "*by* the people," but, he said, this "splendid dream" was more likely to be "realized by the aid of machinery than by any attempt to suppress" its use.[58] The machine was here to stay; it represented "progress." Artists had to take account of it.[59]

The reform platform of industrial designers like Dresser and Day was then that the machine could be a useful, even powerful tool to elevate the taste of the public. A concerted effort at art education was necessary for it to happen. For all their acceptance of the machine, they still rejected imitation and thought the aesthetic issue centered on class and taste. Poor work was "loud and showy," good work was simple, refined and true to the nature of materials. Imitation could only be false, vulgar and a dishonest sham.

AMERICAN ARGUMENTS

In America, meanwhile, two major exhibitions encouraged a closer alliance between artists and manufacturers—the New York Crystal Palace Exhibition of 1853 and the Centennial Exhibition held in Philadelphia in 1876. Like the British Crystal Palace Exhibition of 1851, these American displays were meant as celebrations of industrial progress.

In a small pamphlet called *Art and Industry* (1853), Horace Greeley, editor of the *New York Herald Tribune*, asked what lessons could be learned from the New York fair. He answered, "Stupendous as our advances have been in railroads, steamboats, canals, printing-presses, hotels, and agricultural implements—rapidly as we are growing in excellence in a thousand departments of design and handicraft—astonishing as may be our achievements . . . we have yet few fabrics equal to those of Manchester, few wares equal to those of Birmingham and Sheffield." American machinery was among the best in the world, but its ornamental design lagged behind the standards of Europe. Greeley thought "mere wealth" useless without the "refinements of wealth." If America was to be truly independent of other nations, it was in the national interest for its "ornamental and elegant appliances" to "keep pace with our external development."[60]

Twenty-three years later, the problem was still evident to critics of the American displays at the 1876 Philadelphia Centennial Exhibition. Art educator Isaac Edward Clarke noted a "relative inferiority of Americans in most of the production industries in which the fine arts enter as an important element." The application of "art to industry" was a problem Americans needed to address.[61]

British critics also thought American taste was in need of improvement. Christopher Dresser wrote in 1873 that "nowhere on earth is taste in matters of decorative art so depraved as it is in America." In speaking of carpet designs, he said, "Let the pattern be 'loud' and inharmoniously coloured, and the chances of its sale in the American market are great."[62]

Reformers believed art education could improve American standards of taste. A pioneering effort to do so was made in Boston in 1870 under the leadership of Walter Smith, professor of art education at the Boston Normal School of Art and Massachusetts director of art education. Smith campaigned successfully for state legislation that established public schools of industrial design in the state. Soon after that, the Massachusetts Institute of Technology in conjunction with the Lowell Institute initiated a "free course of practical design for manufactures."[63] By the 1880s and 1890s, most large cities boasted schools of practical arts and design, among them the Cooper Union for the Advancement of Science and Art in New York (1883), the Pratt Institute in Brooklyn (1887), and the Drexel Institute in Philadelphia (1890). All of them were committed to uniting art and industry.[64]

The effort to ally art education and industrial manufacture had some effect. In the early twentieth century, the George Blabon Linoleum Company was a corporate advisor for both the Pennsylvania Museum School of Industrial Art as well as the Philadelphia School of Design for Women, offering prizes for linoleum designs and hiring several of their graduates.[65] The Edwards Manufacturing Company of Ohio, a leading producer of pressed-metal ornament, advertised that their art director was an art school graduate. The larger linoleum and pressed-metal manufacturers usually had in-house design departments staffed by people trained in the professional schools. Free-lance designers regularly supplied ornamental patterns for the industries in the United States just as their counterparts did in England.

Americans seemed more accepting of machine production than Europeans were. And while Americans might be less sure of their taste, they were more willing to experiment with new materials. All of this is evident from the histories of the new materials laid out in the preceding chapters. It is also evident in what happened to the Arts and Crafts Movement in America.

The American Arts and Crafts Movement

Although the Arts and Crafts Movement in Britain was strongly linked to William Morris's socialism, in America, the ties between art and politics were looser from the first. Improvement in taste and revival of craftsmanship seemed to be the key issues for most American adherents. Some believed that mass production and the profit motive were at the root of the problem of poor design, but not the machine itself. To American designer Ernest Batchelder, it was a question of whether machines used workers or workers used machines. He declared that "if Mediaeval craftsmen could return to the world, they would welcome machinery."[66]

One of the most articulate spokesmen for the craftsman ideal in America was Gustav Stickley (1858–1942). As editor and owner of *Craftsman* magazine from 1901 to 1916, and as the master craftsman of his own guild association, United Crafts, as well as his own furniture firm, he did much to democratize the Arts and Crafts Movement. Stickley addressed himself to the professional and middle classes, calling for a simple style without the excesses of decoration popular in the Victorian period. He objected to machine-carved ornament as a sham, but, while his own furniture was largely hand made, Stickley never objected to machine production per se. He was also an active promoter of vocational education believing the worker needed to master the machine as a useful tool.[67]

Stickley published designs in his magazine for concrete-block houses (though he recommended plainface, which could be stuccoed, rather than rockface).[68] He also published a brief history of the development of linoleum, recognizing that it was widely used by his readers.[69] He even carried advertisements for metal ceilings.[70] Technology itself was not the evil. But it had to be used wisely to create a style of simplicity and honesty.

Another mutation of the Arts and Crafts Movement developed in Chicago at Jane Addams's Hull House. Art lectures, classes, exhibits, and a museum of labor were offered to immigrant families. The program was intended to relieve the drudgery of factory work, and foster an understanding of the worker's role in the production of goods. Addams believed that "if a child goes into a sewing factory with a knowledge of the work she is doing in relation to the finished product[,] . . . if she understands the design she is elaborating in its historic relation to art[,] . . . her daily life is lifted."[71] At Hull House, the arts and crafts were part of a program of civic improvement and social uplift, and the machine was an integral part of the reform.[72]

Addams brought many local artists to lecture at the settlement house, including her friend Frank Lloyd Wright, a charter member of the organization. In 1901 Wright gave a lecture that has since become well known for its seminal consideration of art and industrial culture. He took Ruskin's and Morris's craftsman ideal and applied it to the machine.

Frank Lloyd Wright

In his Hull House lecture, "The Art and Craft of the Machine," Wright began with the premise that the machine was a tool for creating art, and proceeded to the conclusion that the machine was the only hope for the future of the arts and crafts. While praising William Morris for his reformist zeal, Wright also claimed that Morris, "the grand democrat," had failed to realize "that the machine was the great forerunner of Democracy." Moreover, "every age has done its work, produced its art with the best tools or contrivances it knew, the tools most successful in saving the most precious thing in the world—human labor." The artist was thus "emancipated to work his will with a rational freedom unknown to the laborious art" of the past.[73]

Wright agreed with Ruskin and Morris that the art produced thus far by the machine was generally of poor quality. With typical hyperbole, he complained that "the magnificent prowess of the machine" had bombarded "the civilized world with the mangled corpses of strenuous horrors that once stood for cultivated luxury." But "the machine is the creature and not the creator of this iniquity." Unfortunately, artists had tried to use the machine to recreate the past while the need was for an art of the "here and now."[74]

Wright's typical example of how the machine had been misused was the machine-cut wood carving on popular Grand Rapids furniture. But rather than reject the machine in favor of expensive, hand-carved ornament as the Arts and Crafts Movement had done, how much more logical was it to "learn from the machine" and exploit the simple, clean cuts that revealed the texture and color of the "true nature" of the wood?[75]

The artist's role was to use the machine to link "Science and Art." The modern artist was like a "leader of an orchestra, where he once was a star performer." Moreover, "once the manufacturers are convinced of due respect and appreciation on the part of the artist, they will welcome him and his counsel gladly."[76]

Although Wright later claimed that he was the lone advocate for the use of the machine, in fact, the argument had deep roots in both the English and American design reform movements.[77] Still, historians often cite this lecture as the beginning of a new, modernist theory. Wright later elaborated his ideas in a series of articles entitled "In the Cause of Architecture" published in the *Architectural Record* in 1927 and 1928.[78]

In this series, Wright again asserted that whether the machine was a good or bad tool depended on how it was used. He explored the proposition in regard to a variety of building materials—stone, brick, wood, steel, concrete, sheet metal, and glass—the modern "tools in the tool box" for the architect. The first necessity was to understand the "nature of materials." He spoke of concrete, for example, as a plastic conglomerate that had not yet found an expression that would allow it to "take plastic form." Instead, it was cast in molds as if it were "tallow, cast iron or plaster."[79] Too often, concrete was simply presented as an artificial stone and had become "the ideal makeshift of this, the vainglorious Makeshift Era."[80] Wright condemned the popular rockface concrete block as "cheap imitation" and relegated it to "the backyard of aesthetic oblivion." But block was not without merit. It could be a "mechanical unit in a quiet, plastic whole."[81] An architect could exploit concrete's potential and create new patterns and forms, as Wright himself did in his experiments with textile blocks.[82]

Another material with great potential was sheet metal. But, Wright claimed, no architect would consider it because it had been degraded in "the cheapest and most insulting fashion." Sheet metal had become the "prime makeshift to his highness the American jerrybuilder." Wright told of a sheet-metal firm in Chicago that produced wooden doors covered with sheet metal grained to imitate wood. The doors were useful as fire stops, but the contortions of forced imitation made the product more expensive than it needed to be. By contrast, Wright demonstrated his own innovative use of sheet metal for a building in Los Angeles. Again, it was the architect's role to discover the nature of the material and to exploit it with imagination.[83]

Wright thus added to the design-reform arguments not only by advocating the exploration of machine potential, but also by condemning imitations of past styles and traditional materials. He called for the creation of a modern architecture where new materials would find modern and innovative expressions.

Wright was not the only one to do this, of course. Parallel efforts by the German Werkbund and others predate Wright's lectures and articles. Yet for all the condemnations of imitation that such movements produced, manufacturers went on making rockface concrete block, pressed-metal imitations of plaster and stone, linoleum marble and parquetry, and Lincrusta "oak" wainscoting. And the public went on buying it. To understand why, the arguments used in promoting the new materials need to be explored. They provide insight into the motivation behind imitation and into the cultural values of the period.

In Defense of New Materials and Their Imitative Qualities

The defenders of the new, imitative materials made certain claims repeatedly: the materials were cheaper, more durable, and easier to keep clean than traditional ornamental forms. Rather than being "shams" or "makeshifts," these new materials, produced by the technological wonders of the Industrial Revolution, were better than the older hand-crafted materials they imitated.

Decorative and attractive substitutes, they represented modernity, democracy, and progress. Imitation done well needed no apology. A closer examination of each of these claims reveals why the public accepted the new materials.

Cheapness

Economist Thorstein Veblen had declared in 1902 that "industry, in so far as it is character-istically modern, means the machine process," since a "democratic culture requires low cost and a large, thoroughly standardized output of goods."[84] The chief advantage of industrial work was that it produced goods more cheaply. As many business historians have noted, the consumer prices of new products often actually declined as orders increased, production became more efficient and factory output expanded.[85] That was true, for example, for the American Linoleum Company on Staten Island. In 1876 the prices for their cheapest plain and printed linoleum ranged from 95 cents to $1.05 a square yard; by 1886 it was 45 to 73.5 cents a square yard, by 1911, the most expensive printed linoleums were only 55 cents a square yard.[86] Mass production in general meant lower prices.

When advertisers claimed new architectural materials were "cheaper," the obvious question was, cheaper than what? Linoleum was not cheaper than floorcloth. Concrete block and pressed metal were not cheaper than simple clapboarding over wood frame. Lincrusta was not cheaper than plain paint, or simple wallpaper. They were cheaper only in relation to the preindustrial ornamental materials they imitated. Linoleum was cheaper than marble or parquet floors. Concrete block was cheaper than stone. Metal ceilings were cheaper than decorative plaster. Lincrusta was cheaper than real oak wainscoting or embossed leather. Hand-crafted ornamental forms cost more because they demanded skilled labor and often, rare, expensive materials with which to work.

Ruskin and Morris had argued that when the "makeshift" was accepted by the public the real thing ceased to be available. But those who turned that argument to criticize the new imitative materials at the turn of the century ignored the fact that people who used linoleum, concrete block, pressed-metal ornament and Lincrusta were, in general, not people who could afford the handmade "real thing." Usually the buyers were the middle class, who were gradually acquiring a level of luxury they would never have had before the industrial expansion of the second half of the nineteenth century made ornamental architectural features widely available and affordable.

Not all new imitative materials were "cheap." A range of goods met every level of the market with differing grades, wide varieties of types and prices to suit every income level. Business historians call the process "product multiplication." Armstrong provides a typical example. The firm diversified their offerings, making low-priced, felt-based Quaker Rugs in the 1920s at the same time that they were also acquiring two Walton rotary presses for making inlaid linoleum, the most expensive floor covering in their line. In England, linoleum was laid both in the backhalls of Buckingham Palace and in the front halls of working-class homes.

Pressed-metal manufacturers such as Berger sold cheap, thin grades of pressed-metal "stone" and "brick" siding at the same time that they marketed their "artistic" and more expensive steel ceilings. Even Walton's Lincrusta company made varying grades of the embossed wall covering from fashionable, artist-designed patterns to "cheap" dado. John Rockefeller had a Lincrusta-Walton embossed leatherlike pattern with gilded accents in his Fifth Avenue home. At the same time, Sears offered Lincrusta wainscoting to middle-class customers at thirteen cents a yard and recommended ordinary housepaint for a change of color. The range of prices and quality grades for these products also reflected the range of social class and income level of the people who used them. It was not all "cheap," only "cheaper" than the ornamental forms being imitated.

What did "cheap" mean to those who used the term in the nineteenth century? The *Oxford English Dictionary* gives the original meaning of the term as bartering, bargaining, or buying and selling. Thus the London area known as Cheapside was a place where such activities took place. By the sixteenth century, the term had come to mean an abundance of goods, something that cost little and was easily attained, or something low priced in relation to its intrinsic value, as in "cheap at any price."[87] All of these are positive connotations.

There was also the possibility of a negative meaning for "cheap" as an item of little worth. When Ruskin and Morris used the term there was no doubt of their pejorative intent. They usually emphasized the negative by calling sham materials "cheap and nasty." Today, "cheap" has a nearly exclusive negative connotation and is rarely used in advertising. Modern imitative materials like vinyl siding might be "low-priced," "economical," or "affordable," but never "cheap." In the nineteenth century, however, when Frederick Walton advertised his shilling a yard dado as "cheap," or when Thomas Palmer called Anaglypta the "cheapest substantial relief decoration," they obviously intended a positive meaning for the term that might be difficult for modern readers, unfamiliar with the original meaning of the word to understand. It was another positive benefit of the industrial revolution that goods were "cheap," that is, abundant, available, and low priced.

Durability

Contrary to all the mid-century rhetoric about "makeshifts," most of the imitative materials considered here were extremely durable. Concrete block could last as long as the stone it imitated, indeed longer than some of the more porous stones. Exterior pressed metal needed regular painting to preserve it, but the many sheet-metal cornices that still line the commercial streets of America are evidence of their longevity. Pressed-metal ceilings lasted longer than plaster ones. Linoleum might not last outlast wood, tile or marble, but it had the longest wearing life of any manufactured hard-surface floor covering. Lincrusta was nearly "indestructible."

Durable as what they imitated, these materials were even more durable than what they replaced. The people who used concrete block or pressed metal did not choose them over stone; they chose them instead of wood. Linoleum was not substituting for marble, but oil floorcloth. The Sears customers who bought Lincrusta most likely had plain walls or wallpaper as an alternative. The new materials were usually vastly superior substitutes in the length of their ornamental life.

The durability of these products made it imperative that manufacturers continue to expand their markets. Since they could not count on replacement demand, they needed new customers. Expanding population and the growing wealth of a middle class ready to buy the new luxuries fueled expanding production.

The example of Armstrong linoleum is instructive. Oil floorcloth had been considered a type of carpet that would be replaced regularly. But Armstrong promoted linoleum as a "permanent" floor covering. Oil floorcloth had been simply laid on the floor like a rug, or tacked down with carpet tacks. Armstrong recommended that its linoleum be laid over building felt and glued down. Although they claimed the resulting floor would "last as long as the house," within the company, official calculations were that linoleum would have an average replacement cycle of twenty years.[88] It could last considerably longer than that—there were reports of the best grades lasting over sixty years—but twenty was the average, partly because the owners grew tired of the pattern in that time.

Armstrong not only expanded linoleum production and sales every year between 1908 and 1930; they also continuously expanded their selection of patterns, introducing new ones annually. How could this idea of fashion with its inherent short-term aspects be reconciled with the durability of the material? Armstrong counted on finding new buyers rather than replacing the old product. That was true for concrete-block, pressed-metal, and embossed wall covering firms as well. The dynamic possibilities of what seemed like an endlessly expanding market fed the mass production of these materials.

Most people thought this new industrialized consumer culture constituted "progress." Yet as T. J. Jackson Lears has documented in his study *No Place of Grace*, a significant minority was uneasy with the dominant culture's uncritical embrace of the new. Calls for a return to hand craft, Ruskin and Morris's fears that the machine had made slaves of workers, the anxiety over modern life and its rapidity of change articulated by Henry Adams[89] and others all formed a strong undercurrent of doubt to the widely held belief that things were getting better and better.

In the midst of such anxieties, the idea of durability offered a promise of permanence. Henry Adams was not one to find comfort in the durability of concrete block, of course, but the advertising emphasis on the long-lived stability of these products reflects a deep cultural desire for such permanence. In the face of change, there were some things on which one could depend. In one's architectural surroundings, change could be a matter of choice.

Cleanliness

Another reflection of Victorian anxiety was an obsession with hygiene. Joseph Lister and Robert Koch had expounded the germ theory in the 1860s, but the general public did not widely understand or accept it until the turn of the century. Instead, they blamed miasmas and sewer gas, garbage and dirt for the spread of disease.[90]

In her book *Chasing Dirt*, Suellen Hoy argued that city dwellers in the 1880s often felt besieged by the deplorable sanitary conditions in the expanding cities and the recurrent outbreaks of typhoid, diphtheria, and influenza. Given the limited understanding of what caused disease, middle- and upper-class residents feared the unsanitary ways of the urban poor. American sanitarian Harriette Plunkett wrote in 1885, "A man may live on the splendid 'avenue,' in a mansion plumbed in the latest and costliest style, but if, half a mile away . . . there is a 'slum,' or even a neglected tenement-house, the zepher will come along and pick up the disease-germs and bear them onward, distributing them to whomsoever it meets, whether he be a millionaire or shillingare, with a perfectly leveling and democratic impartiality."[91] In the face of such jeopardy, cleanliness seemed to be a means of controlling the unpredictable. That was true for both individuals and cities.[92]

In the 1880s and 1890s, American cities mounted major efforts to battle street filth as a source of contamination. Like most sanitarians of his day, reformer George Waring, a commissioner for the National Board of Health, believed public cleanliness could promote public health. In the 1880s he helped build the first American sewage systems to separate waste from storm water. He became New York's street-cleaning commissioner in 1894, and organized a department of white-uniformed "soldiers of cleanliness and health" whose job it was to fight "daily battles with dirt."[93]

Harriette Plunkett's inventively titled 1885 book, *Women, Plumbers, and Doctors,* encouraged women to take responsibility for the health of their homes by checking for leaky drains and contaminated wells. She also encouraged them to emulate Florence Nightingale by looking to the street beyond, and thinking of the health of their cities. One group of New York women did just that in 1887 when they told the mayor that everyone knew dirt was "unsanitary" and "dangerous," but because men had been "derelict in the matter of street cleaning," much of women's time and energy was "spent in removing from floors and walls, furniture, utensils and clothing, the dirt and soil" that invaded "the household at every hour" and threatened their families' survival.[94] If the streets were clean, homemakers could more easily keep their houses clean and safe.

When advertisers promoted pressed-metal ceilings, linoleum and Lincrusta as easy to clean, sanitary materials, they reflected this concern that dirt itself was contaminating. These new products could be weapons in a woman's arsenal to protect her family.

Some feared the home itself was a source of contamination, as Annmarie Adams has recorded in *Architecture in the Family Way.* Contaminated air from leaking sewer pipes could threaten the family; so could arsenic in the wall paper or dirt and filth clinging to rugs and fabrics. New materials such as metal, tile, linoleum, and Lincrusta, it was claimed, were inherently cleaner than wood since they harbored less dust and humidity.[95]

Only against the background of the sanitarians' warnings against dust as a carrier of disease, can the modern reader understand such admonitions as the one a home-advice writer gave in 1908: "Cleanliness is, of course, of the utmost importance in a bedroom, and most people will not on any account use carpets in the rooms that are to be used for sleeping purposes, but have linoleum closely fitted to the skirtings."[96] The fear was not simply that carpets might hold dust, it was that they might hold deadly disease. Linoleum was a safer floor covering.

The sheet-metal industry often promoted metal ceilings as being better than plaster because they did not "promote dust" and could be easily cleaned. That made them suitable for hospitals, restaurants, and schools. Because it was "peerless as a sanitary agent," Lincrusta-Walton won a gold medal for wall covering at the International Health Exposition in London in 1884. Proponents claims that it "would not absorb moisture and give it out" like plaster meant that contamination would not cling to it or be released into the rooms and lungs of the household.

As acceptance of the germ theory grew in the early twentieth century, the idea of an easily cleanable, nonabsorbent surface still seemed an effective means of defeating even the invisible causes of disease. Linoleum received a scientific stamp of approval when in 1912, a German chemist reported on experiments that suggested linoleum emitted a germicidal gas.

Advertisers quickly broadcast the claim that linoleum was antiseptic. In a scientific age, here was scientific evidence that linoleum could protect one's family.[97]

Cleanliness was certainly easier for those who could afford it. Running water and servants helped. For the middle class at the turn of the century, however, cleanliness was not only necessary for health; it was also an expression of class standards. Armstrong's linoleum advertisements such as "The Story of a Woman and a Floor" (fig. 54) played to those values by suggesting that the modern woman met the expectations of her family and her peers only with a spotless house. Linoleum was one way to achieve that goal. At a time when there were fewer servants and middle-class women did the house work themselves, the claims that linoleum, Lincrusta, and metal walls and ceilings were easy to clean reflected less the fear of dirt, germs and disease as the expectation that a virtuous, respectable house was a clean one.

Modernism, Democracy, and Progress

When "Quaker" wrote his 1876 letters defending the imitative nature of sheet metal to the *American Architect and Building News,* he argued that while not everyone could "possess an original Angelo, Raphael or Rubens," still, "we may enjoy a good copy." Should we be denied access to the work of great artists "because we are not able to possess the originals?" He concluded that "It may do for a Ruskin, who would roll the world back a century, but not for this enlightened and progressive age."[98]

The advantage of machines was that they required less labor to make products faster and cheaper. Machine-made materials were often stronger and more durable as well. All this was part of modernism, a world view sure that science and industry were transforming life for the better. When the E. E. Souther Iron Company declared, "This is the age of steel and there is scarcely a purpose heretofore served by a construction of wood which cannot now be replaced by steel," it was proclaiming the gospel of the day.[99] Modern science had provided new materials. God had given humankind dominion over the earth; the machine had increased that dominion. Nature itself could be transformed and even improved upon by use of the machine. Technological development, like a kind of manifest destiny, was both inevitable and inherently good.[100]

Enthusiasts repeatedly claimed that the new machine power would be liberating. Even Morris acknowledged that it could relieve the drudgery of work. Industrial development had spurred vast changes in wealth, comfort, and education. Novelist William Dean Howells described it: "Men's minds and men's hands were suddenly released to an activity unheard of before. Invention followed invention; our rivers and seas became the warp of commerce where the steam-sped shuttles carried the woof of enterprise to and fro with tireless celerity. Machines to save labor multiplied themselves as if they had been procreative forces; and wares of every sort were produced with incredible swiftness and cheapness."[101]

Howells added that this great "accumulation" had also brought "into existence a hapless race of men" to supply the labor to operate the machines. The problem of reconciling the great wealth of the period with its great poverty occupied many reformers. Waves of immigrants swelled the cities. Jacob Riis, Lincoln Steffens and other reformers documented their shocking privations.[102] Still, the inevitability of social progress was an article of faith for most Americans. A democratic uplift based on the country's wealth would eventually improve the lot of everyone.[103]

The defenders of new architectural materials often evoked that belief in democracy. Architect Louis H. Gibson had declared in 1906, "The cement block machine is a great art democrat. It may produce and reproduce artistic forms for the masses."[104] Earlier, in 1888, a writer referred to Lincrusta-Walton and other embossed wall coverings as "a modern idea, the products of a democratic age," and added that "art in the past ministered to but a few. . . . [I]n the future it will be the many and art is rapidly becoming democratic in the consequence."[105] The machine was the means by which art was "becoming democratic"; it made available to the masses ornamentation previously only available to the wealthy.

Another aspect of the social democratization brought by the new technologies was its effect on women. It is a much-studied, well-established fact that women's roles changed profoundly in the 1870–1930 period. The Victorian ideal of a separate sphere for women in the home was challenged by the struggle for women's suffrage and by women's activism in social reform movements. Advertising for the new architectural materials reflected many of these changes.

There was a general tendency to classify exterior materials as a male realm and interior, decorative forms as appropriate to female control. But interesting cross-overs occasionally arose. For example, *Cement World* reported in 1908 that Mrs. Mary Pollock had just finished building a two-and-a-half-story concrete-block residence for herself and her husband in Cincinnati. She had molded the blocks and "her husband placed them as she directed." With a bow to conventional gender roles, the editor added that "Mrs. Pollock is just as deft at embroidery work, or

Fig. 72. "So simple a girl can operate it": a Chamberlain cement-shingle machine. Cement World 3 (Feb. 1909): 792.

making biscuits as she is in concrete work."[106] At a time of social change in women's roles, Mrs. Pollock exemplified both "What a Woman Can Do," as the story was entitled, and a reassurance that in spite of taking on traditionally male work, she was still a "real woman."

Other women, too, undertook concrete-block construction. Wilhelmine Vogl designed and laid out the ornamental plan for her family's concrete-block house in New Kent County, Delaware, in 1915. But Pollock and Vogl were clearly exceptions. When women were associated with concrete products, it was more often as a Chamberlain Cement Shingle Machine advertisement presented her (fig. 72): A young woman operated the machine while below her the caption read, "So Simple a Girl can operate it."[107]

There is much clearer evidence for women's roles in making and buying linoleum. The mid-century design reform movement in England established classes for women at the design schools. In 1880, the London *Art Journal* reporting a great improvement in linoleum designs, cited those of Miss Katherine Moon of the School of Art in Bristol as particularly "worthy of attention."[108] At the Philadelphia School of Design for Women, students submitted linoleum designs for competition[109] and the International Correspondence School 1905 text book recorded that a "large number" of designers for the linoleum trade were women.[110]

Women also worked in the linoleum factories. In response to a civilian labor shortage during World War I, women worked in every department of the Scottish firm of Barry, Ostelere and Sheperd (fig. 73).

Manufacturers, however, always perceived women's role primarily as that of consumer.

Fig. 73. Women working at Barry, Ostlere and Shepherd's linoleum factory, Kirkcaldy, Scotland, c. 1915. During WWI women took over most of the jobs at the plant, including the packing and shipping department. Kirkcaldy Museum and Art Gallery, Kirkcaldy, Scotland.

Armstrong advertised principally in "women's magazines" and directed their ads to women. Even their in-house *Salesmanship Guidebook* began with "Mrs. Average Customer, You Must Know Her Before You Can Sell Her," because "nine out of ten customers who come to your sales floor are women."[111] The guidebook's gender assumptions were clear: Women customers were "emotional" and "afraid to trust their own judgment"; that was "why so many women shop with a friend." The center of a woman's life was family and home. Her social life and status with her peers depended on the attractiveness of her home; she shopped not for "yards of linoleum, but for *home beautification.*" Confronting the woman customer's uncertainty, the linoleum salesman needed to take manly charge, to establish himself as an authority figure

Fig. 74. A photograph from Armstrong's Salesmanship Guidebook, *1936, p. 44. The salesman as authority figure stands before his seated woman customer. Hagley Museum and Library.*

Linoleum should always be displayed for the customer by unrolling it on the floor so that it can be seen to best advantage.

(fig. 74). Still, for all the gender stereotyping implied in the text, a clear message was that women made the decisions about the home's interior.

The woman consumer was another expression of democratic empowerment. Long before she gained the right to vote, she had a significant control over her home and a flood of new consumer goods expanded her choices. Historian William Leach has argued in *The Land of Desire* that this power to choose was a new kind of democracy in the late nineteenth century. Previous concepts of democracy had involved voting rights and land ownership, but the people of the consumer age also saw the possibility of material possession itself as empowering. Growing incomes, a rising standard of living, and an infinite supply of goods promised comfort and prosperity for everyone.[112]

All of this was part of progress. If there was one concept the nineteenth and early twentieth centuries held dear, it was the idea that things could and would improve. Robert Nisbet, in his comprehensive *History of the Idea of Progress* summarized Herbert Spencer's late-nineteenth-century view that "all forms of authoritarianism—religious, caste, racial, moral, and political—are destined to decline and eventually become extinct."[113] Progress was an underlying concept for nineteenth-century ideas of equality, social justice and popular sovereignty. It made them seem not only desirable but inevitable. All history was a slow, gradual, but continual growth toward social betterment. What ever small steps one generation made achieved a wider significance when they were cast as "the inexorable march of mankind."[114]

Of course, one of the ironies of the period is that the majority of Americans could believe in social progress while at the same time they also upheld laws that ensured white supremacy, women's subordination, and the preservation of the privilege's status quo. As Alan Dawley has shown, these contradictory ideas coexisted at the heart of the American experience. As unequal as things were, most people still believed adamantly in the concepts of equality, liberty, freedom and social betterment.[115]

The idea of progress was so pervasive that defenders of the new architectural materials often cited it as a sort of ultimate justification for their products. There was no arguing it. Progress was progress; it was good and inevitable; the new architectural materials were part of it. Quaker pronounced the period that had produced sheet metal an "enlightened and progressive age."[116] Metal ceilings were perfect for any "progressive contractor" smart enough to recognize the value of this "modern material."[117] They represented "the progressive spirit" of one "enterprising and successful" Virginia bank.[118] In advertisement after advertisement, machine-made, low-cost materials that were widely available to the masses were linked with the concept of progress. Progress was the driving force behind both democracy and modernism.

A Culture of Imitation

Defenders of the new, imitative architectural materials usually met objections with the arguments just discussed: Imitation did not matter when one considered the advantages of the materials' low-cost, their durability and cleanliness, and their embodiment of the concepts of modernism, democracy and progress. As for the aesthetic debate, it seemed far more important to the educated elite minority writing their treatises than it did to the consuming, middle-class majority. The former were decrying common practice. The latter were unselfconsciously participating in what historian Miles Orvell has called "a culture of imitation."[119]

Orvell notes that nineteenth-century consumers were fascinated by reproductions, replicas, and imitations. Period styles in furniture and architecture, reproductions of art works, even photographs blurred the boundary between "the real thing" and the imitation.

One of the most stunning late-nineteenth-century examples of materials parading as what they were not was the 1893 Columbian Exposition in Chicago (fig. 75). On the shores of Lake Michigan, a formal city was laid out around connecting lagoons. The classically inspired architecture and its profusion of ornamental sculpture looked like gleaming marble, but all of it was "staff"—plaster-soaked burlap layered into molds to form the outer skin of both buildings and sculpture. Painted white, staff gave the fair its nickname, the "White City." The buildings were temporary, the staff sheathing was only expected to last about a year, but the effect was spectacular. The exhibits housed in these makeshift buildings demonstrated the industrial wonders of American progress. People flocked to the sham city and few objected to its fake marble or theatrical, temporary display; they were used to the idea of imitation. It pervaded the culture.

In *Life on the Mississippi* (1883), Mark Twain described the forms of imitation found in a typical river mansion: There was usually a "big, square, two-story 'frame' house, painted

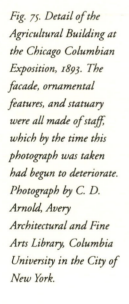

Fig. 75. Detail of the Agricultural Building at the Chicago Columbian Exposition, 1893. The facade, ornamental features, and statuary were all made of staff, which by the time this photograph was taken had begun to deteriorate. Photograph by C. D. Arnold, Avery Architectural and Fine Arts Library, Columbia University in the City of New York.

white and porticoed like a Grecian temple—with this difference, that the imposing fluted columns and Corinthian capitals were a pathetic sham, being made of white pine, and painted." Inside on the mantel was "a large basket of peaches and other fruits, natural size, all done in plaster, rudely or in wax, and painted to resemble the originals—which they don't." Hanging on the wall was an engraving of *Washington Crossing the Delaware*. On another wall were lithographs. On a table, under a glass dome was a "large bouquet of stiff flowers done in corpsy white wax."[120] Everywhere were imitations; the columns, fruit, flowers, engravings and prints spoke of a society that accepted the idea of one material masquerading as another, even while Twain found ironic humor in the spectacle.

The popularity of chromolithographs offers an another example of the acceptance of imitation. "Chromos," as they were called, could be won as prizes in art lotteries, purchased from catalogues or stores, or given out as insurance promotions. Twain made reference to them in *Connecticut Yankee* when his hero spoke of his home in East Hartford where "all unpretending as it was, you couldn't go into a room but you would find an insurance chromo, or at least a three-color God-Bless-Our Home over the door; and in the parlor we had nine."[121] Chromos offered a whole range of subject matter from Louis Prang's reproductions of well-known masterpieces, to popular Currier and Ives genre scenes. They were not only cheap, they were good quality reproductions. The Beecher sisters recommended them in *The American Woman's Home* for tasteful decoration.[122]

One defender of sheet metal cited this wide dissemination and acceptance of chromos when he declared that stamped metal ornament held the same "position which the chromo holds relative to the costly painting of which it is a faithful reproduction."[123] When Quaker said, "We cannot all expect to possess an original" work of art, but can "enjoy a good copy" he was most likely referring to chromolithographs and using them as an argument for imitation.[124] Since chromolithographs were accepted reproductions, so too should metal cornices and building fronts.

Machines had made all this imitation possible. In fact, to most nineteenth-century viewers, the purpose of the machine was to imitate. Moreover, popular taste demanded it.

Class and Taste

A recurring theme in the arguments against imitative materials was the issue of class and taste. British writers in particular were alarmed not only by materials that imitated their betters, but by people who did so too. Pugin warned that "cheap deceptions of magnificence" encouraged "persons to assume a semblance of decoration far beyond either their means or their station."[125] Ruskin feared manufacturers were liable to cause "class confusion" and dismissed those who accepted sham materials as participating in "vulgarity" and "impertinence."[126]

Americans seemed less concerned with social pretension, but equally attached to the idea that judgments about aesthetic taste were the province of the educated elite. Taste was the ultimate weapon of the *American Architect and Building News* editors in their 1876 debate with Quaker over the propriety of sheet-metal ornament. "If a man has not a natural disgust for shams," they wrote, "it is difficult to argue him into it."[127] One either had it or one didn't, and Quaker's defense of the imitative material proved he didn't.

Elite observers argued that sophisticated taste, whether innate as the *AABN* suggested, or acquired through education as the design reformers held, was based on absolutes of beauty and truth. Thorstein Veblen challenged this view in 1899 in his classic study, *The Theory of the Leisure Class*. About the concept of taste, Veblen argued that while the leisure class might think they liked a more expensive, handmade item better than a machine produced replica because of its "beauty," in fact, unconscious cultural associations influenced their evaluation.[128]

Veblen gave an example of two spoons. One was hand-wrought of silver and cost twenty dollars, the other was machine-made of aluminum and cost twenty cents. Both served their purposes though the machine-made one was more perfectly made. But the silver spoon gratified the viewer's taste and sense of the beautiful. Was the silver spoon really more beautiful? Veblen said that, in fact, it did not greatly excel in "intrinsic beauty of grain or color" and had no appreciable degree of superiority in "mechanical serviceability." Moreover, he argued that if on closer inspection, the silver spoon proved to be a "clever imitation," then its so-called beauty would be immediately diminished. His conclusion was that the "superior gratification derived from the use and contemplation of the costly and supposedly beautiful product" was in great measure a gratification of our sense of costliness masquerading under the name of beauty. Our higher appreciation of the silver spoon was in reality, only "an appreciation of its superior honorific character" not its supposed "beauty."[129]

Veblen also attacked the Arts and Crafts Movement, arguing that machine-made goods were generally superior to handmade goods in "perfection of workmanship" and greater "accuracy of detail." But "honorific values" had stood good sense on its head by teaching "well-bred people" to prefer the "crudity and wasted effort" of handmade work.[130]

The real sin of machine-made work was simply that it cost less, and therefore was common. "What is common is within the (pecuniary) reach of many people. Its consumption is therefore not honorific, since it does not serve the purpose of a favorable invidious comparison with other consumers." Veblen concluded that "the marks of cheapness or commonness are accepted as definitive marks of artistic unfitness, and a code or schedule of aesthetic proprieties on the one hand, and of aesthetic abominations on the other, is constructed on this basis for guidance in questions of taste."[131]

Veblen concluded that taste was not based on absolutes of beauty and truth, but was an indicator of the wealthy class' desire to assert their social status by owning and displaying expensive goods. It was an example of "conspicuous consumption."

The defenders of imitative architectural materials had anticipated some of Veblen's arguments. In 1876, Quaker had asked, "Must the fact that these forms can be produced so as to be within the reach of almost our entire building-community" be the sole reason for rejection? Demands that embellishments be in stone smacked "strongly of wanton waste of people's money" when pressed-metal ornaments were "equally good and appropriate."[132] Quaker believed, as Veblen later said, that the only reason for the rejection of machine-made imitative decoration was that it was inexpensive and commonly used.

The Authenticity of Imitation

Some admirers didn't bother defending the imitative qualities of the new materials; they simply said how good the imitation was. The editors of *Queen* praised the embossed wall covering Cordelova in 1896 for its artistic reproductions of "leather, old oak, and plaster," which they found "very beautiful." They particularly noted Cordelova's "exact and deceptive imitation of old oak."[133]

Deception was a positive quality of the material. British interior designer Arthur Jennings recommending the embossed metal "Emdeca" in 1908, claimed it gave "the effect of real tiles very closely" and that "some really charming patterns may be had."[134] In 1898, the Reeve Company installed linoleum floors in the Library of Congress. They boasted that the French and Florentine mosaic designs reproduced "not only the finest details of the stone work, but also the rare old tints" of the older material.[135] In the same year, the Potter Company of Philadelphia advertised that their inlaid linoleum "succeeded in faithfully reproducing" stone tiling effects.[136] Armstrong advertised in 1918 that its inlaid marble linoleum offered "the charm and effectiveness of marble" at a fraction of the cost.[137] To all these people, imitation and even "deception" recommended the materials rather than condemned them.

Undoubtedly one reason the new materials so often appeared in the guise of older ones was that similarity itself made the new forms more acceptable. Human nature prefers the familiar. A product might be "new and improved," but if it also looked like something old and traditional, the public accepted it more readily.

Frank Lloyd Wright and other reformers urged that new materials should look modern. But popular taste was consistently reluctant to accept modernism. Concrete block that looked like rough-cut stone referred symbolically to an "authentic" building material, an association that lent credence to the new product. No one would mistake concrete block for stone, but the fact that rockface block reminded one of a more expensive, high style material meant an associational transfer of meaning from the old form to the new. Defenders of the new products referred to this associational process when they claimed concrete block and pressed metal simply "alluded" to the things they copied.

A related argument was that even though the new materials might allude to older forms, the new products were unique and deserved to be considered in their own right. A *Sheet Metal Builder* contributor wrote in 1874 that sheet metal was not "mock-wood" or "mock-stone" but a material unto itself.[138] A Tynecastle tapestry defender wrote in 1896 that the wall covering did not seek to "simulate leather"; but had its own modern designs suited to its special nature.[139] Frank A. Parsons wrote in 1918 that linoleum was a special material, "recent in conception and suited to particular conditions," which made it capable of standing "on its own legs as a practical and attractive floor."[140]

This point of view remained a staple of rhetoric surrounding the new imitative materials. A 1921 critic claimed that Lincrusta-Walton's leather effects were so close to the original that "one's impression is, in short that it is not so much a material which aims at simulating the surface effects of leather as a real leather substitute, kind of a synthetic."[141] In other words, if the imitation was good enough, one would accept the material in its own right, eventually no longer thinking of it as imitation. That is just what happened to some of these materials. Elite critics might wince at linoleum parquet, but the public at large accepted linoleum marble and tile effects simply as modern floor covering. Metal ceilings that imitated decorative plaster deceived few; most people knew exactly what they were and accepted them as practical and attractive modern ceilings.

Ada Louise Huxtable was right. The popularity of "substitute gimcrackery" in the latter half of the nineteenth century was fueled by the "desire to find ways of doing things that were 'cheap, quick, and easy.'" It was also the result of what she and a long line of elite critics called "the tastelessness of a new middle class society." But simply to dismiss the popularity of concrete block, pressed metal, Linoleum, and Lincrusta as "bad taste" misses the larger issues of what they represented to the people who made and used them. They were not dishonest "shams" and "makeshifts." They were the products of the industrial age. They were better than the materials they replaced. Cheaper, more durable, cleaner, and safer, the new, imitative architectural ornaments were also expressions of aspirations for democracy, modernism, and progress. As the material culture of their age, they embody some of the most deeply held values of their period.

NOTES

CHEAP, QUICK, AND EASY: INTRODUCTION

1. Ada Louise Huxtable, "Concrete Technology in USA: Historical Survey," *Progressive Architecture* 41 (Oct. 1960): 144.

2. Robert Tressell, *The Ragged Trousered Philanthropists* (1906; reprint, London: Panther Books, 1967), 49–50. A novel about a group of house decorators.

3. W. A. Slagle, interview by author, Emporia, Va., 8 Oct. 1991. Notes in possession of the author.

4. Troy Weimer, interview by author, Fairfield, Va., 16 Apr. 1996. Notes in possession of the author.

5. Jules D. Prown, "Mind in Matter: An Introduction to Material Culture Theory and Method," in *Material Life in America 1600–1860,* ed. Robert Blair St. George (Boston: Northeastern Univ. Press, 1987), 17–37.

6. Dell Upton, "The Power of Things: Recent Studies in American Vernacular Architecture," in *Material Culture: A Research Guide,* ed. Thomas J. Schlereth (Lawrence: Univ. Press of Kansas, 1985), 57–78.

7. Philip Scranton, "Manufacturing Diversity: Production Systems, Market, and an American Consumer Society, 1870–1930," *Technology and Culture* 35 (July 1994): 476–505.

8. The building slowdown of the 1930s Depression era is one reason for ending the study there, but there is also the extraordinary number of new synthetic materials that were developed during the World War II period and its aftermath. That would be the subject of a separate study.

9. Scranton, "Manufacturing Diversity," 477–78, 482.

10. David Hounshell, *From the American System to Mass Production, 1800–1932* (Baltimore: Johns Hopkins Univ. Press, 1983).

11. Thomas K. McCraw, ed., *The Essential Alfred Chandler: Essays Toward a Historical Theory of Big Business* (Boston: Harvard Business School Press, 1988).

12. Scranton, "Manufacturing Diversity," 477, 486.

13. Ruth S. Cowan, *More Work for Mother* (New York: Basic Books, 1983); Susan Strasser, *Satisfaction Guaranteed: The Making of the American Mass Market* (New York: Pantheon Books, 1989).

14. Charles W. Calhoun, ed., *The Gilded Age: Essays on the Origin of Modern America* (Wilmington, Del.: Scholarly Resources, 1996).

15. Roland Marchand, *Advertising the American Dream: Making Way for Modernity, 1920–1940* (Berkeley and Los Angeles: Univ. of California Press, 1985).

16. Frank Luther Mott, *A History of American Magazines, 1885–1905* (Cambridge: Harvard Univ. Press, Belknap Press, 1957), 20–34.

17. John Kasson, *Civilizing the Machine, Technology and Republican Values in America, 1776–1900* (New York: Viking, 1976), 183.

18. Ibid.

19. Calhoun, *Gilded Age,* xiii.

1. Stone for the Masses

1. William A. Radford, *Cement Houses and How to Build Them* (Chicago: Radford Architectural, 1909), 3.

2. A. J. Fraries, *The Cement Industry, 1796–1914: A History* (London: David and Charles, 1977), is the source for much of this section. See also Carl Condit, *America Building: Materials and Techniques from the First Settlements to the Present* (Chicago: Univ. of Chicago Press, 1968).

3. H. C. Badder, "The Invention and Early Development of Portland Cement," *Concrete* 25, no. 4 (Oct. 1924): 119–27.

4. Edison Portland Cement Company, *The Romance of Cement* (Boston: Lovermore and Knight, 1926).

5. The earliest suggestion for concrete block appears to be a British patent given Thomas Grant in 1632. John Francis Watt received a patent in 1814 for a solid block. In 1832, William Ranger took a patent on "Ranger's Artificial Stone" and constructed the College of Surgeons in Lincoln's Inn Fields and some houses in Pall Mall. Joseph Gibbs took a patent in 1850 for hollow blocks in wooden molds, but he made it clear that the cavities should be filled during construction. L. D. Owen proposed large blocks with holes for drying in 1856. In 1866 C. S. Hutchenson took out a U.S. patent on a hollow block, and in 1868 both Thomas J. Lowry and George A. Frear received similar patents. F. Ransome took a provisional English patent in 1866 for large hollow blocks, but again, they were to be filled during construction. In the 1870s the patents were most numerous and for the first time proposed preserving the hollow cavities. T. B. Rhodes was granted a U.S. patent on hollow block in 1874, but no method of molding was stated. In England, H. P. Holt took a full patent on the hollow block in 1875. He was followed by J. C. Sellars, who in 1877 proposed a machine for compressing hollow block in metal rather than wooden molds. Harmon S. Palmer's 1900 U.S. patent was the "first modern type machine for making hollow concrete blocks." H. Kempton Dyson, "Concrete Block Making in Great Britain," pts. 1–4, *Concrete and Constructional Engineering* 3, nos. 3–6 (1908–9): 224–30, 291–98, 383–90, 463–66; and William M. Torrance, "Types of Hollow Concrete Blocks Used in the States and Their Patents," *Concrete and Constructional Engineering* 1, no. 3 (July 1906): 206–14. The latter is reprinted from *Cement Age.*

6. This idea is presented in Carl W. Condit, *American Building Art: The Nineteenth Century* (Oxford: Oxford Univ. Press, 1960), 226–27, and repeated in Ann Gillespie, "Early Devel-

opment of Artistic Concrete Block: The Case of the Boyd Brothers," *APT* 11, no. 2 (1979): 30; and in J. Randall Cotton, "Ornamental Concrete Block Houses," *Old House Journal,* 12, no. 8 (Oct. 1984): 180.

7. Joseph Bell, *From the Carriage Age to the Space Age: The Birth and Growth of the Concrete Masonry Industry* (Herndon, Va.: National Concrete Masonry Association, 1969).

8. S. B. Newberry, "Hollow Concrete Block Building Construction in the United States," *Concrete and Constructional Engineering* 1, no. 2 (May 1906): 118.

9. Ibid., 122.

10. Maurice M. Sloan, *The Concrete House and Its Construction* (Philadelphia: Association of American Portland Cement Manufacturers, 1912), 206; Radford, *Cement Houses,* 14, 34; and William A. Radford, *Dykema Cement Stone Molds, Cement Stone Machines, Cement Appliances, Cement Building Plans* (Grand Rapids, Mich.: K. Dykema and Son, 1905), 5–7.

11. Newberry, "Hollow Concrete Block Building Construction," 118.

12. *Concrete Machinery, Specialty Catalogue* (Chicago: Sears, Roebuck, 1917), 2. The same arguments also appeared in the 1907 Sears Catalogue No. 117, 424.

13. Ibid., 1.

14. Carolyn Murray-Wooley, "Stamper House," Kentucky Historic Resources Inventory, Site No. Lw. 13. An I-house is a two-story, single-pile, central-passage plan with two rooms on each floor. It was a traditional house form throughout the nineteenth century.

Frances H. Hurt, "The Virginia Years of Georgia O'Keeffe," *Commonwealth* 47, no. 9 (Oct. 1980): 24–26; Roxanna Robinson, *Georgia O'Keeffe: A Life* (New York: Harper and Row, 1989), 55, 73–76; and Benita Eisler, *O'Keeffe and Stieglitz: An American Romance* (New York: Penguin Books, 1991), 52–53. The four-square house, popular at the turn of the century, is a two-story, square-shaped house with a hipped roof.

August Kuhlman, was a German immigrant to Colorado in the 1880s. His ranch was in an isolated valley area. HABS Survey, Kuhlmam-Periman Ranch, Delores Valley, Montezuma County, Colorado, 1981.

15. Katherine Cole Stevenson and H. Ward Jandl, *Houses by Mail* (Washington, D.C.: Preservation Press, 1968), 241. "The Canton," an example of the concrete-block plan, was published in catalogs from 1911, 1913, 1916, 1917, and 1918.

16. Margaret Stevenson, "C. K. Harvey" (paper presented at Symposium on Virginia Architecture, Univ. of Virginia, Nov. 1994). Notes supplied by the author.

17. Bell, *From Carriage Age,* 5.

18. Thomas Brenton Burrell to the Nebraska State Historical Society, 30 June 1987. Nebraska State Historical Society, Lincoln, Nebraska.

19. Paul Baker Touart, *Building the Backcountry: An Architectural History of Davidson County, North Carolina* (Davidson County, N.C.: Davidson County Historical Association, 1987), 93–94; and Paul Baker Touart, letter to author, 23 Jan. 1987. Letter in possession of the author.

20. David Dickey, "Manly Brown's Blacksmith Shop," student paper, Washington and Lee Univ., 1981, Leyburn Library Special Collections, Washington and Lee Univ., Lexington, Va.

21. "Organization of Bank of Fairfield Told in Rhyme," *Rockbridge County News,* 22 Feb. 1923, p. 1. Typescript of poem supplied to the author by the poet's grandson, Royster Lyle Jr.

22. Dyson, "Concrete Block Making in Great Britain," pt. 3, 386.

23. "Concrete Block Church in Cairo," *Construction and Engineering* 4, no. 2 (May 1909): 140–41. It was a Church of Scotland denomination. The architect was W. J. Dilley, and the blocks were made on the site by the Artificial Stone Company on a Hercules Machine with an Italian gang of masons. The Nairobi hospital was cited in Dyson, "Concrete Block Making in Great Britain," pt. 3, 388.

24. "Two Boys from Osgoode," in *Ideal Ideas* (London: Ideal Concrete Machinery, 1913), 4, Boyd Brothers Papers, vol. 1, file 2, National Archives of Canada (hereafter cited as Boyd Papers).

25. Boyd Papers, vol. 1, file 5.

26. Cash Book, Boyd Papers, vol. 10, file 1.

27. *Ideal Ideas,* 5.

28. Oscar and Grace Kingston, interview by author, Osgoode, Ontario, Canada, 16 June 1996. Grace is the daughter of Harry Boyd, and her husband, Oscar, was the office manager for the company from 1945 to 1981. Notes in possession of the author.

29. *Ideal Ideas,* 4.

30. Radford, *Cement Houses,* 12.

31. Bell, *From Carriage Age,* 6.

32. *Ideal Ideas,* 5.

33. Janet Hutchison, "The Cure for Domestic Neglect: Better Homes in America, 1922–1955," in *Perspectives in Vernacular Architecture,* ed. Camille Wells (Columbia: Univ. of Missouri Press, 1986), 2:168–78.

34. Bell, *From Carriage Age,* 4.

35. Radford, *Cement Houses,* 12.

36. John P. White, "The Vogl House," Historic American Building Survey (HABS), Aug. 1975. Copy in Delaware State Historic Preservation Office.

37. Bell, *From Carriage Age,* 6.

38. Oswald C. Herring, *Concrete and Stucco Houses* (New York: Robert M. McBride, 1912), 52.

39. "Report of AIA Committee," *American Architect and Building News* (hereafter cited as *AABN*) 92 (Dec. 1907): 214.

40. Ibid.

41. Bruce Brooks Pfeiffer, ed., *Frank Lloyd Wright: Collected Writings* (New York: Rizzoli, 1992), 1:304. For Wright's experiments with textile block, see Robert L. Sweeney, *Wright in Hollywood: Visions of a New Architecture* (Cambridge, Mass.: Architectural History Foundation and MIT Press, 1993).

42. Pfeiffer, *Frank Lloyd Wright: Collected Writings,* 1:213. The essay was published in 1925. Also see Katheryn Smith, *Hollyhock House and Olive Hill: Buildings and Projects for Aline Barnsdall* (New York: Rizzoli, 1992), 166.

43. "Report of AIA Committee," 214.

44. Herring, *Concrete and Stucco Houses,* 55.

45. James F. Hobart, "Some Thoughts on Concrete Block Construction," *Building Age* 32 (June 1910): 246.

46. Harvey Whipple, *Concrete Stone Manufacture,* 2d ed. (Detroit: Concrete-Cement Age, 1918), 230.

47. For the St. Louis development, see Mary M. Stiritz, "Oakherst Place Concrete Block District," National Register of Historic Places Nomination Form, 5 May 1987. For Mineville, see "Concrete Cottages for Workingmen," *Building Age* 32 (Apr. 1910): 169. The article notes that tailings from the mining company operation were used to make the concrete blocks for the workers' cottages.

48. Louis H. Gibson, "Cement Block Architecture," *AABN* 89 (Feb. 1906): 72. Gibson made his pronouncement of the block machines as "art democrats" within the context of an argument for better architect-designed buildings that would improve the taste of the masses.

49. *Better Buildings with Straub's Patented Cinder Concrete Building Block* (Philadelphia: Philadelphia Partition and Building Block, [1927?]).

50. Bell, *From Carriage Age,* 96–98.

51. For a detailed discussion of the history of the curing process, see Bell, *From Carriage Age,* 103–25.

52. Dan Pezzoni, *The History and Architecture of Lee County, North Carolina* (Sanford, N.C.: Railroad House Historical Association, 1995), 335.

53. Matt Beebe, interview by author, Lexington, Va., 6 Dec. 1986. Notes in possession of the author.

2. Embossed Facades

1. "Sheet Metal Pavilion," *Centennial Eagle* (July–Sept. 1876): 134.

2. "Centennial Architecture," *AABN* 1 (10 June 1876): 187.

3. For general background on the history of metal in building, see Margot Gayle, David W. Look, and John G. Waite, *Metals in America's Historic Buildings* (Washington, D.C.: U.S. Dept. of Interior Heritage Conservation and Recreation Service Technical Preservation Services Division, 1980). Also, David Chase and Carolyn Laray, *Sheet Metal Craftsmanship: Progress in Building* (Washington, D.C.: National Building Museum, 1988).

4. W. H. Mullins, *Sheet Metal Architectural Ornaments, Statuary, Cornices, Building Fronts, Finials, etc.* (Salem, Ohio: W. H. Mullins, 1894).

5. Gayle, Look, and Waite, *Metals in America's Historic Buildings,* 74.

6. Thomas Jefferson to Charles Yancey, 23 July 1821, Jefferson Papers, Library of Congress.

7. Diana S. Waite, *Nineteenth Century Tin Roofing and Its Use at Hyde Hall* (New York: New York State Historic Trust, 1971).

8. Ibid., 5–7.

9. Ibid., 2. Also Carroll W. Pursell Jr., "Tariff and Technology: The Foundation and Development of the American Tin-Plate Industry, 1872–1900," *Technology and Culture* 3 (1962): 267–84; and Jeannette Lasansky, *To Cut, Piece and Solder: The Work of the Rural Pennsylvania Tinsmith, 1778–1908* (College Park, Pa.: Keystone Books, Pennsylvania State Univ. Press, 1982).

10. "Tin Plates," *Metal Worker* 42 (13 Oct. 1894): 52.

11. For an excellent discussion of this background, see Ann H. Gillespie, "Decorative Sheet-Metal Building Components in Canada 1870–1930" (master's thesis, Carleton Univ., 1985).

12. Chase and Laray, *Sheetmetal Craftsmanship,* 29; and Gayle, Look, and Waite, *Metals in American's Historic Buildings,* 18.

13. John Harboe, "History and Technology of the Sheet Metal Cornice" (master's thesis, Columbia Univ., 1984).

14. Mary B. Dierickx, "Decorative Metal Roofing in the United States," in *The Technology of Historic American Building,* ed. H. Ward Jandl (Washington, D.C.: Foundation for Preservation Technology, 1983), 153–87. She cites an article in the English magazine, the *Builder* (31 July 1869): 57, which refers to a new kind of metal roofing in France as the earliest mention of metal shingles. Articles on metal shingles produced in the United States appear in *Sheet Metal Builder* 2 (15 July 1875): 71, and *Carpentry and Building* 1 (Mar. 1879): 51.

15. Margaret Carter and Julian S. Smith, "The Metallic Roofing Co. Showroom, A Look at Preservation," report for Ontario Heritage Foundation, Nov. 1987–Jan. 1988. Also see "New Metallic Tile," *Carpentry and Building* 6 (July 1884): 132.

16. Advertisement, *Carpentry and Building* 1 (Mar. 1879): ii, and "Metallic Shingles," *Carpentry and Building* 2 (July 1880): 130.

17. "New Roofing Tile," *Carpentry and Building* 5 (Nov. 1883): 228; "New Metallic Shingle," *Carpentry and Building* 6 (Jan. 1884): 11; and "Novelties, A New Sheet-Metal Tile," *Carpentry and Building* 9 (Mar. 1887): 52.

18. *Carpentry and Building* 6 (Jan. 1884): 11.

19. *Pedlar People Catalogue* (c. 1914), 13.

20. Metallic Roofing Company of Canada, Ltd., *Illustrated Catalogue of Eastlake Metallic Shingles and Sheet Steel Pressed Brick* (Toronto: Metallic Roofing, 1890).

21. *The Pedlar People, Ltd., Sheet Metal Products Reference Book ND22R* (Oshawa, Ont.: Pedlar People, n.d.).

22. John W. Evans, "Slater Building, La Grande, Oregon," National Register of Historic Places Inventory-Nomination Form, (14 Dec. 1982), Oregon State Historic Preservation Office.

23. Catherine W. Bishir and Michael T. Southern, *A Guide to the Historic Architecture of Eastern North Carolina* (Chapel Hill: Univ. of North Carolina Press, 1996), 132.

24. George L. Mesker and Company, *Architectural Iron Works Catalogue* (Evansville, Ind.: George L. Mesker, 1902), 2.

25. Mullins, *Sheet Metal Architectural Ornaments,* 1.

26. *Bakewell and Mullins Designs of Architectural Ornaments* (Salem, Ohio: Bakewell and Mullins, 1887), 49.

27. The journal started in 1874 and was bought by Kittredge in 1876. See Harboe, "History and Technology," 5.

28. See Arthur A. Hart, "Sheet Iron Elegance, Mail Order Architecture in Montana," *Montana: The Magazine of Western History* 40 (Autumn 1990): 26–31; and "Design by Mail Order: Mt. Carroll, IL," *National Building Museum Blueprints* 3, no. 1 (Fall 1984): 10–11. There are good collections of Mesker trade catalogues at the Winterthur Museum and Library, the Avery Library at Columbia University, and an important archival collection at the Missouri Historical Society Library in St. Louis.

29. *The Story: A Story of People, the Story of Mullins, the Story of Your Job* (Salem, Ohio: Mullins Manufacturing, 1947). Seventy-fifth anniversary pamphlet history of the company. Hagley Collection.

30. *Metal Worker* 35 (3 Jan. 1891): 24

31. Neal Quinto, "A Case for the Historic Preservation of the W. F. Norman Corporation in Nevada, Missouri," typescript, Missouri Department of Natural Resources, Division of Historic Preservation Office.

32. Slagle, interview.

33. See Alfred D. Chandler Jr., *The Visible Hand: The Managerial Revolution in American Business* (Cambridge: Harvard Univ. Press, 1977), for the nature of this shift. More recent business historians have challenged Chandler's assumptions about the universality of the change, but his analysis still seems well suited to what happened in the sheet-metal industry.

34. *Edwards Metal Roofing, Siding, Ceiling, etc., Catalogue* (Cincinnati: Edwards Manufacturing, 1912), 3.

35. Mott, *History of American Magazines*, 21–22.

36. "No-Co-Do Steel Ceilings," *National Builder* 41 (Mar. 1910): 16.

37. "Hardware Association Show," *National Builder* 43 (Apr. 1912): 54.

38. Trade catalogues were important for many manufacturers, especially in the hardware and building trades. See "How Catalogues Should Look and What They Should Contain," *Canadian Manufacturer* 134, no. 1 (June 1914): 39–40.

39. "Catalogues," *National Builder* 36 (Sept. 1905): 48.

40. *Edwards Metal Roofing, Siding, Ceilings*, 3.

41. *What People Say: General Testimonials for "Eastlake" Galvanized Steel Shingles* (Toronto: Metallic Roofing Company of Canada, 1894), 9.

42. Mesker and Company, *Architectural Iron Works Catalogue*, 27.

43. *Mikor Sheet Metal Products* (Milwaukee: Milwaukee Corrugating, 1915), 246.

44. H. M. Sanders to the editor, *Sheet Metal Builder* 1 (Dec. 1874): 134. Sanders refers to "servile imitation" as if the term is already a cliché and argues that the industry has to project a more positive image.

45. "Servile Imitation," *Metal Worker* 23, no. 26 (17 June 1885): 20.

46. "Centennial Architecture," *AABN* 1 (3 June 1876): 187, 179.

47. "An Argument for Sheet-Metal in Architecture," *AABN* 1 (22 July 1876): 239.

48. Ibid.

49. Ibid., 234.

50. Ibid.

51. "Sheet-Metal Architecture," *AABN* 1 (11 Nov. 1876): 366.

52. Ibid., 365–66.

53. Ibid., 367.

54. T. Claxton Fidler, "The Architectural Use of Iron and Steel," *Carpentry and Building* 13 (May 1891): 114.

55. Frank Lloyd Wright, "In the Cause of Architecture, VII: Sheet Metal and a Modern Instance," *Architectural Record* 64 (Oct. 1928): 334.

56. Huxtable, "Concrete Technology."

57. "Sheet-Metal Architecture," 365.

58. "Cornice Work: The Relative Advantages of Stamped Ornaments for Architectural Purposes," *Carpentry and Building* 1 (Feb. 1879): 34.

59. Ibid.

60. Editorial, *Sheet Metal Builder* 1 (Apr. 1874): 5.

61. *E. E. Souther Iron Company Catalogue No. 18* (St. Louis: E. E. Souther, [1910?]).

62. The firms include Shanker Steel, Secaucus, N.J. (founded 1912); W. F. Norman Corporation, Nevada, Mo.; Old Jefferson Tile Company, Jefferson, Tex.; A. A. Abingdon Affiliates, Brooklyn, N.Y., and Chelsea Decorative Metal Company, Houston, Tex.

3. Artful Interiors

1. "How Casey Came to Sell Ceilings," *Metal Worker* 84 (22 Oct 1915): 528–29.

2. Ibid.

3. See Mary Dierickx, "Metal Ceilings in the U.S.," *APT Bulletin* 7, no. 2 (1975): 83–98; and Gillespie, "Decorative Sheet-Metal Building Components."

4. Diana Waite, *Architectural Elements: The Technological Revolution* (New York: Bonanza Books, 1976), fig. 7.

5. "Metallic Ceilings," *Metal Worker* 3 (6 Feb. 1875): 2.

6. Mary Dierickx, "Metal Ceilings in the U.S."

7. "Sheet-Metal Ceiling," *Carpentry and Building* 8 (Oct. 1886): 188.

8. "Northrop's Embossed Patent Ceilings," *Building: An Architectural Weekly* 10, no. 3 (19 Jan. 1889): trade supplement, first page.

9. "Northrop's Paneled Ceiling," *Carpentry and Building* 11 (Mar. 1889): 53.

10. "The Beginning of Metal Ceilings," *Sheet Metal Worker* 25 (Jan. 1934): 23–24.

11. "Sheet-Metal Ceilings and Center Pieces," *Carpentry and Building* 11 (Mar. 1889): 63.

12. Small pieces of ornamental zinc had been used for decoration on exterior cornices and building fronts since the 1870s; see chapter 3. They had also been used on interiors in conjunction with plaster to make ornamental centerpieces for ceilings in the 1870s. See "Cornice Work," 34.

13. "Sheet Metal Ceiling Work," *Carpentry and Building* 9 (Dec. 1887): 244–45; and "Sheet-Metal Ceilings and Center Pieces," 63–64.

14. "Metal for Ceilings," *Architecture and Building* 8 (27 Dec. 1890): 358.

15. Mesker and Company, *Architectural Iron Works* (1903), 30.

16. *Seventy-Fifth Penn Metal Year, 1869–1944* (Philadelphia: Penco, 1944).

17. "The Art of Making Steel Ceilings," *National Builder* 43 (Aug. 1912): 104–6.

18. *Northrop, Coburn and Dodge Co., Manufacturers of Northrop's Metal Ceilings and Walls, Catalogue No. 9* (New York: Northrop, Coburn and Dodge, 1905).

19. While the advertisements seemed to disappear in the 1930s from builders' journals like the *National Builder,* specialist trade magazines like the *Sheet Metal Worker* continued to publish articles on the metal ceiling trade throughout the decade. There was a "boosterish" tone encouraging Depression-era contractors that even though times were tough, there was money to be made. The author of several of the articles was the manager of the Steel Ceiling Division of Edwards Manufacturing Company, Cincinnati, Ohio.

20. *National Builder* 46 (Dec. 1915): 131.

21. Ibid., 16.

22. *National Builder* 40 (Oct. 1909): 72.

23. See, for example, "Metallic Relief Ceilings," *Metal Worker* 36 (18 July 1891): 36; "Metal Ceilings," *National Builder* 43 (Jan. 1912): 62; or "Here Is the Evidence," *Sheet Metal Worker* 26 (Jan. 1935): 15–16.

24. "The Record & Guide of New York," 14 Nov. 1914, newspaper account reproduced in *Mikor Sheet Metal Products*, 246.

25. B. D. Hodges, "Metal Ceilings for Residences," *Metal Worker* 77 (15 Mar. 1912): 383. Hodges, a Hubbard, Texas, contractor, wrote to the magazine in response to a series of articles on using metal ceilings in homes.

26. Drop Press, "Sheet Metal Ceilings," *Metal Worker* 43 (20 Apr. 1895): 48.

27. Quoted in *All about the Iron Ceilings, Side Walls, etc., Manufactured by A. Northrop & Co.* (Pittsburgh: A. Northrop, 1890), back cover.

28. The headline was from the *Boston American*, 16 May 1931, and was reproduced in Howard E. Jones, "Steel Ceiling Selling Suggestions," *Sheet Metal Worker* 22 (7 Aug. 1931): 470. Another similar point was made in "Even When It Falls Metal Ceiling Is Best," *Sheet Metal Worker* 20 (14 June 1929): 381.

29. *Berger Architectural Sheet Metal Work* (Canton, Ohio: Berger Manufacturing, 1895), 88, 92.

30. *Sears, Roebuck, Steel Ceilings* (Chicago: Sears, Roebuck, 1910), 151.

31. *Berger's "Classik" Steel Ceilings, Catalogue 21* (Canton, Ohio: Berger, 1915), 1.

32. *Steel Ceilings* (Ottawa: McFarland-Douglas, n.d.), 1.

33. "Milwaukee Artistic Metal Ceiling Co.," *National Builder* 43 (Jan. 1912): 57.

34. Brian Powell, "Canterbury Shaker Village, Introduction," graduate student paper submitted to Richard Candee, Boston Univ. Preservation Studies Program. Copy supplied to the author.

35. *Canton Line Steel Ceilings, Catalogue F* (Canton, Ohio: Canton Manufacturing, 1915).

36. *Edwards Manufacturing Company, Catalogue No. 68* (Cincinnati: Edwards Manufacturing, 1923), 204.

37. *National Builder* 42 (Sept. 1911): 70–71.

38. V. Moesleins, *Stamped Steel Ceilings Catalogue* (New York: V. Moesleins, 1894), 15.

39. Ibid.

40. *National Builder* 32 (1 Aug. 1901): 21.

41. Interview by author, 8 Oct. 1991. Notes in the possession of the author.

42. "Metal Ceilings and Metal Construction in South America," *National Builder* 42 (May 1911): 56; and "Metal Ceilings in Rio de Janeiro," *Metal Worker* 83 (11 June 1915): 846.

43. See Carter and Smith, "The Metallic Roofing Co. Showroom." Also see Gillespie, "Decorative Sheet-Metal Building Components," and Ann H. Gillespie, "Ceilings of Metal," *Canadian Heritage* 9 (May–June 1983): 8–10, 48.

44. Henry Simpson (1864–1926) was the Toronto architect who designed both the showroom and the factory behind it. See Carter and Smith, "Metallic Roofing Co. Showroom."

45. *Pedlar Art Steel Ceilings, Catalogue No. 21-C* (Oshawa, Ont.: Pedlar People, [1921?]), 4. The National Archives of Canada have extensive archives of Pedlar Company papers and catalogues.

46. *Pedlar's Perfect Art Steel Ceilings and Wall Designs* (Oshawa, Ont.: Pedlar People, 1930).

47. *Australasian Builder & Contractor's News* (23 Aug. 1890): n.p., quoted in Terence Lane

and Jessie Serle, *Australians at Home: A Documentary History of Australian Domestic Interiors from 1788–1914* (Oxford: Oxford Univ. Press, 1990), 376–77.

48. See Lane and Serle, *Australians at Home,* 45, 47, 49, and 376–77; Miria Worthington, "Pressed Metal Ceilings in Western Australia," *Heritage Australia* 5 (Autumn 1986): 31–32; and *Forty Years of Wunderlich Industry, 1887–1927* (Sydney: Wunderlich, 1927).

49. "Building World News," *Building World* 9, no. 222 (13 Jan. 1900): 225.

50. "British Stamped Metal Ceiling Co., Ltd.," *Decorator* 3 (22 Oct. 1904): 128.

51. Ibid.

52. Jeremy Cragg, House Manager of Erddig, a National Trust property in Wales, to the author, 31 Dec. 1995. Letter in the possession of the author.

53. Helen C. Long, *The Edwardian House: The Middle-Class Home in Britain, 1880–1914* (Manchester: Manchester Univ. Press, 1993), 139–41.

54. The reason for this may have been the competition from Lincrusta-Walton, Anaglypta and other embossed wall coverings. See chapter 5 for a fuller discussion.

55. A number of how-to articles regarding the installation of metal ceilings appeared in the 1970s and 1980s, reflecting a new preservation interest in the material. See David Bell, "Patterns Overhead," *Americana* (July/Aug. 1979): 52–59; Barbara Schiller, "Metal Ceilings," *Old-House Journal* 7 (Mar. 1979): 1, 29–33; or John Kosmer, "Tin Ceiling, An Installation Guide," *Victorian Homes* 7 (Winter 1988): 56–61.

56. W. A. Slagle, owner of the Klugel Architectural Metal Works in Emporia, Va., says that "most people who walk into the shop and want any sort of metal work, ask for 'tin'" and that the shops themselves were called "tin shops" and the workers, "tinners" well into the twentieth century, even when most of the work was done in steel. Interview by author.

57. *Oxford English Dictionary,* 2d ed., s.v. "Tin."

58. *All about the Iron Ceilings.*

59. "An Object Lesson in Getting Business: Why Sheet Metal Was Used So Generously in Remodeling St. Paul's Lutheran Church at Waterloo," *Sheet Metal Worker* 22 (25 Dec. 1931): 738–39.

60. *House Beautiful* 33 (Apr. 1913): iv. It was fairly unusual for metal ceilings to be advertised in anything other than building journals. While ads do occasionally appear in magazines aimed at the consuming public, and in this case, women, they were not common.

61. *Carpentry and Building* 21 (Dec. 1899): xvii.

62. Lane and Serle, *Australians at Home,* 377.

63. *The Illustrated Carpenter and Builder,* advertising supplement 46 (15 June 1900): 4.

64. "Unlimited Opportunities for Steel Ceilings," *Sheet Metal Worker* 27 (Jan. 1936): 18.

65. *All about the Iron Ceilings.*

66. *Lexington (Va.) Gazette,* 17 Feb. 1915, p. 3.

67. *National Builder* 48 (July 1917): 105.

4. Fashion Floors

1. Frederick Walton, *The Infancy and Development of Linoleum Floorcloth* (London: Simpkin, Marshall, Hamilton, Kent, 1925), 13–14.

2. Helene Von Rosenstiel, *American Rugs and Carpets from the Seventeenth Century to Modern Times* (New York: William Morrow, 1978); Helene Von Rosenstiel and Gail Casky, *Floor Coverings for Historic Buildings* (Washington, D.C.: Historic Preservation Education Foundation, 1993); Bonnie Parks, "Floorcloths to Linoleum: The Development of Resilient Flooring," and John Wilson Jr., "Floorcloths in America: 18th Century to Present" in *The Interiors Handbook for Historic Buildings,* vol. 2, ed. Michael J. Auer, Charles E. Fisher III, Thomas C. Jester, and Marilyn E. Kaplan (Washington, D.C.: Historic Preservation Education Foundation, 1993).

3. Von Rosenstiel, *American Rugs and Carpets,* 51.

4. Ibid.

5. Wilson, "Floorcloths in America," 24.

6. M. W. Jones, *The History and Manufacture of Floorcloth and Linoleum* (Bristol: Walter R. Powell, 1918).

7. Augustus Muir, *Nairns of Kirkcaldy: A Short History of the Company* (Cambridge: W. Heffer and Sons for Michael Nairn and Company, 1956), 13.

8. Ibid., 28–33.

9. "A Day at a Floorcloth Factory," *Penny Magazine* (Aug. 1842): 337–44, also gave a full account of the manufacturing process. The magazine was published in London by the Society for the Diffusion of Useful Knowledge.

10. Muir, *Nairns of Kirkcaldy,* 41–46, and Parks, "Floorcloths to Linoleum," 2–3.

11. Ibid., 32.

12. Charles Dickens, "Gin-shops" and "Our Next-Door Neighbour," in *Sketches by Boz* (1838); also *Martin Chuzzelwit* (1844; Macmillan, 1892), 140, 412–13. Cited in Philip Gooderson, *Lord Linoleum, Lord Ashton, Lancaster and the Rise of the British Oilcloth and Linoleum Industry* (Keele, England: Keele Univ. Press, 1996), 39.

13. *Mrs. Beeton's Book of Household Management,* pt. 2 (London, 1869), 1936–37. Cited in Gooderson, *Lord Linoleum,* 40.

14. Catherine E. Beecher and Harriet Beecher Stowe, *The American Woman's Home* (1869; reprint, New York: Arno Press, 1971), 371.

15. Tressell, *Ragged Trousered Philanthropists,* 49–50.

16. Gooderson, *Lord Linoleum,* 30–31.

17. Ibid., 33.

18. Jones, *History and Manufacture of Floorcloth,* 26–31.

19. Linda Parry, ed., *William Morris Textiles* (New York: Viking Press, 1983), 74–75.

20. G. W. Yapp, ed., *Art Industry: Furniture, Upholstery, and House-Decoration* (London: J. S. Virtue, 1880), 60.

21. This was for "linoxyn." British Patent 290, 1860.

22. British Patent 3210, 1863 for "Improvement of the Manufacture of a Wax Cloth for Floors."

23. William B. Coleman, "Frederick Walton, Inventor of Machinery for the Manufacture of Linoleum and Founder of the Linoleum Industry," *Mechanical Engineering* 57 (May 1935): 298; and William B. Coleman, "Frederick Walton, Centenary of the Birth of the Inventor of Linoleum," *Industrial and Engineering Chemical News* 12 (10 Apr. 1834): 119.

24. Linoleum Manufacturing Company, Ltd., Record Books 1865–1905, Greater London Record Office.

25. Walton, *Infancy and Development of Linoleum,* 34.

26. While Walton usually explained the meaning of linoleum with the implication that he came up with the idea himself, Muir, writing a company history of Walton's rival firm, claimed that an "imaginative English parson" suggested the name. Muir, *Nairns of Kirkcaldy,* 70.

27. Ibid., 28. Also *London Times,* 2 Feb. 1877 and 31 Jan. 1878, cited in Gooderson, *Lord Linoleum,* 34.

28. Adrian Room, *Directory of Trade Name Origins* (London: Routledge and Kegan Paul, 1982), 110; and *Fife Free Press,* 2 Feb. 1878, clipping file, Kirkcaldy Museum and Library, Kirkcaldy, Scotland (hereafter cited as Kirkcaldy Museum).

29. Charles L. Sachs, *Made on Staten Island,* exhibition catalogue (Richmondtown, N.Y.: Staten Island Historical Society, 1988). Also, Charles L. Sachs, Curator's Files, Staten Island Historical Society.

30. "Floorcloth," *Carpet Trade* 10 (Oct. 1879): 17–18.

31. The Linoleum Manufacturing Company, Record Books, 1881. "Your Directors have made arrangements with their manufacturing Manager, Mr. Leake to work his patent for through Inlaid Pattern Linoleum which promises to be a great success." Leake's 1880 patent was No. 2307. In 1888, he took out another, No. 18110, with Godfrey and Lucas for machinery to produce the molded inlay. Greater London Record Office.

32. Sachs, *Made on Staten Island,* 90. Melvin (1875–1914) was a Scottish-born engineer. His U.S. patent was No. 412,279, 8 Oct. 1889.

33. Coleman, "Frederick Walton, Inventor," 297–302; Coleman, "Frederick Walton, Centenary," 119, 128; Barry, Ostlere and Shepherd, "Linoleum, Historical Development," typescript, n.d. [after 1929], Kirkcaldy Museum.

34. Coleman, "Frederick Walton, Inventor," 297–302; Walton gave the date of 1898 for the opening of Greenwich Inlaid; the British Trade Register gives 1895, as do Muir and Coleman.

35. Sachs, Curator's Files.

36. Edward C. Dearden, *A Historical Sketch of the George W. Blabon Co., 1851–1915* (Philadelphia: George W. Blabon, 1915).

37. "How Linoleums and Oilcloths Are Made," *Scientific American* (13 July 1907): 28–30.

38. Muir, *Nairns of Kirkcaldy,* 85–90.

39. H. W. Prentis Jr., *Thomas Morton Armstrong (1836–1908), Pioneer in Cork* (New York: Newcomen Society, 1950) and *The First 125 Years* (Lancaster, Pa.: Armstrong, 1985).

40. "Linoleum Makers Face Shortages," *Dry Goods Economist* 69 (31 July 1915): 7.

41. Robert F. Lanzillotti, *The Hard-Surface Floor-Covering Industry: A Case Study of Market Structure and Competition in Oligopoly* (N.p.: State College of Washington Press, 1955).

42. "Armstrong Fiberlin," *Carpet and Upholstery Trade Review* 46, no. 21 (1 Nov. 1915): 7.

43. "Linoleum Production Curtailed," *Carpet and Upholstery Trade Review* 49, no. 9 (1 May 1918): 33.

44. Ibid. (1 Oct. 1915): 51.

45. *Ladies Home Journal* (Jan. 1918): 45.

46. "Federal Trade Commission," *Carpet and Upholstery Trade Review* 49, no. 10 (15 May 1918): 48; and *Blabon Art Linoleums, Styles for 1924* (Philadelphia: George W. Blabon, 1924), 19.

47. Weimer, interview.

48. *Jute Year Book: Annual Directory of the Jute, Canvas and Linoleum Industries and Trade* (London: British-Continental Trade Press, 1935), 53.

49. Hazel Dell Brown, *The Attractive Home: How to Plan Its Decoration* (Lancaster, Pa.: Armstrong Bureau of Interior Decoration, 1928), 38. Armstrong's "Quaker Rugs" evoked an image of simple modesty and thrift.

50. Lanzillotti, *Hard-Surface Floor-Covering Industry*, 15.

51. Bonnie Parks Snyder, "Chronology of Linoleum Production," typescript, 1995, copy supplied to the author.

52. Lanzillotti, *Hard-Surface Floor-Covering Industry*, 26–28.

53. *H. W. Prentis, Jr., 1884–1959* (Lancaster, Pa.: Armstrong Cork, 1961), 7–9.

54. *Armstrong Linoleum Pattern Book* (Lancaster, Pa.: Armstrong Cork, 1923), 6.

55. *Armstrong Linoleum Pattern Book* (Lancaster, Pa.: Armstrong Cork, 1918), 5–6; *Armstrong Linoleum Pattern Book* (Lancaster, Pa.: Armstrong Cork, 1926), 4.

56. *Jute Year Book: Annual Directory* (1935), 53.

57. *Business Floors of Armstrong Linoleum* (Lancaster, Pa.: Armstrong Cork, 1924), 4.

58. *Linotile Floors* (Lancaster, Pa.: Armstrong Cork, 1920), 8.

59. "Germs vs. Linoleum," *Dry Goods Economist* 68 (29 Nov. 1913): 23; and *Helpful Hints for Linoleum Salesmen* (Lancaster, Pa.: Armstrong Cork, 1918), 11.

60. Brown, *Attractive Home*, 13.

61. Ibid., 18.

62. *Sweets Architectural Catalogue* (New York: Architectural Record, 1927–28), B1576–77, B1576–72; and "Linoleum in Warfare," *Carpet and Upholstery Trade Review* 26, no. 13 (1 July 1895): 42.

63. "Paris Exposition, Compagnie Rouennaise," *Carpet and Upholstery Trade Review* 31, no. 17 (1 Sept. 1900): 58.

64. Marilyn Irvin Holt, *Linoleum, Better Babies and the Modern Farm Woman, 1890–1930* (Albuquerque: Univ. of New Mexico Press, 1995), 89.

65. *Helpful Hints for Linoleum Salesmen*, 2–3.

66. Muir, *Nairns of Kirkcaldy*, 57–58.

67. Christopher Dresser, *Modern Ornamentation: A Series of Original Designs* (London: B. T. Batsford, 1886), plates 29 and 40.

68. Nicholas Pevsner, "Christopher Dresser, Industrial Designer," *Architectural Review* 81 (1937): 183–86.

69. Joan Campbell, *The German Werkbund: The Politics of Reform in the Applied Arts* (Princeton: Princeton Univ. Press, 1978); and Stuart Durant, *Ornament from the Industrial Revolution to Today* (Woodstock, N.Y.: Overlook Press, 1986).

70. "Panama Pacific Exposition," *Dry Goods Economist* 68 (20 June 1914): 267.

71. *International Correspondence School Reference Library*, sec. 9, "Oilcloth and Linoleum Designing" (Scranton, Pa.: International Textbook, 1905), 6–7.

72. Ibid., 10–13.

73. Leo Blackman and Deborah Dietsch, "A New Look at Linoleum: Preservation's Rejected Floor Covering," *Old House Journal* 10 (Jan. 1982): 9–12; and Leo Blackman and Deborah Dietsch "Linoleum: How to Repair It, Install It, and Clean It," *Old House Journal* 10 (Feb. 1982): 36–38.

74. *Floors, Utile and Beautiful* (London: Jas. F. Ebner, 1882), 1.

75. Interviews with author: Doreen Cross, Ottawa, Canada, 1993; Myrle E. Hemenway, Boulder, Colo., 1993; Ted Seder, Hot Springs Village, Ark., 1993; Winifred Hadsel, Lexington, Va., 1994; and David Blair, Canterbury, England, 1995. All revealed memories of an hierarchy in room-use appropriateness for linoleum. Notes to interviews in possession of the author.

76. *International Correspondence School Reference Library*, sec. 9, p. 13.

77. Cited in C. D. Edwards, "A Unique Floorcovering: An Investigation into Technology and Changes in Design, Using the Linoleum Industry as a Case Study" (master's thesis, VA/RCA, Apr. 1987), 39. Typescript, Kirkcaldy Museum.

78. Ibid., 41.

79. *Carpet and Upholstery Trade Review* 42, no. 7 (1 Apr. 1911): 1, 7.

80. Hazel H. Adler, *Planning the Color Scheme for Your Home* (Philadelphia: George W. Blabon, 1926), 7.

81. Margaret McElroy, *Color and Charm in Home Interiors* (Kearney, N.J.: Congoleum-Nairn, 1930), 21.

82. Frank Alvah Parsons, *The Art of Home Furnishing and Decoration* (Lancaster, Pa.: Armstrong Cork, 1918), 26.

83. Paul Vaughan, *Something in Linoleum* (London: Sinclair-Stevenson, 1994), 62.

5. GOOD IMPRESSIONS

1. Clarence Cook, *What Shall We Do with our Walls?* (New York: Warren Fuller, 1880).

2. Lesley Hoskins, ed., *The Papered Wall* (New York: Harry N. Abrams, 1994) and Joanna Banham, "The History of Anaglypta," typescript, 1988, Crown Decorative Products, Ltd., Darwen, England.

3. Walton, *Infancy and Development of Linoleum*. Also see Parks, "Floorcloths to Linoleum," and Joni Monnich, "Embossed Wallcoverings: The Ideal Choice for Your Walls," in Auer et al., *Interiors Handbook*, vol. 2.

4. The Wallpaper Manufacturers, Ltd., "The Lincrusta Walton, Caméoid, and Cordelova Branch," *Journal of Decorative Art* 25 (Sept. 1905): 29, special supplement, "Wallpaper News."

5. Ibid., 30, and Bruce Bradbury, "Lincrusta-Walton: Can the Democratic Wallcovering Be Revived?" *Old House Journal* 10 (Oct. 1982): 203–6; W. G. Sutherland, *Modern Wall Decoration* (London: Simpkin, Marshall, Hamilton and Kent, 1893); Alan V. Sugden and John L. Edmondson, *A History of English Wallpaper, 1509–1914* (New York: Charles Scribner's Sons, 1925).

6. Wallpaper Manufacturers, Ltd., "Lincrusta Walton," 29. The Record Books of the Linoleum Manufacturing Company indicate that Walton resigned his active management of the works because "of the state of his health," but it seems more likely that he simply wanted to devote his time to developing his new product.

7. Walton, *Infancy and Development of Linoleum*, 45.

8. Coleman, "Frederick Walton, Inventor."

9. Room, *Directory*, 110; *Fife Free Press* (2 Feb. 1878). Clipping File, Kirkcaldy Museum.

10. *Lincrusta-Walton: The Sunbury Wall Decoration, a New Linoleum Product* (London: Waterlow and Sons, 1880), 8.

11. Coleman, "Frederick Walton, Inventor," 299.

12. Ibid.

13. "Lincrusta-Walton," *Journal of Decorative Art* 4 (Mar. 1884): 472.

14. Referred to in advertisements in *Journal of Decorative Art* 17 (June 1897), ad section, and *Building World* 3, no. 76 (27 Mar. 1897): 6.

15. *Builder* (26 Dec. 1896): iv.

16. A. S. G. Butler, *Recording Ruin* (London: Constable, 1942), 139.

17. Mme. Le Prince, *Lincrusta-Walton Decoration* (New York: Frederick Beck, 1884), 2.

18. "Extracts from the Press," *A New Decorative Material: Lincrusta-Walton* (New York: Lincrusta-Walton Manufacturing, [1883?]), 9.

19. *Lincrusta-Walton Designs* (New York: Frederick Beck, [1889?]).

20. "New Mexico Capitol," *Santa Fe Daily New Mexican,* 24 Dec., 1886, p. 1.

21. *Sears, Roebuck, Wallpaper Catalogue* (Chicago: Sears, Roebuck, 1918), 20, and *Sears, Roebuck Catalogue,* Fall 1915, 1594.

22. "Lincrusta-Walton," *Journal of Decorative Art* 15 (Jan. 1895): 20, and (July 1895): 170.

23. Ibid., 20.

24. "Lincrusta-Walton," *Journal of Decorative Art* 1 (Mar. 1881): 29.

25. Philippe Thiébaut, Claude Frontisi, Georges Vigne, and Marie-Madeleine Massé, *Guimard* (Paris: Réunion des Musées Nationaux, 1992), 137.

26. The Wallpaper Manufacturers, Ltd., "The Anaglypta Branch," *Journal of Decorative Art* 25 (Sept. 1905), special supplement, "Wallpaper News," 8–9; and Banham, "History of Anaglypta," 6–7.

27. The Wallpaper Manufacturers, Ltd., "The Anaglypta Branch," Ibid., 8

28. Ibid. Also Bruce Bradbury, "Anaglypta and Other Embossed Wallcovering: Their History and Their Use Today," *Old House Journal* 10 (Nov. 1982): 231–34; Sugden and Edmondson, *History of English Wallpaper,* 283.

29. "Anaglypta Catalogue," *Journal of Decorative Art* 17 (July 1897): 186.

30. "Anaglypta," *Decorator* 2 (22 Apr. 1904): 310.

31. Hoskins, *Papered Wall,* 160–63.

32. *Building News and Engineering Journal* 68 (Jan. 1895): vi.

33. Sugden and Edmondson, *History of English Wallpaper,* 53.

34. Elspeth Hardie, "William Scott Morton," *Antique Collector* 59 (Mar. 1988): 70–79; and Elspeth Hardie, "Tynecastle Tapestry in the United States," *Antique Collector* 60 (May 1989): 108–15.

35. Elspeth Hardie, "Tynecastle Tapestry," 114–15.

36. Wallpaper Manufacturers, Ltd., "Lincrusta Walton," 30–31.

37. Ibid.

38. Sugden and Edmondson, *History of English Wallpaper,* 252.

39. *Journal of Decorative Art* 18 (Jan. 1898): 42.

40. Sutherland, *Modern Wall Decoration,* 48.

41. Hoskins, *Papered Wall,* 158.

42. Wallpaper Manufacturers, Ltd., "Wallpaper News," *Journal of Decorative Art* 25 (Sept. 1905), special supplement, 1–32.

43. Crown Decorative Products, Ltd., Akzo Nobel, P.O. Box 37, Darwen, Lancashire BB3 OBG, England.

44. Le Prince, *Lincrusta-Walton,* 12.

45. "Tynecastle Tapestry at the Albert Works, Edinburgh," *Art Journal* n.s. (Mar. 1896): 81–85.

46. William Morris, "The Arts and Crafts Today," address delivered in Edinburgh, 1889, in Morris, *Collected Works,* 23:366.

47. Butler, *Recording Ruin,* 139.

48. "Anaglypta," *Decorator* 2 (22 Apr. 1904): 310.

49. "Lincrusta-Walton," *Journal of Decorative Art* 4 (Mar. 1884): 473.

50. Le Prince, *Lincrusta-Walton,* 12.

51. *Journal of Decorative Art* 17 (June 1897): ad section.

52. *Lincrusta-Walton: The Sunbury Wall Decoration,* 10.

53. *Wallpaper Trade Department* (Mar. 1888): 109.

54. Ibid.

6. Grand Illusions

1. Jonathan Thornton and William Adair, "Applied Decoration for Historic Interiors, Preserving Composition Ornament," *Preservation Briefs,* no. 34 (Washington, D.C.: National Parks Service, May 1994); Jonathan Thornton, "'Compo': The History and Technology of 'Plastic' Compositions," American Institute for Conservation of Historic and Artistic Works, Preprints of papers presented at the thirteenth annual meeting, Washington, D.C., 22–26 May 1985; and J. Randall Cotton, "Composition: Restoring and Caring for Molded 'Carvings,'" *Old-House Journal* 21 (Jan./Feb. 1993): 28–33.

2. William Adair, "An Investigation of Composition Ornamentation," in Auer et al., *Interiors Handbook,* vol. 2.

3. Cotton, "Composition," 29.

4. Mark Reinberger, "Robert Wellford and the Southeast Composition Ornament Trade" (paper presented to Southeastern Society of Architectural Historians, Clemson, S.C., 5 Nov. 1993). Typescript supplied by the author.

5. Ibid., 6.

6. Ibid., 7–8.

7. *Sweet's Catalogue of Building Construction* (New York: Architectural Record, 1906), 322.

8. Thornton and Adair, "Applied Decoration for Historic Interiors," 2, 8.

9. *Lombard Company Catalogue* (New York: Lombard, 1918).

10. Jacobson and Company, *A Second Book of Old English Designs* (New York: Jacobson, 1928). A 1915 catalogue in the collection claimed the company had been in business for twenty-five years and advertised decorative, artificial materials that imitated stucco.

11. George Jackson and Sons, *Carton-Pierre, Papier-mâché, and Patent Fibrous Plaster Works* (London, [1900?]).

12. Jonathan Thornton, "The History, Technology and Conservation of Architectural *Papier*

Mâché," *Journal of American Institute for Conservation* 32, no. 2 (Summer 1993): 165–76. The spelling of papier-mâché varies widely even in modern scholarly writing. Sometimes it has a hyphen, sometimes not. Occasionally the "a" in mâché is unaccented, sometimes "papier" is "paper." Sometimes the name is italicized as a foreign term, usually it is not.

13. Quoted in Charles Bielefeld, *Ornaments Manufactured in the Improved Papier Mâché* (London: published by the author, 1850); also cited in Thornton, "History, Technology and Conservation," 166.

14. Thornton, "History, Technology and Conservation," 166.

15. Ibid., and *Oxford English Dictionary*, s.v. "Papier-mâché," 439–40.

16. John Thomas Smith, *Nollekens and His Times* (London: Henry Colburn, 1828), 191. Also cited in Ada K. Longfield, "The Manufacture of 'Raised Stucco' or *'Papier-Mâché'* Papers in Ireland c. 1750–70," *Journal of the Royal Society of Antiquaries of Ireland* 78 (July 1948): 55–62, as well as in Charles Frederick Bielefeld, *On the Use of the Improved Papier Mâché in Furniture, in the Interior Decoration of Buildings, and in Works of Art* (London: J. Rickerby, 1840), 4.

17. Bielefeld, *On the Use of the Improved Papier Mâché*, 3.

18. Shirley Spaulding DeVoe, *English Papier-Mâché of the Georgian and Victorian Periods* (Middletown, Conn.: Wesleyan Univ. Press, 1971), 25–27.

19. Thornton and Adair, "Applied Decoration for Historic Interiors," 15.

20. Yapp, *Art Industry*, 26.

21. Longfield, "The Manufacture of 'Raised Stucco,'" 57.

22. Bielefeld, *On the Use of the Improved Papier Mâché*, 5.

23. Ibid., 8.

24. DeVoe, *English Papier-Mâché*, 30.

25. "Relief Decoration," *Decorator's and Painter's Magazine* 3 (15 Mar. 1904): 380.

26. David Hayles to the author, 5 Mar. 1997. Hayles's account differs from that presented by Jeff Greene in "Architectural Scagliola in Significant American Interiors," in Auer et al., *Interiors Handbook,* 2:4–9, 4–10.

27. Greene, "Architectural Scagliola," 4–9.

28. Margaret Jourdain, *English Interior Decoration, 1500 to 1830* (London: B. T. Batsford, 1950), 66–67.

29. Ibid.

30. Greene, "Architectural Scagliola," 4–10.

31. Ibid., 4–11.

32. Ibid.

33. *Sweet's Catalogue,* 1906, 748.

34. Ibid., 750–52.

35. *Moreau Marble Co. Ltd.* (London: Moreau Marble, 1902), trade pamphlet, Bodleian Ephemera Collection, Box 1, Housing and Houses.

36. *Sani Onyx* (Indianapolis; Marietta Manufacturing, 1927), 3.

37. *Building Age and National Builder* 49 (Sept. 1927): 40.

38. Walker C. Johnson, "Terrazzo," in *Twentieth Century Building Materials, History and Conservation,* ed. Thomas C. Jester (New York: McGraw-Hill, 1995), 234–39.

39. Ibid., 237.

40. Ibid., 235.

41. Paul N. Hasluck, *Practical Graining and Marbling* (Philadelphia: David McKay, 1915), 155.

42. *Marbleized Slate Mantels* (Philadelphia: Keystone Slate and Soapstone Works, 1880), 2, 71, and *Marbleized Slate Mantels* (Philadelphia: Enterprise Slate and Soapstone Works, 1886), 2.

43. *Lexington (Va.) Gazette,* 29 May 1869, cited in Royster Lyle and Pamela H. Simpson, *The Architecture of Historic Lexington* (Charlottesville: Univ. Press of Virginia, 1977), 189.

44. Adrienne B. Cowden and David P. Wessel, "Cast Stone," in Jester, *Twentieth Century Building Materials,* 86–93.

45. Benedict Stone, Curator's File, National Building Museum, Washington, D.C., compiled by Brenda Doyle, 1991.

46. Cowden and Wessel, "Cast Stone," 91.

47. *House Beautiful* 33 (Apr. 1913): v.

48. Ibid.

49. Michael Stratton, *The Terracotta Revival: Building Innovation and Image of the Industrial City in Britain and North America* (London: Victor Gollancy; North Pomfret, Vt.: Peter Crawley, Trafalgar Square, 1993). The British usually spell terra cotta as one word, while American usage separates it into two. I use the American form here.

50. Allison Kelly, *Mrs. Coade's Stone* (Upton-upon-Severn, Worcs.: Self Publishing Association, in conjunction with the Georgian Group, 1990), 23–24.

51. Ibid., 58–60.

52. Allison Kelly, "Coade Stone in Georgian Architecture," *Architectural History* 28 (1985): 71, and Kelly, "Sir John Soane and Mrs. Eleanore Coade," *Apollo* 129 (Apr. 1989): 247–53.

53. Kelly, *Mrs. Coade's Stone,* 37.

54. *Building News* 19 (1870): 55, cited in Stratton, *Terracotta Revival,* 62.

55. Stratton, *Terracotta Revival,* 12.

56. Ibid., 148.

57. Deborah Slaton and Harry J. Hunderman, "Terra Cotta," in Jester, *Twentieth Century Building Materials,* 156–61, and Stratton, *Terracotta Revival,* 233–34.

58. Stratton, *Terracotta Revival,* 163.

59. Ibid. 159.

60. Ian C. Bristow, *Architectural Colour in British Interiors, 1615–1840* (New Haven: Paul Mellon Center, Yale Univ. Press, 1996), 1–13, 28–32, 67, 175–82.

61. H. R. McIlwain, ed., *Journals of the House of Burgess of Virginia, 1702–1712,* 13 vols. (Richmond: Virginia State Library, 1912), 4:118.

62. Nina Fletcher Little, *American Decorative Wall Painting, 1700–1850* (Old Sturbridge Village, Mass., 1952).

63. Laura Phillips, "Grand Illusions: Decorative Interior Painting in North Carolina," *Perspectives in Vernacular Architecture,* ed. Thomas Carter and Bernard Herman (Columbia, Mo.: Univ. of Missouri Press, 1991): 4:155–62.

64. Ann McCleary, "Preach a Little, Paint a Little, Drink a Little: The Work of Itinerant

Painter Green Berry Jones," *Augusta Historical Bulletin* 22 (Staunton, Va.: Augusta County Historical Society, 1986), 31–39.

65. Bristow, *Architectural Colour,* 67.

66. Ian C. Bristow, *Interior House-Painting Colours and Technology, 1615–1840* (New Haven: Paul Mellon Center, Yale Univ. Press, 1996), 133. See also A. Ashman Kelly, *The Standard Grainer, Stainer and Marbler* (Philadelphia: David McKay, 1933); William E. Wall, *Graining Ancient and Modern,* revised by F. N. Vanderwaller (New York: Drake, 1955, 1972); W. L. Savage, *Graining and Marbling, Complete and Practical Guide* (London: Austin Rogers, 1925); John Parry, *Graining and Marbling* (London: Crosby, Lockwood and Son, 1949); and Jourdain, *English Interior Decoration,* 38, 68.

67. Allen Freeman, "Faux Arts," *Historic Preservation* 43 (Jan./Feb. 1991): 48.

68. E. W. Hudnall, New Canton, Va. to William Massie, Nelson County, Va., 19 Mar. 1815. William Massie Papers, 1747–1865, Univ. of Texas at Austin.

69. "The Art of Painting," *Scientific American* 2 (8 Jan. 1846): 2.

70. Andrew Jackson Downing, *The Architecture of Country Houses* (New York: D. Appleton, 1850), 367.

71. Hasluck, *Practical Graining and Marbling,* 9.

72. John Ruskin, *The Seven Lamps of Architecture* (London: Smith, Elder, 1849), 43.

73. John Ruskin, *The Stones of Venice* (1851–53; reprint, London: John Wiley and Sons, 1885), 30.

74. "Imitation," *Carpentry and Building* 2 (22 Feb. 1878): 114.

75. Ibid.

76. Parry, *Graining and Marbling,* 2.

77. Quoted in Jourdain, *English Interior Decoration,* 68. The recommendation comes from J. C. Loudon, *Cottage, Farm, and Villa Architecture* (1833), 277.

78. Hasluck, *Practical Graining and Marbling,* 10.

7. SUBSTITUTE GIMCRACKERY

1. Huxtable, "Concrete Technology," 144.

2. A. Welby Pugin, *The True Principles of Pointed or Christian Architecture* (1841; reprint, London: Academy Editions, St. Martin's Press, 1973), 34.

3. Ibid., 53.

4. Ibid., 42

5. *New York Ecclesiologist* 1 (Oct. 1848): 5.

6. Pugin, *True Principles,* 34.

7. Julie Wosk, *Breaking Frame: Technology and the Visual Arts in the Nineteenth Century* (New Brunswick, N.J.: Rutgers Univ. Press, 1992).

8. Pugin, *True Principles,* 65–66.

9. Eileen Boris, *Art and Labor: Ruskin, Morris, and the Craftsman Ideal in America* (Philadelphia: Temple Univ. Press, 1985), 4.

10. Ibid.

11. E. T. Cook and Alexander Wedderburn, *The Works of John Ruskin* (London: George Allen, 1903), 8:75–76.

12. Ruskin, *Stones of Venice,* 30.

13. Cook and Wedderburn, *Works of John Ruskin,* 8:72.

14. Ibid., 81.

15. Ibid., 219.

16. Ibid., 82.

17. Ibid., 83.

18. Cook and Wedderburn, *Works of John Ruskin,* 16:344.

19. George Gilbert Scott, *Remarks on Secular and Domestic Architecture, Present and Future* (London: John Murray, 1858), vi.

20. Ibid., 56–57.

21. Ibid., 239.

22. Ibid., 240.

23. Ibid.

24. Ibid., 242.

25. Ibid., 243.

26. Ibid., 244.

27. Ibid., 245.

28. Ibid., 246–47.

29. Ibid., 261.

30. Charles Eastlake, *Hints on Household Taste* (London: Longmans, Green, 1878), 43.

31. Ibid., 51.

32. May Morris, ed., *The Collected Works of William Morris* (London: Longmans, 1910–15), 22:323. Also Boris, *Art and Labor,* 7.

33. Morris, *Collected Works,* 23:164–91, 192–214.

34. Ibid., 23:192–214.

35. Charles Harvey and Jon Press, "The Businessman," and Linda Parry, "Textiles," in Parry, *William Morris* (London: Philip Wilson for Victoria and Albert Museum, 1996), 49–55, and 224–34.

36. Morris, ed., *Collected Works,* 2:392.

37. Ibid., 1:246.

38. Ibid., 1:242.

39. Ibid., 2:469–70.

40. Ibid., 2:470.

41. Ibid., 22:331–41.

42. James Morrison, "Report of Select Committee of 1835," quoted in Wosk, *Breaking Frame,* 120.

43. Wosk, *Breaking Frame,* 120–21, and A. I. F. Bøe, *From Gothic Revival to Functional Form: A Study of Victorian Theories of Design* (Oslo: Oslo Univ. Press, 1954), 73–74.

44. Malcolm Baker and Brenda Richardson, eds., *A Grand Design* (Harry N. Abrams for Baltimore Museum of Art, 1997). This catalogue traces the history of the Victoria and Albert Museum.

45. Quoted in Stuart Durant, "Chronological Outline of the Life of Christopher Dresser," in *Principles of Decorative Design,* by Christopher Dresser (1873; reprint, London: Academy Editions, St. Martin's Press, 1973), n.p.

46. Christopher Dresser, "Hindrances to the Progress of Applied Art," *Journal of the Society of Arts* 20 (12 Apr. 1872): 435.

47. Ibid.

48. Ibid., 437.

49. Christopher Dresser, *The Art of Decorative Design* (1862; reprint, Watkins Glen, N.Y.: American Life Foundation, 1977), 137.

50. Dresser, *Principles of Decorative Design*, 89.

51. Ibid., 16.

52. Ibid., 89.

53. Ibid., 24.

54. Ibid., 25.

55. "The Year's Advance in Art Manufactures," *Art Journal*, n.s. (1883): 353.

56. Lewis F. Day, "Machine-Made Art," *Art Journal*, n.s. (1885): 107–10.

57. Ibid., 107.

58. Ibid., 109.

59. Ibid., 108.

60. Horace Greely, ed., *Art and Industry* (New York: Redfield, 1853): 50.

61. Isaac Edwards Clark, ed., *Art and Industry: Education in the Industrial and Fine Arts in the United States* (Washington, D.C.: GPO, 1885–98), 1:xciii, xcv.

62. Dresser, *Principles of Decorative Design*, 104.

63. Wosk, *Breaking Frame*, 121.

64. Clark, *Art and Industry*, 3:xiii–xix.

65. Nina de Angeli Walls to the author, 15 July 1996. Letter in possession of the author.

66. Ernest Batchelder, "Arts and Crafts Movement in America: Work or Play?" *Craftsman* 16 (Aug. 1902): 122–23, quoted in Boris, *Art and Labor*, 29.

67. Boris, *Art and Labor*, 74–75; and Miles Orvell, *The Real Thing: Imitation and Authenticity in American Culture, 1880–1940* (Chapel Hill: Univ. of North Carolina Press, 1989), 160.

68. "Concrete Bungalows, Showing Economy of Construction: By the editor," *Craftsman* 21 (Mar. 1912): 663–75. He also included a concrete block design in *Craftsman Homes* (New York: Craftsman, 1909).

69. "Linoleum: A Page from the Storybook of Modern Industry," *Craftsman* 26 (May 1914): 238–39.

70. Advertisement, Northrop, Coburn, Dodge, Company, *Craftsman* 20 (Feb. 1911): 34a.

71. Jane Addams, *Twenty Years at Hull House* (1910), quoted in T. J. Jackson Lears, *No Place of Grace: Antimodernism and the Transformation of American Culture, 1880–1920* (New York: Pantheon Books, 1981), 81.

72. Boris, *Art and Labor*, 46.

73. Bruce Brooks Pfieffer, ed., *Frank Lloyd Wright Collected Writings* (New York: Rizzoli, 1992), 1:59–61.

74. Ibid., 62–63.

75. Ibid., 64–65.

76. Ibid., 66.

77. Eileen Boris claims it also had deep roots in Chicago's intellectual and cultural world. *Art and Labor*, 47.

78. Pfeiffer, *Frank Lloyd Wright Collected Writings*, 1:225–316.

79. Ibid., 301.

80. Ibid., 304.

81. Ibid.

82. Sweeney, *Wright in Hollywood*, gives a full discussion of the development of the textile block system.

83. Pfeiffer, *Frank Lloyd Wright Collected Writings*, 1:305–9.

84. Thorstein Veblen, "Arts and Crafts," *Journal of Political Economy* 11 (Dec. 1902): 108–10.

85. Scranton, "Manufacturing Diversity," 476–505. Scranton quotes David Hounshell that the cycle of mass production involves technological innovation, diminished prices, effective marketing, and massive orders as well as industrial manufacture of objects on a mass scale.

86. Curator's Files, Staten Island Historical Society.

87. *Oxford English Dictionary*, s.v. "Cheap," 306–7.

88. Lanzillotti, *Hard-Surface Floor-Covering Industry*, 69.

89. Henry Adams, *The Education of Henry Adams* (1918; reprint, New York: Random House, 1931).

90. Annmarie Adams, *Architecture in the Family Way, Doctors, Houses, and Women, 1870–1900* (Montreal: McGill Queen's Univ. Press, 1996), 29.

91. Harriette M. Plunkett, *Women, Plumbers, and Doctors; or, Household Sanitation* (New York: Appelton, 1885), 203, 40.

92. Suellen Hoy, *Chasing Dirt: The American Pursuit of Cleanliness* (New York: Oxford Univ. Press, 1995), 69.

93. Ibid., 79.

94. Ibid., 74.

95. Adams, *Architecture in the Family Way*, 91–92.

96. Arthur Seymour Jennings, *The Home Beautiful* (London: Greening, 1908), 75.

97. "Germs vs. Linoleum," 23; and *Helpful Hints for Linoleum Salesmen*, 11.

98. "Argument for Sheet-Metal in Architecture," 239.

99. *E. E. Souther Iron Co., Catalogue No. 18*.

100. Orvell, *Real Thing*, xv–xvi.

101. William Dean Howells, *A Traveler from Alturia* (1894; reprint, New York: Sagamore Press, 1957), 274.

102. Jacob Riis, *How the Other Half Lives: Studies among the Tenements of New York* (Williamstown, Mass.: Corner House, 1890) and Lincoln Steffens, *The Shame of the Cities* (New York: McClure, Phillips, 1904).

103. Simon J. Bronner, *Consuming Visions: Accumulation and Display of Goods in America, 1880–1920* (New York: W. W. Norton, 1989).

104. Gibson, "Cement Block Architecture," 72.

105. *Wallpaper Trade Department* (Mar. 1888): 109.

106. "What a Woman Can Do," *Cement World* 2 (Dec. 1908): 618.

107. *Cement World* 2 (Feb. 1909): 792.

108. "Linoleum and Borders," *Art Journal* 19 (1880): 176.

109. Nina de Angeli Walls, "Educating Women for Art and Commerce: The Philadelphia School of Design," *History of Education Quarterly* 34 (Fall 1994): 329–55; and letter to the author, 15 July 1996.

110. *International Correspondence School Reference Library,* sec. 9, p. 6–7.

111. *The Salesmanship Guidebook* (Lancaster, Pa.: Armstrong Cork, 1936), 7.

112. William Leach, *Land of Desire: Merchants, Power, and the Rise of a New American Culture* (New York: Pantheon Books, 1993).

113. Robert Nisbet, *History of the Idea of Progress* (New York: Basic Books, 1980), 230.

114. Ibid., 171.

115. Alan Dawley, *Struggles for Justice: Social Responsibility and the Liberal State* (Cambridge: Harvard Univ. Press, Belknap Press, 1991).

116. "Argument for Sheet-Metal in Architecture," 239.

117. "Unlimited Opportunities for Steel Ceilings," 18.

118. *Lexington (Va.) Gazette,* 17 Feb. 1915, p. 3.

119. Orvell, *Real Thing,* 40–72.

120. Mark Twain, *Life on the Mississippi* (1883; reprint, New York: American Classics Society, 1977), 233–36.

121. Mark Twain, *A Connecticut Yankee in King Arthur's Court* (1889; reprint, New York: New Amsterdam Library, 1963), 46–47. Cited in Orvell, *Real Thing,* 38.

122. Beecher and Stowe, *American Woman's Home,* 91–94. Cited in Orvell, *Real Thing,* 37.

123. "Cornice Work," 34.

124. "Argument for Sheet-Metal in Architecture," 239.

125. Pugin, *True Principles,* 34

126. Cook and Wedderburn, *Works of John Ruskin,* 26:344, 8:239.

127. "Sheet-Metal Architecture," *AABN* 1 (22 July 1876): 234.

128. Thorstein Veblen, *The Theory of the Leisure Class* (1899; reprint, New Brunswick, N.J.: Transaction, 1992), 94–95.

129. Ibid.

130. Ibid., 115.

131. Ibid.

132. "Sheet-Metal Architecture," *AABN* 1 (11 Nov. 1876): 366.

133. "New Relief Wall Decorations," *Queen* 20 (1 Feb. 1896): 189.

134. Jennings, *Home Beautiful,* 79.

135. *Carpet and Upholstery Trade Review* 28 (15 May 1898): 45.

136. Ibid., 50.

137. *Ladies Home Journal* 35 (Mar. 1918): 112.

138. Editorial, *Sheet Metal Builder* 1 (Apr. 1874): 5.

139. "Tynecastle Tapestry at the Albert Works," 81.

140. Parsons, *Art of Home Furnishing and Decoration,* 26.

141. "Lincrusta Leather," *Journal of Decorative Art* 41 (Jan. 1921): 25.

Glossary

AMERICAN CLOTH. Oilcloth imitations of leather. Used in the mid- and late nineteenth century for inexpensive upholstery, especially for carriages.

ANAGLYPTA. Paper pulp–based embossed wall covering, patented in Great Britain in 1886 by Thomas J. Palmer and still made today. (See fig. 63.)

ARTIFICIAL MARBLE. Several materials that imitated marble, such as enameled slate, concrete with a high portion of marble dust and chips, and, usually, the materials known as scagliola or marezzo, which are plaster-based.

ARTIFICIAL STONE. Any form of concrete block cast to imitate stone effects.

ART STONE. Concrete with high portions of marble or granite dust and chips for aggregate. Cast into decorative forms, it was sometimes also carved to create greater depth. Also called cast stone.

ASPHALT TILE. A type of hard-surface, manufactured flooring. When introduced in the 1920s, it was made with asphalt, but later asbestos was substituted. Often used over cement slabs since it was impervious to moisture.

BOULINIKON. One of the more bizarre floor coverings of the 1870s, it used buffalo hide, wool, and hair as the binder in an oil base.

BRITISH CEMENT. A type of artificial cement invented by Isaac Johnson in the early nineteenth century.

CALENDERS. Heavy metal revolving cylinders used in the production of oilcloth and linoleum. (See fig. 43.)

CAMÉOID. Paper-based embossed wall covering invented in Great Britain by D. M. Southerland in 1888. Frederick Walton manufactured it beginning in 1896 as a lightweight, less-expensive alternative to Lincrusta-Walton.

CARTON PIERRE. Pulped paper material hardened with glue, whiting, and gypsum and pressed into molds to imitate plaster ornament.

CAST IRON. Metallic blast-furnace product cast into decorative forms. Commonly used for nineteenth-century commercial building fronts and ornamental detail.

CEMENT. Mixture of clay and lime fired at a high temperature and then ground into a fine powder, used for the binder in concrete.

CINDER BLOCK. Lightweight concrete block patented in 1917 by F. J. Straub, so-called for the aggregate of coal furnace cinders. In later production, other lightweight materials were substituted.

COADE STONE. A terra cotta or kiln-fired clay substance named for its late-eighteenth-century inventor and manufacturer, Eleanore Coade. She called it an artificial stone.

Cobble block. Concrete block units cast to imitate a cobblestone finish.

Compo. Also called composition. A plasterlike substance made from glue, linseed oil, resin, and chalk. Usually pressed into molds to form sculptural relief decoration. (See fig. 66.)

Concrete. Mixture of cement, stone aggregates, sand, and water that can be cast in its fluid state in molds or forms. Sets to a stonelike hardness and strength.

Concrete block. A hollow, cast building unit usually measuring eight by eight by sixteen inches. (See fig. 4.)

Congoleum. Commercial name for a felt-based flooring first manufactured in the 1910s.

Cordelova. An embossed wallpaper manufactured in Edinburgh in the 1890s.

Cornice brake. Machine used for bending sheets of metal into decorative profiles for the upper terminus of a wall. (See fig. 15.)

Corrugated metal. Metal formed into alternating ridges and valleys to increase tensile strength. (See fig. 27.)

Corticine. Hard-surface floor covering patented in 1871, with a polymerized linseed oil base and compressed cork filling. Also an embossed wall covering. The floor covering was later known as cork carpet.

Emdeca. Commercial name for a stamped and enameled sheet-metal product made in Britain from 1894 and promoted as a substitute for bathroom tiles.

Faience. Glazed terra cotta.

Felt-base floor covering. Floor covering composed of a felt base saturated with a petroleum derivative and covered with a coat of enamel and a painted pattern. First produced in 1910s, considered a cheap alternative to linoleum. Commercial names were Feltoleum, Fiberlin, Floortex, Congoleum, Quaker Rugs. (See fig. 51.)

Floor oilcloth. Floor covering made up of layers of sizing and paint over a canvas base. Produced by hand in the eighteenth century, the process was increasingly mechanized in the early nineteenth century. Other names include floorcloth, painted floorcloth, oilcloth, waxcloth. (See fig. 40.)

Galvanized iron or steel. Iron or steel coated by immersion in molten zinc to prevent rust.

Graining. Art of painting illusionistic wood grain patterns, usually on interior woodwork. (See fig. 71.)

Hard-surface floor covering. Term for floor oilcloth, linoleum, felt-base, asphalt-tile, and vinyl floor covering, distinguishing them from fabric carpets and rugs.

Hydraulic cement. A type of cement that sets under water.

Inlaid linoleum. Linoleum composed of various colored pieces of linoleum fit together by hand or machine to form decorative patterns and then reheated and rolled to fuse the material. (See figs. 49, 50.)

Kamptulican. Hard-surface floor covering composed of India rubber, gutta percha (tree sap gum), and cork. Patented in Great Britain by Elijah Galloway in 1844.

Keene's cement. Patented plaster made from gypsum and alum, it sets slowly to a very hard surface; used in artificial marbles.

Lignomur. Embossed wall covering first produced in the United States in 1880. In 1896 taken over by a London firm, which changed the formula from a wood fiber to a paper-pulp base.

Lincrusta-Walton. Embossed wall covering similar to linoleum in composition but with a wood-pulp binder. Invented by Frederick Walton in 1877. Could imitate plaster, wood, leather, or tile effects. (See fig. 57.)

LINOLEUM. Hard-surface floor covering composed of an oxidized linseed-oil base with ground cork dust, rosin, and gum filler pressed between heavy rollers onto a canvas backing. Invented by Frederick Walton in the 1860s. (See figs. 44, 45, 53.)

MARBLING. Art of imitating the appearance of marble by painting. Frequently found on interior woodwork.

MAREZZO. Artificial marble made with plaster, animal glue, and pigments mixed in a fluid state.

MOREAU MARBLE. Artificial marble manufactured in Great Britain in early 1900s. Limestone treated and baked in a patented process.

PAPIER-MÂCHÉ. Paper pulp or layers of paper mixed with glue and other materials and pressed into molds, hardened, and painted. Used for decorative objects, furniture, clock cases, and architectural ornament.

PORTLAND CEMENT. Mixture of clay and lime fired at a high temperature and ground to a fine powder, a binder in concrete. Invented by Joseph Aspdin in 1824, named for the gray Portland stone it resembled.

POZZOLANA. A naturally occurring form of cement found in volcanic deposits.

PRESS. Machine for embossing sheets of metal. Draw press employed mechanical pressure; drop press, the force of a drop hammer to stamp the decorative design. Hence, pressed-metal ceilings or stamped-metal ceilings, referring to the process of manufacture.

REINFORCED CONCRETE. Concrete cast in temporary forms and reinforced with metal bars or mesh to add tensile strength.

ROCKFACE BLOCK. Cement block units cast to imitate quarried stone. (See figs. 4, 5, 6.)

ROMAN CEMENT. An early type of manufactured cement invented by James Parker in 1796.

SALAMANDER. Embossed wall covering patented in Great Britain in 1896 made of asbestos.

SANI ONYX. Artificial marble produced by the Marietta Manufacturing Company of Indianapolis in the 1920s. A vitreous building material of rock fused at a high temperature. (See fig. 67.)

SANTORIN. A naturally occurring form of cement found in volcanic deposits.

SCAGLIOLA. Artificial marble made from plaster, animal glue, and pigments, dried to a hard, stonelike surface and polished.

SHEET METAL. Iron, copper, steel, and other metals flattened between metal rollers into thin sheets. Used for pressed and stamped ceilings, shingles, siding, and roofing.

STRAUBLOX. The commercial name for F. J. Straub's early cinder block.

TABLE-BAIZE. Light form of oilcloth used as waterproof table and sometimes wall covering.

TERNEPLATE. Thin sheets of iron or steel dipped in a molten lead-tin alloy to prevent rust. Much used in the nineteenth century for roofing, hence sometimes called roofing plate.

TERRA COTTA. Hard, fired clay used for architectural ornament. Usually reddish brown or gray in color. (See fig. 70.)

TERRAZZO. Flooring made of marble or other stone chips embedded in Portland cement, with sections separated by metal strips. Ground and polished to a stonelike finish when set.

TEXTILE BLOCK. Decorative concrete block units created by Frank Lloyd Wright in the 1920s.

Tin ceiling. Slang term for pressed-metal ceilings, probably in reference to the thinness of the metal, which was usually steel, never tin.

Tinplate. Thin sheets of iron or steel dipped in molten tin to prevent rust. (See fig. 14.)

Trass. A naturally occurring form of cement found in volcanic deposits.

Tynecastle tapestry. Embossed wall and ceiling covering made from paper pulp pressed onto canvas. Manufactured in Edinburgh beginning in the 1880s by William Scott Morton. (See fig. 64.)

Tynecastle vellum. A papier-mâché wall and ceiling covering.

Vinyl flooring. Synthetic material made from polymerized resins. Patented in 1934, first produced in 1947. A substitute for linoleum.

Selected Bibliography

UNPUBLISHED SOURCES

Collections and Archives

Barnett Papers. National Archives of Canada.

Boyd Brothers Papers. National Archives, Canada.

Curator's Files. National Building Museum, Washington, D.C.

Curator's Files. Staten Island Historical Society, Richmond Town, Staten Island.

Ephemera Collection. Bodleian Library, Univ. of Oxford.

Johnson Collection. Bodleian Library, Univ. of Oxford.

Linoleum Manufacturing Company, Ltd. Record Books, 1865–1905, Greater London Record Office.

Nairn Collection. Kirkcaldy Museum and Art Gallery, Kirkcaldy, Scotland.

Patent Design Records. London Record Office, Kew.

Pedlar People Papers. National Archives, Canada.

Walter J. Thompson Archives. Duke Univ., Durham, N.C.

Interviews and Letters

Notes to all interviews and letters to the author are in her possession.

Beebe, Matt. Interview by author. Lexington, Va., 6 Dec. 1986.

Blair, David. Interview by author. Canterbury, Kent, England, 25 July 1995.

Burrell, Thomas Brenton to the Nebraska State Historical Society, 30 June 1987, Lincoln, Neb.

Cragg, Jeremy. Letter to the author. 31 Dec. 1995.

Cross, Doreen. Interview by author. Ottawa, Canada, 16 Aug. 1993 and 17 June 1996.

Hadsel, Winifred. Interview by author. Lexington, Va., 27 Jan. 1994.

Hemenway, Myrle, and Leone Hemenway. Interview by author. Boulder, Colo., 5 Jan. 1993.

Hudnall, E. W., New Canton, Va., to William Massie, Nelson County, Va., 19 Mar. 1815. William Massie Papers, 1747–1865. Univ. of Texas at Austin.

Jefferson, Thomas, to Charles Yancey, 23 July 1821. Jefferson Papers, Library of Congress.

Kingston, Oscar, and Grace Kingston. Interview by author. Osgoode, Ontario, Canada, 16 June 1995.

Seder, Ted, and Sally Seder. Interview by author. Hot Springs Village, Ark., 23 Oct. 1993.

Slagle, W. A. Interview by author. Emporia, Va., 8 Oct. 1991.

Walls, Nina de Angeli. Letter to author. 15 July 1996.

Weimer, Troy. Interview by author. Fairfield, Va., 16 Apr. 1996.

Papers, Reports, and Theses

Banham, Joanna. "The History of Anaglypta." Typescript, 1988. Crown Berger Ltd., Darwen, England.

Barry, Ostlere, and Shepherd, Ltd. "Linoleum, Historical Development." Typescript, n.d. [after 1929]. Kirkcaldy Museum and Library, Kirkcaldy, Scotland.

Carter, Margaret, and Julian S. Smith. "The Metallic Roofing Co. Showroom, A Look at Preservation." Report for the Ontario Heritage Foundation, Ottawa, Ontario, Canada. Nov. 1987–Jan. 1988.

Dickey, David. "Manly Brown's Blacksmith Shop." Student paper, 1981. Leyburn Library Special Collections, Washington and Lee Univ., Lexington, Va.

Edwards, C. D. "A Unique Floorcovering: An Investigation into Technology and Changes in Design, Using the Linoleum Industry as a Case Study." Master's thesis, VA/RCA, Apr. 1987. Kirkcaldy Museum and Library, Kirkcaldy, Scotland.

Evans, John W. "Slater Building, La Grande, Oregon." National Register of Historic Places Inventory-Nomination Form, 14 Dec. 1982. Oregon State Historic Preservation Office.

Gillespie, Ann H. "Decorative Sheet-metal Building Components in Canada 1870–1930." Master's thesis, Carleton Univ., Canada, 1985.

Harboe, John. "History and Technology of the Sheet Metal Cornice." Master's thesis, Columbia Univ., 1984.

Hudlow, Scott M., and Anna Gray. "Phase II Architectural Evaluation of Hoxton Hall (36–171)." Virginia Department of Transportation, Oct. 1991, Richmond, Va.

Murray-Wooley, Carolyn. "Joshua Stamper House." Kentucky Historic Resources Inventory, Site No. Lw. 17, Mar. 1984, Kentucky Heritage Council, Frankfurt, Ky.

Neiswander, Judith A. "Liberalism, Nationalism and the Evolution of Middle Class Values: Literature on Interior Decoration in England, 1875–1914." Ph.D. diss., Univ. of London, 1988.

Powell, Brian. "Canterbury Shaker Village, Introduction." Graduate student paper submitted to Richard Candee, Boston Univ. Preservation Studies Program, 1981.

Quinto, Neal. "A Case for the Historic Preservation of the W. F. Norman Corporation in Nevada, Missouri." Typescript supplied by the Norman Corp. Copy in the Missouri Department of Natural Resources, Division of Historic Preservation Office.

Reinberger, Mark. "Robert Wellford and the Southeast Composition Ornament Trade." Paper presented to Southeastern Society of Architectural Historians, Clemson, S.C., 5 Nov. 1993. Typescript supplied by the author.

Sandiford, Mark. "Embossed Wallpapers, Infilling in Situ." Final Project, RCA/V&A M.A. course, 1993. Decorative Arts Dept., Victoria and Albert Museum, London.

———. "Materials and Techniques: Embossed Wallpapers, the Creation and Impression of Relief." RCA/V&A M.A. course, 1992. Decorative Arts Dept., Victoria and Albert Museum, London.

Snyder, Bonnie Parks. "Chronology of Linoleum Production." Typescript, 1995. Supplied by the author.

Stevenson, Margaret. "C. K. Harvey." Paper presented to Symposium on Virginia Architecture, Univ. of Virginia, 1994. Notes supplied by the author.

Stiritz, Mary M. "Oakherst Place Concrete Block District, St. Louis, Mo." National Register of Historic Places Nomination Form, 5 May 1987.

Swanson, Betsy. "Artificial Stone houses of Artesia, New Mexico, Thematic Group." National Register of Historic Places Nomination Form, 6 Jan. 1984.

Thornton, Jonathan. "'Compo': The History and Technology of 'Plastic' Compositions." Preprints of papers presented to American Institute for Conservation of Historic and Artistic Works, Washington, D.C., 22–26 May 1985. Copy supplied by the author.

White, John P. "Vogl House." Historic American Building Survey, Aug. 1975.

PUBLISHED SOURCES

Builders' and Decorators' Trade Journals

Whole runs of the following were read:

American Architect and Building News, 1876–1930.

American Artisan, Tinner and House Furnisher, 1893–97.

Art Journal, 1874–1905.

Builder, 1888–1922.

Building Age and National Builder, 1925–30.

Building News, 1895–1905.

Building World, 1895–1902.

Carpenter and Builder, 1880–1906.

Carpentry and Building, 1879–1925.

Carpet and Upholstery Trade Review, 1876–7, 1895–1926.

Concrete and Constructional Engineering, 1906–9.

Craftsman, 1890–1915.

Decorator, 1902–21.

Dry-Goods Economist, 1911–15.

House Beautiful and American Suburbs, 1902–3, 1910–13.

Jute Year Book: Annual Directory of the Jute, Canvas and Linoleum Industries and Trade, 1930–35.

Journal of Decorative Arts, 1895–1931.

Ladies Home Journal, 1897–1912, 1917–20.

Metal Worker, 1875–1920.

National Builder, 1895–1930.

Sheet Metal Builder, 1874–75.

Southern Architect and Building News, 1904–5, 1914, 1922–26.

Trade Catalogue Collections

Extensive collections of trade catalogues were consulted at the following institutions:

Avery Architectural Library. Columbia Univ., New York.

Bodleian Library. Oxford.
Canadian Centre for Architecture. Montreal, Canada.
Crown-Berger Decorative Division. Akzu-Nobel, Darwen, England.
Duke Univ. Durham, N.C.
Hagley Museum and Library. Wilmington, Del.
Kirkcaldy Museum and Library. Kirkcaldy, Scotland.
Library of Congress. Washington, D.C.
Museum of Science and Technology. Ottawa, Canada.
National Archives. Ottawa, Canada.
National Art Library. Victoria and Albert Museum, London.
Winterthur Museum and Library. Wilmington, Del.

Periodical Articles

"Argument for Sheet-Metal in Architecture." *American Architect and Building News* 1 (22 July 1876): 239–40.

"Armstrong Fiberlin." *Carpet Trade and Upholstery Review* 46, no. 21 (1 Nov. 1915): 7.

"The Art of Making Steel Ceilings." *National Builder* 43 (Aug. 1912): 104–6.

"The Art of Painting." *Scientific American* 2 (8 Jan. 1846): 2.

Badder, H. C. "The Invention and Early Development of Portland Cement." *Concrete* 25 (Oct. 1924): 119–27.

Batchelder, Ernest. "Arts and Crafts Movement in America: Work or Play?" *Craftsman* 16 (Aug. 1902): 122–23.

"The Beginning of Metal Ceilings." *Sheet Metal Worker* 25 (Jan. 1934): 23–24.

Bell, David. "Patterns Overhead." *Americana* 7 (July/Aug. 1979): 52–59.

Blackman, Leo, and Deborah Dietsch. "Linoleum: How to Repair It, Install It, and Clean It." *Old House Journal* 10 (Feb. 1982): 36–38.

———. "A New Look at Linoleum, Preservation's Rejected Floor Covering." *Old House Journal* 10 (Jan. 1982): 9–12.

Bradbury, Bruce. "Anaglypta and Other Embossed Wallcovering: Their History and Their Use Today." *Old House Journal* 10 (Nov. 1982): 231–34.

———. "Lincrusta-Walton, Can the Democratic Wallcovering Be Revived?" *Old House Journal* 10 (Oct. 1982): 203–6 and (Nov. 1982): 231–34.

"British Stamped Metal Ceiling Co., Ltd." *Decorator* 3 (22 Oct. 1904): 128.

"Building World News." *Building World* 9, no. 222 (13 Jan. 1900): 225.

"Catalogues." *National Builder* 36 (Sept. 1905): 48.

"Centennial Architecture." *American Architect and Building News* 1 (3 June 1876): 178–79, (10 June 1876): 186–87, (25 Nov. 1876): 378.

Coleman, William B. "Frederick Walton, Centenary of the Birth of the Inventor of Linoleum." *Industrial and Engineering Chemical News* 12 (Apr. 1834): 119.

———. "Frederick Walton, Inventor of Machinery for the Manufacture of Linoleum and Founder of the Linoleum Industry." *Mechanical Engineering* 57 (May 1935): 298.

"Concrete Block Church in Cairo." *Construction and Engineering* 4, no. 2 (May 1909): 140–41.

"Concrete Cottages for Workingmen." *Building Age* 32 (Apr. 1910): 169.

"Cornice Work." *Metal Worker* 35 (3 Jan. 1891): 24.

"Cornice Work: The Relative Advantages of Stamped Ornaments for Architectural Purposes." *Carpentry and Building* 1 (Feb. 1879): 34.

Cotton, J. Randall. "Composition, Restoring and Caring for Molded 'Carvings.'" *Old-House Journal* 21 (Jan./Feb. 1993): 28–33.

———. "Ornamental Concrete Block Houses." *Old House Journal* 12 (Oct. 1984): 165, 180–83.

———. "Return to Concrete Block Houses." *Old House Journal* 13 (Mar. 1995): 33–37.

"A Day at a Floorcloth Factory." *Penny Magazine* (Aug. 1842): 337–44.

Day, Lewis F. "Machine-Made Art." *Art Journal,* n.s. (1885): 107–10.

Dierickx, Mary. "Decorative Metal Roofing in the United States." In *The Technology of Historic American Building,* edited by H. Ward Jandl, 153–87. Washington, D.C.: Foundation for Preservation Technology, 1983.

———. "Metal Ceilings in the U.S." *APT Bulletin* 7 (1975): 83–98.

Dresser, Christopher. "Hindrances to the Progress of Applied Art." *Journal of the Society of Arts* 20 (12 Apr. 1872): 435.

Drop Press. "Sheet Metal Ceilings." *Metal Worker* 43 (20 Apr. 1895): 48.

Dyson, H. Kempton. "Concrete Block Making in Great Britain." Pts. 1–4. *Concrete and Constructional Engineering* 3, nos. 3–6 (1908–9): 224–30, 291–98, 383–90, 463–66.

Editorial. *New York Ecclesiologist* 1 (Oct. 1848): 5.

Editorial. *Sheet Metal Builder* 1 (Apr. 1874): 5.

"Even When It Falls Metal Ceiling Is Best." *Sheet Metal Worker* 20 (14 June 1929): 381.

"Federal Trade Commission." *Carpet and Upholstery Trade Review* 48, no. 10 (15 May 1918): 48.

Fidler, T. Claxton. "The Architectural Use of Iron and Steel." *Carpentry and Building* 13 (May 1891): 114.

"Floorcloth." *Carpet Trade* 10 (Oct. 1879): 17–18.

"Floor Coverings: Their History and Manufacture." *Carpet and Upholstery Trade Review* 29, no. 19 (1 Oct. 1898): 41.

Freeman, Allen. "Faux Arts." *Historic Preservation* 43 (Jan./Feb. 1991): 48.

"Germs vs. Linoleum." *Dry Goods Economist* 68 (29 Nov. 1913): 23.

Gibson, Louis H. "Cement Block Architecture." *American Architect and Building News* 89 (Feb. 1906): 72.

Gillespie, Ann H. "Ceilings of Metal." *Canadian Heritage* 9 (May–June 1983): 8–10, 48.

———. "Early Development of Artistic Concrete Block: The Case of the Boyd Brothers." *APT Bulletin* 11, no. 2 (1979): 30.

Hagloch, Fred W. "Cement Building Construction." *American Carpenter and Builder* 1 (Nov. 1905): 553–54 and (Apr. 1905): 20–21.

Hardie, Elspeth. "Tynecastle Tapestry in the United States." *Antique Collector* 60 (May 1989): 108–15.

———. "William Scott Morton." *Antique Collector* 59 (Mar. 1988): 70–79.

"Hardware Association Show." *National Builder* 43 (Apr. 1912): 54.

Hart, Arthur A. "Design by Mail Order: Mt. Carroll, IL." *National Building Museum Blueprints* 3, no. 1 (Fall 1984): 10–11.

———. "Sheet Iron Elegance, Mail Order Architecture in Montana." *Montana: The Magazine of Western History* 40 (Autumn 1990): 26–31.

"Here Is the Evidence." *Sheet Metal Worker* 26 (Jan. 1935): 15–16.

Hobart, James F. "Some Thoughts on Concrete Block Construction." *Building Age* 32 (June 1910): 246–47.

"How Casey Came to Sell Ceilings." *Metal Worker* 84 (22 Oct. 1915): 528–29.

"How Catalogues Should Look and What They Should Contain." *Canadian Manufacturer* 134, no. 1 (June 1914): 39–40.

"How Linoleums and Oilcloths Are Made." *Scientific American* 100 (13 July 1907): 28–30.

Hurt, Frances H. "The Virginia Years of Georgia O'Keeffe." *Commonwealth* 47, no. 9 (Oct. 1980): 24–26.

Hutchinson, Janet. "The Cure for Domestic Neglect: Better Homes in America, 1922–1955." In *Perspectives in Vernacular Architecture II,* edited by Camille Wells, 168–79. Columbia: Univ. of Missouri Press, 1986.

Huxtable, Ada Louise. "Concrete Technology in USA: Historical Survey." *Progressive Architecture* 41 (Oct. 1960): 144–49.

"Imitation." *Carpentry and Building* 2, no. 22 (22 Feb. 1878): 114.

"Inlaid Linoleum at St. Louis." *Cabinet Maker and Complete Home Furnisher* 25 (Dec. 1904): 175.

Jones, Howard E. "Steel Ceiling Selling Suggestions." *Sheet Metal Worker* 22 (7 Aug. 1931): 470.

Kelly, Allison. "Coade Stone in Georgian Architecture." *Architectural History* 28 (1985): 71.

———. "Sir John Soane and Mrs. Eleanore Coade." *Apollo* 129 (Apr. 1989): 247–53.

"Kinnear's Metallic Ceiling." *Carpentry and Building* 10 (Nov. 1888): 229–30.

"Kinnear's Paneled Ceiling." *Carpentry and Building* 11 (Sept. 1889): 193.

Kosmer, John. "Tin Ceiling, An Installation Guide." *Victorian Homes* 7 (Winter 1988): 56–61.

"Lincrusta Leather." *Journal of Decorative Art* 41 (Jan. 1921): 25, 27.

"Lincrusta-Walton." *Journal of Decorative Art* 1 (Mar. 1881): 29–30.

"Lincrusta-Walton." *Journal of Decorative Art* 4 (Mar. 1884): 472–77.

"Linoleum and Borders." *Art Journal* 19 (1880): 176.

"Linoleum: A Page from the Storybook of Modern Industry." *Craftsman* 26 (May 1914): 238–39.

"Linoleum in Warfare." *Carpet and Upholstery Trade Review* 26 (1 July 1895): 42.

"Linoleum Makers Face Shortages." *Dry Goods Economist* 69 (31 July 1915): 7.

"Linoleum Production Curtailed." *Carpet and Upholstery Trade Review* 48, no. 9 (1 May 1918): 33.

Longfield, Ada K. "The Manufacture of 'Raised Stucco' or *'Papier-Mâché'* Papers in Ireland c. 1750–70." *Journal of the Royal Society of Antiquaries of Ireland* 78 (July 1948): 55–62.

"Making Concrete Building Blocks." *American Carpenter and Builder* 1 (Nov. 1905): 366.

McCleary, Ann. "Preach a Little, Paint a Little, Drink a Little: The Work of Itinerant Painter Green Berry Jones." *Augusta Historical Bulletin* 22 (Staunton, Va.: Augusta County Historical Society, 1986): 31–39.

"Metal Ceilings." *National Builder* 43 (Jan. 1912): 62.

"Metal Ceilings and Metal Construction in South America." *National Builder* 42 (May 1911): 56.

"Metal Ceilings for Residences." *Metal Worker* 77 (15 Mar. 1912): 383.

"Metal Ceilings in Rio de Janeiro." *Metal Worker* 83 (11 June 1915): 846.

"Metal for Ceilings." *Architecture and Building* 8 (27 Dec. 1890): 358.

"Metallic Ceilings." *Metal Worker* 3 (6 Feb. 1875): 2.

"Metallic Relief Ceilings." *Metal Worker* 15, no. 3 (18 July 1891): 36.

"Metallic Shingles." *Carpentry and Building* 2 (July 1880): 130.

Newberry, S. B. "Hollow Concrete Block Building Construction in the United States." *Concrete and Constructional Engineering* 1, no. 2 (May 1906): 118.

"New Metallic Shingle." *Carpentry and Building* 6 (Jan. 1884): 11.

"New Metallic Tile." *Carpentry and Building* 6 (July 1884): 132.

"New Relief Wall Decorations." *Queen* 20 (1 Feb. 1896): 189.

"New Roofing Tile." *Carpentry and Building* 5 (Nov. 1883): 228.

"No-Co-Do Steel Ceilings." *National Builder* 41 (Mar. 1910): 16.

"Northrop's Embossed Patent Ceilings." *Building: An Architectural Weekly* 10, no. 3 (19 Jan. 1889): trade supplement.

"Northrop's Paneled Ceiling." *Carpentry and Building* 11 (Mar. 1889): 53.

"Novelties, A New Sheet-Metal Tile." *Carpentry and Building* 9 (Mar. 1887): 52, and 6 (Jan. 1884): 11.

"An Object Lesson in Getting Business: Why Sheet Metal Was Used So Generously in Remodeling St. Paul's Lutheran Church at Waterloo." *Sheet Metal Worker* 22 (25 Dec. 1931): 738–39.

"Oilcloth and Linoleum Designing." *International Correspondence School Reference Library.* Sec. 9, 6–13. Scranton, Pa.: International Textbook, 1905.

"On the Materials and Tools Used by the House Painter and Decorator: Lincrusta-Walton." *Journal of Decorative Art* 4 (Mar. 1881): 29–30.

"Panama Pacific Exposition." *Dry Goods Economist* 68 (20 June 1914): 267.

"Paneled Iron Ceilings." *Carpenter and Builder* 26 (8 Aug. 1890): 123–24.

"Paris Exposition, Compagnie Rouennaise." *Carpet and Upholstery Trade Review* 31, no. 17 (1 Sept. 1900): 58.

Pevsner, Nicholas. "Christopher Dresser, Industrial Designer." *Architectural Review* 81 (1937): 183–86.

Phillips, Laura. "Grand Illusions: Decorative Interior Painting in North Carolina." In *Perspectives in Vernacular Architecture IV,* edited by Thomas Carter and Bernard Herman, 155–62. Columbia: Univ. of Missouri Press, 1991.

Porter, Rufus. "Imitation Painting." *Scientific American* 2 (8 Jan. 1846): 2.

"Potter Page." *Carpet and Upholstery Trade Review* 46, no. 19 (1 Oct. 1915): 51

Prown, Jules. "Mind in Matter: An Introduction to Material Culture Theory and Method." In *Material Life in America 1600–1860,* edited by Robert Blair St. George, 17–37. Boston: Northeastern Univ. Press, 1987.

Pursell, Carroll W., Jr. "Tariff and Technology: The Foundation and Development of the American Tin-Plate Industry, 1872–1900." *Technology and Culture* 3 (1962): 267–84.

"Recent Development in Decoration." *Canadian Architect and Builder* 3 (Mar. 1890): 32.

"Report of AIA Committee." *American Architect and Building News* 92 (Dec. 1907): 214.

Sanders, H. M. "Servile Imitation." *Sheet Metal Builder* 1 (Dec. 1874): 134.

Schiller, Barbara. "Metal Ceilings." *Old House Journal* 7 (Mar. 1979): 1, 29–33.

Scranton, Philip. "Manufacturing Diversity: Production Systems, Market, and an American Consumer Society, 1870–1930." *Technology and Culture* 35 (July 1994): 476–505.

"Servile Imitation." *Metal Worker* 23 (17 June 1885): 20.

"Sheet-Metal Architecture." *American Architect and Building News* 1 (22 July 1876): 234–35 and (11 Nov. 1876): 365–66.

"Sheet-Metal Ceiling." *Carpentry and Building* 8 (Oct. 1886): 188.

"Sheet-Metal Ceiling Work." *Carpentry and Building* 9 (Dec. 1887): 244–45.

"Sheet Metal Pavilion." *Centennial Eagle* (July–Sept. 1876): 134.

Simpson, Pamela H. "Cheap, Quick and Easy: Embossed Wallcoverings at the Turn of the Century." *Wallpaper History Review* (1996–97): 22–26.

———. "Cheap, Quick and Easy: The Early History of Concrete Block Building." In *Perspectives in Vernacular Architecture III,* edited by Thomas Carter and Bernard Herman, 108–18. Columbia: Univ. of Missouri Press, 1991.

———. "Cheap, Quick and Easy Part II: The History of Pressed Metal Ceilings." In *Gender, Class and Shelter, Perspectives in Vernacular Architecture V,* edited by Elizabeth C. Cromley and Carter L. Hudgins, 152–63. Knoxville: Univ. of Tennessee Press, 1995.

———. "Concrete Block." In *Twentieth Century Building Materials, History and Conservation,* edited Thomas C. Jester, 80–85. New York: McGraw-Hill, 1995.

———. "The Early History of Concrete Block." *Building Renovation Magazine* (Mar.–Apr. 1995): 49–53.

———. "Linoleum and Lincrusta: Democratic Coverings for Floors and Walls." In *Exploring Everyday Landscapes, Perspectives in Vernacular Architecture, VII,* edited by Annmarie Adams and Sally McMurry, 281–92. Knoxville: Univ. of Tennessee Press, 1997.

———. "Ornamental Sheet Metal in the United States, 1870–1930." *Journal of Architectural and Planning Research* 11 (Winter 1994): 294–310.

———. "Pressed Metal Ceilings, 1890–1930." *Building Renovation Magazine* (Nov.–Dec. 1992): 69–72.

Stickley, Gustav. "Concrete Bungalows, Showing Economy of Construction: By the editor." *Craftsman* 21 (Mar. 1912): 663–75.

Thornton, Jonathan, and William Adair. "Applied Decoration for Historic Interiors, Preserving Composition Ornament." *Preservation Briefs* 34. Washington, D.C.: National Parks Service, May 1994.

———. "The History, Technology and Conservation of Architectural *Papier Mâché.*" *Journal of American Institute for Conservation* 32, no. 2 (Summer 1993): 165–76.

"Tin Plates." *Metal Worker* 42 (13 Oct. 1894): 52.

Torrance, William M. "Types of Hollow Concrete Blocks Used in the States and Their Patents." *Concrete and Constructional Engineering* 1, no. 3 (July 1906): 206–14.

"Tynecastle Tapestry at the Albert Works, Edinburgh." *Art Journal* n.s. (Mar. 1896): 81–85.

"Unlimited Opportunities for Steel Ceilings." *Sheet Metal Worker* 27 (Jan. 1936): 18–19.

Upton, Dell. "The Power of Things: Recent Studies in American Vernacular Architecture." In *Material Culture: A Research Guide,* edited by Thomas J. Schlereth, 57–78. Lawrence: Univ. of Kansas, 1985.

Veblen, Thorstein. "Arts and Crafts." *Journal of Political Economy* 11 (Dec. 1902): 108–10.

"Wallpaper Manufacturers Ltd." *Journal of Decorative Art* 25, pt. 297 (Sept. 1905): supplement, 1–32.

Walls, Nina de Angeli. "Educating Women for Art and Commerce: The Philadelphia School of Design." *History of Education Quarterly* 34 (Fall 1994): 329–55.

Walsh, George Ethelbert. "Metals for Interior Decoration." *Architects and Builders Magazine* 4 (Oct. 1902): 454–56.

"What a Woman Can Do." *Cement World* 2 (Dec. 1908): 618.

Worthington, Miria. "Pressed Metal Ceilings in Western Australia." *Heritage Australia* 5 (Autumn 1986): 31–32.

Wright, Frank Lloyd. "In the Cause of Architecture, VII: Sheet Metal and A Modern Instance." *Architectural Record* 64 (Oct. 1928): 334.

"The Year's Advance in Art Manufactures." *Art Journal,* n.s. (1883): 353.

Books

Adams, Annmarie. *Architecture in the Family Way: Doctors, Houses, and Women, 1870–1900.* Montreal: McGill-Queen's Univ. Press, 1996.

Adams, Henry. *The Education of Henry Adams.* 1918. Reprint, New York: Random House, 1931.

Adler, Hazel H. *Planning the Color Scheme for Your Home.* Philadelphia: George W. Blabon, 1926.

Auer, Michael J., Charles E. Fisher III, Thomas C. Jester, and Marilyn E. Kaplan, eds. *The Interiors Handbook for Historic Buildings.* Vol. 2. Washington, D.C.: Historic Preservation Education Foundation, 1993.

Baker, Malcolm, and Brenda Richardson, eds. *A Grand Design.* New York: Harry N. Abrams for Baltimore Museum of Art, 1997.

Beecher, Catherine E., and Harriet Beecher Stowe. *The American Woman's Home.* 1869. Reprint, New York: Arno, 1971.

Bell, Joseph. *From the Carriage Age to the Space Age: The Birth and Growth of the Concrete Masonry Industry.* Herndon, Va.: National Concrete Masonry Association, 1969.

Bielefeld, Charles Frederick. *On the Use of the Improved Papier Mâché in Furniture, in the Interior Decoration of Buildings, and in Works of Art.* London: J. Rickerby, [1840?].

———. *Ornaments Manufactured in the Improved Papier Mâché.* London: published by the author, 1850.

Bishir, Catherine W., and Michael T. Southern. *A Guide to the Historic Architecture of Eastern North Carolina.* Chapel Hill: Univ. of North Carolina Press, 1996.

Bøe, A. I. F. *From Gothic Revival to Functional Form: A Study of Victorian Theories of Design.* Oslo: Oslo Univ. Press, 1954.

Boris, Eileen. *Art and Labor: Ruskin, Morris, and the Craftsman Ideal in America.* Philadelphia: Temple Univ. Press, 1985.

Bristow, Ian C. *Architectural Colour in British Interiors, 1615–1840.* New Haven: Yale Univ. Press, 1996.

————. *Interior House-Painting Colours and Technology, 1615–1840.* New Haven: Yale Univ. Press, 1996.

Bronner, Simon J. *Consuming Visions: Accumulation and Display of Goods in America, 1880–1920.* New York: W. W. Norton, 1989.

Brown, Hazel Dell. *The Attractive Home: How to Plan Its Decoration.* Lancaster, Pa.: Armstrong Bureau of Interior Decoration, 1926.

Butler, A. S. G. *Recording Ruin.* London: Constable, 1942.

Calhoun, Charles W., ed. *The Gilded Age: Essays on the Origin of Modern America.* Wilmington, Del.: Scholarly Resources, 1996.

Campbell, Joan. *The German Werkbund: The Politics of Reform in the Applied Arts.* Princeton, N.J.: Princeton Univ. Press, 1978.

Chandler, Alfred D., Jr. *The Visible Hand: The Managerial Revolution in American Business.* Cambridge: Harvard Univ. Press, 1977.

Chase, David, and Carolyn Laray. *Sheet Metal Craftsmanship: Progress in Building.* Washington, D.C.: National Building Museum, 1988.

Clark, Clifford E. *The American Family Home, 1800–1960.* Chapel Hill: Univ. of North Carolina Press, 1986.

Clark, Isaac Edwards, ed. *Art and Industry: Education in the Industrial and Fine Arts in the United States.* Washington, D.C.: GPO, 1885–98.

Condit, Carl. *America Building: Materials and Techniques from the First Settlements to the Present.* Chicago: Univ. of Chicago Press, 1968.

Cook, Clarence. *What Shall We Do with our Walls.* New York: Warren Fuller, 1880.

Cook, E. T., and Alexander Wedderburn. *The Works of John Ruskin.* London: George Allen, 1903.

Cowan, Ruth S. *More Work for Mother.* New York: Basic Books, 1983.

Dawley, Alan. *Struggles for Justice: Social Responsibility and the Liberal State.* Cambridge: Harvard Univ. Press, Belknap Press, 1991.

Dearden, Edward C. *A Historical Sketch of the George W. Blabon Co., 1851–1915.* Philadelphia: George W. Blabon, 1915.

DeVoe, Shirley Spaulding. *English Papier-Mâché of the Georgian and Victorian Periods.* Middletown, Conn.: Wesleyan Univ. Press, 1971.

Downing, Andrew Jackson. *The Architecture of Country Houses.* New York: D. Appleton, 1850.

Dresser, Christopher. *The Art of Decorative Design.* 1862. Reprint, Watkins Glen, N.Y.: American Life Foundation, 1977.

————. *Modern Ornamentation: A Series of Original Designs.* London: B. T. Batsford, 1886.

————. *Principles of Decorative Design.* 1873. Reprint, London: Academy Editions, St. Martin's Press, 1973.

Durant, Stuart. *Ornament from the Industrial Revolution to Today.* Woodstock, N.Y.: Overlook Press, 1986.

Eastlake, Charles. *Hints on Household Taste*. London: Longmans, Green, 1878.

Edison Portland Cement Company. *The Romance of Cement*. Boston: Lovermore and Knight, 1926.

Eisler, Benita. *O'Keeffe and Stieglitz: An American Romance*. New York: Penguin Books, 1991.

Entwisle, E. A. *A Literary History of Wallpaper*. London: B. T. Batsford, 1960.

Fraries, A. J. *The Cement Industry, 1796–1914: A History*. London: David and Charles, 1977.

Gayle, Margot, David W. Look, and John G. Waite. *Metals in America's Historic Buildings*. Washington, D.C.: U.S. Dept. of Interior Heritage Conservation and Recreation Service Technical Preservation Services Division, 1980.

Giedion, Sigfried. *Mechanization Takes Command*. New York: Oxford, 1948.

Gooderson, Philip. *Lord Linoleum, Lord Ashton, Lancaster and the Rise of the British Oilcloth and Linoleum Industry*. Keele, England: Keele Univ. Press, 1996.

Greely, Horace, ed. *Art and Industry*. New York: Redfield, 1853.

Harvey, Charles, and Jon Press. *William Morris: Design and Enterprise in Victorian Britain*. Manchester: Manchester Univ. Press, 1991.

Hasluck, Paul N. *Practical Graining and Marbling*. Philadelphia: David McKay, 1915.

Herring, Oswald C. *Concrete and Stucco Houses*. New York: Robert M. McBride, 1912.

Heschong, Lisa. *Thermal Delight in Architecture*. Cambridge, Mass.: MIT Press, 1979.

History and Manufacture of Floor Coverings. New York: Review Publishing, 1899.

Holbrook, Christine. *My Better Homes and Gardens Home Guide*. Des Moines, Iowa: Meredith Publishing, 1933.

Horsfall, Mrs. *Pretty Homes*. London: European Mail, 1897.

Hoskins, Lesley, ed. *The Papered Wall*. New York: Harry N. Abrams, 1994.

Hounshell, David. *From the American System to Mass Production, 1800–1932*. Baltimore: Johns Hopkins Univ. Press, 1983.

Howe, Harrison E. *The New Stone Age*. London: Univ. of London Press, 1921.

Howells, William Dean. *A Traveler from Alturia*. 1894. Reprint, New York: Sagamore Press, 1957.

Horowitz, Daniel. *The Morality of Spending: Attitudes toward the Consumer Society in America, 1875–1940*. Baltimore: Johns Hopkins Univ. Press, 1985.

Hoy, Suellen. *Chasing Dirt: The American Pursuit of Cleanliness*. New York: Oxford Univ. Press, 1995.

H. W. Prentis, Jr., 1884–1959. Lancaster, Pa.: Armstrong Cork, 1961.

Jandl, H. Ward, ed. *The Technology of Historic American Building*. Washington, D.C.: Foundation for Preservation Technology, 1983.

Jennings, Arthur Seymour. *The Home Beautiful*. London: Greening and Company, 1908.

Jester, Thomas C., ed. *Twentieth Century Building Materials, History and Conservation*. New York: McGraw-Hill, 1995.

Jones, M. W. *The History and Manufacture of Floorcloth and Linoleum*. Bristol: Walter R. Powell, 1918. Originally a paper read before the Bristol section of the Society of Chemical Industry, 21 Nov. 1918.

Jourdain, Margaret. *English Interior Decoration, 1500 to 1830*. London: B. T. Batsford, 1950.

Kasson, John. *Amusing the Millions: Coney Island at the Turn of the Century.* New York: Hill and Wang, 1978.

————. *Civilizing the Machine: Technology and Republican Values in America, 1776–1900.* New York: Viking, 1976.

Katzman, David M. *Seven Days a Week.* New York: Oxford Univ. Press, 1978.

Kelly, A. Ashman. *The Standard Grainer, Stainer and Marbler.* Philadelphia: David McKay, 1933.

Kelly, Allison. *Mrs. Coade's Stone.* Upton-upon-Severn, Worcs.: Self Publishing Association, Ltd., for the Georgian Group, 1990.

Lane, Terence, and Jessie Serle. *Australians at Home: A Documentary History of Australian Domestic Interiors from 1788–1914.* New York: Oxford Univ. Press, 1990.

Lanzillotti, Robert F. *The Hard-Surface Floor-Covering Industry: A Case Study of Market Structure and Competition in Oligopoly.* Pullman: State College of Washington Press, 1955.

Lasansky, Jeannette. *To Cut, Piece and Solder: The Work of the Rural Pennsylvania Tinsmith, 1778–1908.* College Park: Pennsylvania State Univ. Press, Keystone Books, 1982.

Leach, William. *Land of Desire: Merchants, Power, and the Rise of a New American Culture.* New York: Pantheon Books, 1993.

Lears, T. J. Jackson. *No Place of Grace: Antimodernism and the Transformation of American Culture, 1880–1920.* New York: Pantheon Books, 1981.

Little, Nina Fletcher. *American Decorative Wall Painting, 1700–1850.* Sturbridge, Mass.: Old Sturbridge Village, 1952.

Loeb, Lori Anne. *Consuming Angels: Advertising and Victorian Women.* New York: Oxford Univ. Press, 1994.

Long, Helen C. *The Edwardian House: The Middle-Class Home in Britain, 1880–1914.* Manchester: Manchester Univ. Press, 1993.

Lyle, Royster, and Pamela H. Simpson. *The Architecture of Historic Lexington.* Charlottesville: Univ. Press of Virginia, 1977.

Lynn, Catherine. *Wallpaper in America.* New York: Cooper-Hewitt Museum, 1980.

Marchand, Roland. *Advertising the American Dream: Making Way for Modernity, 1920–1940.* Berkeley and Los Angeles: Univ. of California Press, 1985.

McCraw, Thomas A., ed. *The Essential Alfred Chandler: Essays Toward a Historical Theory of Big Business.* Boston: Harvard Business School Press, 1988.

McElroy, Margaret. *Color and Charm in Home Interiors.* Kearney, N.J.: Congoleum-Nairn, 1930.

McIlwain, H. R., ed. *Journals of the House of Burgess of Virginia, 1702–1712.* Vol. 4. Richmond: Virginia State Library, 1912.

Mehler, William A., Jr. *Let the Buyer Have Faith.* Lancaster, Pa.: Armstrong World Industries, 1987.

Morris, May, ed. *The Collected Works of William Morris.* 24 vols. London: Longmans, 1910–15.

Mott, Frank Luther. *A History of American Magazines, 1885–1905.* Cambridge: Harvard Univ. Press, Belknap Press, 1957.

Muir, Augustus. *Nairns of Kirkcaldy: A Short History of the Company.* Cambridge: W. Heffer and Sons for Michael Nairn, 1956.

Mumford, Lewis. *Roots of Contemporary American Architecture.* New York: Dover, 1972.

Nisbet, Robert. *History of the Idea of Progress.* New York: Basic Books, 1980.

Orvell, Miles. *The Real Thing: Imitation and Authenticity in American Culture, 1880–1940.* Chapel Hill: Univ. of North Carolina Press, 1989.

Oxford English Dictionary. Oxford: Clarendon Press, 1970.

Parry, John. *Graining and Marbling.* London: Crosby, Lockwood and Son, 1949.

Parry, Linda, ed. *William Morris.* London: Philip Wilson Publishers for Victoria and Albert Museum, 1996.

———. *William Morris Textiles.* New York: Viking Press, 1983.

Parsons, Frank Alvah. *The Art of Home Furnishing and Decoration.* Lancaster, Pa.: Armstrong Cork, 1918.

Pevsner, Nikolaus. *Pioneers of Modern Design from William Morris to Walter Gropius.* New York: Museum of Modern Art, 1949.

Pezzoni, Dan. *The History and Architecture of Lee County, North Carolina.* Sanford, N.C.: Railroad House Historical Association, 1995.

Pfeiffer, Bruce Brooks, ed. *Frank Lloyd Wright: Collected Writings.* New York: Rizzoli, 1992.

Plunkett, Harriette M. *Women, Plumbers, and Doctors; or, Household Sanitation.* New York: Appelton, 1885.

Prentis, H. W., Jr. *Thomas Morton Armstrong (1836–1908), Pioneer in Cork.* New York: Newcomen Society, 1950.

Pugin, A. W. N. *The True Principles of Pointed or Christian Architecture.* 1841. Reprint, London: Academy Editions, St. Martin's Press, 1973.

Radford, William A. *Cement Houses and How to Build Them.* Chicago: Radford Architectural, 1909.

Rice, Harmon Howard. *Concrete Block Manufacturing Process and Machines.* New York: John Wiley and Sons, 1908.

Robinson, Roxanna. *Georgia O'Keeffe: A Life.* New York: Harper and Row, 1989.

Room, Adrian. *Directory of Trade Name Origins.* London: Routledge and Kegan Paul, 1982.

Rosenberg, Nathan. *Technology and American Economic Growth.* New York: Harper and Row, 1972.

Sachs, Charles L. *Made on Staten Island.* Richmondtown, N.Y.: Staten Island Historical Society, 1988.

St. George, Robert Blair, ed. *Material Life in America 1600–1860.* Boston: Northeastern Univ. Press, 1987.

The Salesmanship Guidebook. Lancaster, Pa.: Armstrong Cork, [1930?].

Savage, W. L. *Graining and Marbling, Complete and Practical Guide.* London: Austin Rogers, 1925.

Schlereth, Thomas, J., ed. *Material Culture: A Research Guide.* Lawrence: Univ. of Kansas Press, 1985.

Scott, George Gilbert. *Remarks on Secular and Domestic Architecture, Present and Future.* London: John Murray, 1858.

Sloan, Maurice M. *The Concrete House and Its Construction.* Philadelphia: Association of American Portland Cement Manufacturers, 1912.

Smith, John Thomas. *Nollekens and His Times*. London: Henry Colburn, 1828.

Smith, Katheryn. *Hollyhock House and Olive Hill, Buildings and Projects for Aline Barnsdall*. New York: Rizzoli, 1992.

Stevenson, Katherine Cole, and H. Ward Jandl. *Houses by Mail*. Washington, D.C.: Preservation Press, 1968.

Stevenson, Louise L. *The Victorian Homefront: American Thought and Culture, 1860–1880*. New York: Twayne Publishers, 1991.

Stickley, Gustav. *Craftsman Homes*. New York: Craftsman Publishing, 1909.

Strasser, Susan. *Satisfaction Guaranteed: The Making of the American Mass Market*. New York: Pantheon Books, 1989.

Stratton, Michael. *The Terracotta Revival: Building Innovation and Image of the Industrial City in Britain and North America*. London: Victor Gollancy; North Pomfet, VT: Peter Crawley, Trafalgar Square, 1993.

Sugden, Alan V., and John Ludlam Edmondson. *A History of English Wallpaper, 1509–1914*. New York: Charles Scribner's Sons, 1925.

Susman, Warren I. *Culture as History: The Transformation of American Society in the Twentieth Century*. New York: Pantheon Books, 1984.

Sutherland, W. G. *Modern Wall Decoration*. London: Simpkin, Marshall, Hamilton and Kent, 1893.

Sweeney, Robert L. *Wright in Hollywood: Visions of a New Architecture*. New York: Architectural History Foundation and MIT Press, 1993.

Sweet's Catalogue of Building Construction. New York: Architectural Record, 1906, 1927–28.

Thiébaut, Philippe, Claude Frontisi, Georges Vigne, and Marie-Madeleine Massé. *Guimard*. Paris: Réunion des Musées Nationaux, 1992.

Touart, Paul Baker. *Building the Backcountry: An Architectural History of Davidson County, North Carolina*. Davidson County, N.C.: Davidson County Historical Association, 1987.

Tressell, Robert. *The Ragged Trousered Philanthropists*. 1906. Reprint, London: Panther Books, 1967.

Twain, Mark. *Connecticut Yankee in King Arthur's Court*. 1889. Reprint, New York: New Amsterdam Library, 1963.

———. *Life on the Mississippi*. 1883. Reprint, New York: American Classics Society, 1977.

Vaughan, Paul. *Something in Linoleum*. London: Sinclair-Stevenson, 1994.

Veblen, Thorstein. *The Theory of the Leisure Class*. 1899. Reprint, New Brunswick, N.J.: Transaction Publishers, 1992.

Von Rosenstiel, Helene, and Gail Caskey Winkler. *American Rugs and Carpets from the Seventeenth Century to Modern Times*. New York: William Morrow, 1978.

———. *Floor Coverings for Historic Buildings*. Washington, D.C.: Historic Preservation Education Foundation, 1993.

Waite, Diana. *Architectural Elements: The Technological Revolution*. New York: Bonanza Books, 1976.

———. *Nineteenth Century Tin Roofing and Its Use at Hyde Hall*. New York: New York State Historic Trust. 1971.

Wall, William E. *Graining Ancient and Modern.* Revised by F. N. Vanderwaller. New York: Drake, 1972.

Walton, Frederick. *The Infancy and Development of Linoleum Floorcloth.* London: Simpkin, Hamilton, Kent, 1925.

Whipple, Harvey. *Concrete Stone Manufacture.* 2d ed. Detroit: Concrete-Cement Age Publishing, 1918.

Winkler, Gail Caskey, and Roger W. Moss. *Victorian Interior Decoration, American Interiors, 1830–1900.* New York: Henry Hart, 1986.

Wosk, Julie. *Breaking Frame: Technology and the Visual Arts in the Nineteenth Century.* New Brunswick, N.J.: Rutgers Univ. Press, 1992.

Wright, Gwendolyn. *Moralism and the Model Home.* Chicago: Univ. of Chicago Press., 1980.

Yapp, G. W. *Art Industry: Furniture, Upholstery, and House-Decoration.* London: J. S. Virture and Company, 1880.

———. *Art Industry: Metal Work.* London: J. S. Virtue and Company, 1877.

Trade Catalogues, Pamphlets, and Ephemera

All about the Iron Ceilings, Side Walls, etc., Manufactured by A. Northrop & Co. Pittsburgh: A. Northrop, 1890. Avery Library, Columbia Univ.

Anaglypta and Salamander Decorations. Darwen, England: Wallpaper Manufacturing, 1909. National Art Library, London.

A New Decorative Material: Lincrusta-Walton. New York: Lincrusta-Walton Manufacturing [1883?]. Canadian Centre for Architecture.

Armstrong Handbook for Linoleum Mechanics. Lancaster, Pa.: Armstrong Cork, 1939. Library of Congress.

Armstrong Linoleum AIA Classification, Detailed Specifications. Lancaster, Pa.: Armstrong Cork, 1924. Canadian Centre for Architecture.

Armstrong Linoleum Pattern Book. Lancaster, Pa.: Armstrong Cork, 1918. Avery Library, Columbia Univ., and Hagley Museum and Library.

Armstrong Linoleum Pattern Book. Lancaster, Pa.: Armstrong Cork, 1923. Winterthur Museum and Library.

Armstrong Linoleum Pattern Book. Lancaster, Pa.: Armstrong Cork, 1926. Avery Library, Columbia Univ., Hagley Museum and Library.

Artistic Interiors in Sheet Metal. Pittsburgh, Pa.: Keighley Metal Ceiling and Manufacturing, [1910?]. Avery Library, Columbia Univ.

Bakewell and Mullins Designs of Architectural Ornaments. Salem, Ohio: Bakewell and Mullins, 1887. Metropolitan Museum of Art Print Department.

Bakewell and Mullins Galvanized Iron Cornices, Window Caps, Architectural Ornaments and Statuary. Salem, Ohio: Bakewell and Mullins, [1887?]. Hagley Museum and Library.

Berger Architectural Sheet Metal Work. Canton, Ohio: Berger Manufacturing, 1895. Winterthur Museum and Library.

Berger's "Classik" Steel Ceilings, Catalogue 21. Canton, Ohio: Berger Manufacturing, 1915. Avery Library, Columbia Univ.

Berloy Steel Ceilings Catalogue No. 22. Kansas City: Berloy, 1927. Avery Library, Columbia Univ.

Better Buildings with Straub's Patented Cinder Concrete Building Block. Philadelphia: Philadelphia Partition and Building Block, [1927?]. Author's collection.

Blabon Art Linoleums, Styles for 1924. Philadelphia: George W. Blabon, 1924. Avery Library, Columbia Univ.

Business Floors of Armstrong Linoleum. Lancaster, Pa.: Armstrong Cork, Jan. 1924. Avery Library, Columbia Univ.

C. H. Pepper's Linoleum. Boston: C. H. Pepper, [1900?]. Avery Library, Columbia Univ.

Canton Line Steel Ceilings, Catalogue F. Canton, Ohio: Canton, 1915. Avery Library, Columbia Univ.

Ceiling Catalogue No. 300. Nevada, Mo.: W. F. Norman Sheet Metal Manufacturing, [1900?]. Avery Library, Columbia Univ.

Concrete Machinery, Specialty Catalogue. Chicago: Sears, Roebuck, 1917. Sears Archives.

Congoleum-Nairn Book of Beautiful Rooms. Kearny, N.J.: Congoleum-Nairn, 1934. Avery Library, Columbia Univ.

Cook's Linoleum. Trenton, N.J.: Trenton Oil Cloth and Linoleum, [1910?]. Hagley Museum and Library.

Corticine Wall Decoration. N.p.: Corticine Floor Covering, [1900?]. Crown Berger Division, Akzu-Nobel, Darwen.

Directions for Laying Linoleum Floors. Lancaster, Pa.: Armstrong Cork, 1918. Avery Library, Columbia Univ.

Dominion Linoleum. Montreal: Dominion, 1926. Canadian Centre for Architecture.

Dykema Cement Stone Molds, Cement Stone Machines, Cement Appliances, Cement Building Plans. Grand Rapids, Mich.: K. Dykema and Son, 1905. Author's collection.

Edwards Manufacturing Company, Catalogue No. 68. Cincinnati: Edwards Manufacturing, 1923. Avery Library, Columbia Univ., and Hagley Museum and Library.

Edwards Metal Roofing, Siding, Ceilings, etc., Catalogue. Cincinnati: Edwards Manufacturing, 1912. Hagley Museum and Library and Avery Library, Columbia Univ.

E. E. Souther Iron Company, Catalogue No. 18. St. Louis: E. E. Souther, [1910?]. Avery Library, Columbia Univ.

The First 125 Years. Lancaster, Pa.: Armstrong, 1985. Author's collection.

Floor Beauty for New Homes and Old. Lancaster, Pa.: Armstrong Cork, 1934. Winterthur Museum and Library.

Floors, Utile and Beautiful. London: Jas. F. Ebner, 1882. Canadian Centre for Architecture.

George Jackson and Sons. *Carton-Pierre, Papier-mâché, and Patent Fibrous Plaster Works.* London: George Jackson and Sons, [1900?]. National Art Library, London.

George L. Mesker and Company. *Architectural Iron Works.* Evansville, Ind.: George L. Mesker, 1903. Hagley Museum and Library.

———. *Architectural Iron Works Catalogue.* Evansville, Ind.: George L. Mesker, 1902. Metropolitan Museum and Hagley Museum and Library.

Helpful Hints for Linoleum Salesmen. Lancaster, Pa: Armstrong Cork, 1918. Avery Library, Columbia Univ., and Library of Congress.

How to Lay and Care for Linoleum. Lancaster, Pa.: Armstrong Cork, 1914. Avery Library, Columbia Univ.

Illustrated Catalogue of Eastlake Metallic Shingles. Toronto: Metallic Roofing Company of Canada, 1890. National Science and Technology Museum Library, Ottawa, Canada.

Illustrated Catalogue of Eastlake Metallic Shingles and Sheet Steel Pressed Brick. Toronto: Metallic Roofing Company of Canada, 1890. National Science and Technology Museum Library, Ottawa, Canada.

Jacobson and Company. *A Second Book of Old English Designs.* New York: Jacobson, 1928. Winterthur Museum and Library.

Le Prince, Mme. *Lincrusta-Walton Decoration.* New York: Fr. Beck, 1884. Library of Congress.

Lincrusta-Walton, Caméoid. Darwen, England: Wallpaper Manufacturers, [1906?]. Crown-Berger Division, Akzu-Nobel, Darwen, England.

Lincrusta-Walton Designs. New York: Frederick Beck and Company, 1888. Avery Library, Columbia Univ.

Lincrusta-Walton: The Sunbury Wall Decoration, a New Linoleum Product. London: Waterlow and Sons, 1880. Library of Congress.

Linotile Floors. Pittsburgh: Armstrong Cork, 1920. Avery Library, Columbia Univ.

Lombard Company Catalogue. New York: Lombard, 1918. Winterthur Museum and Library.

Mikor Sheet Metal Products. Milwaukee: Milwaukee Corrugating, 1915. Avery Library, Columbia Univ.

Moesleins, V. *Stamped Steel Ceilings Catalogue.* New York: V. Moesleins, 1894. Canadian Centre for Architecture.

Moreau Marble Company Ltd. Pamphlet. London: Moreau Marble, 1902. Ephemera Collection, Box 1, Housing and Houses. Bodleian Library, Oxford.

Mullins, W. H. *Sheet Metal Architectural Ornaments.* Salem, Ohio: W. H. Mullins, 1894. Winterthur Museum and Library.

———. *Sheet Metal Architectural Ornaments, Statuary, Cornices, Building Fronts, Finials, etc.* Salem, Ohio: W. H. Mullins, 1894. Winterthur Museum and Library.

Nairn Linoleums. Kearny, N.J.: W. J. Sloan, 1890. Avery Library, Columbia Univ.

Northrop, Coburn and Dodge Co., Manufactures of Northrop's Metal Ceilings and Walls, Catalogue No. 9. New York: Northrop, Coburn and Dodge, 1905. Metropolitan Museum of Art.

Pedlar Art Steel Ceilings, Catalogue No. 21-C. Oshawa, Ont.: Pedlar People, [1921?], National Science and Technology Museum Library, Ottawa, Canada.

Pedlar People Catalogue. Oshawa, Ont.: Pedlar People, [1914?]. National Science and Technology Museum Library, Ottawa, Canada.

Pedlar People, Ltd., Sheet Metal Products Reference Book ND22R. Oshawa, Ont.: Pedlar People, n.d. Canadian Centre for Architecture.

Pedlar's Perfect Art Steel Ceilings and Wall Designs. 1930. Oshawa, Ont.: Pedlar People, n.d. National Archives of Canada.

Penn Metal Catalogue. Philadelphia: Penn Metal and Roofing, 1902. Hagley Museum and Library.

Penn Metal Ceiling and Roofing Company. Philadelphia: Penn Metal and Roofing, 1906. Hagley Museum and Library.

Penn Metal Ceiling and Roofing Company. Boston: Penn Metal and Roofing, 1911–12. Hagley Museum and Library.

Penn Metal Company Penco Metal Ceiling Catalogue. Philadelphia: Penco, 1927. Hagley Museum and Library.

Relief Decoration. Darwen, England: Wallpaper Manufacturers Company, [1920?]. Winterthur Museum and Library.

Salamander Catalogue. N.p.: United Asbestos, June 1896. Crown Berger Division, Akzu-Nobel, Darwen, England.

Salesmanship Guidebook. Lancaster, Pa.: Armstrong Cork, 1936. Avery Library, Columbia Univ. and Hagley Museum and Library.

Sani Onyx. Indianapolis, Ind.: Marietta Manufacturing Company, 1927. Canadian Centre for Architecture.

Sears, Roebuck and Co. Catalogue. Chicago: Sears, Roebuck, 1907. Sears Archives.

Sears, Roebuck and Co. Catalogue. Chicago: Sears, Roebuck, 1917. Sears Archives.

Sears, Roebuck and Co. Catalogue. Chicago: Sears, Roebuck, Fall 1915. National Building Museum.

Sears, Roebuck, Steel Ceilings. Chicago: Sears, Roebuck, 1910. Hagley Museum and Library and Avery Library, Columbia Univ.

Sears, Roebuck, Wallpaper Catalogue. Chicago: Sears, Roebuck, Spring 1918. Duke Univ.

Seventy-Fifth Penn Metal Year, 1869–1944. Philadelphia: Penco, 1944. Hagley Museum and Library.

Sheet Metal Architectural Ornaments. Salem, Ohio: W. H. Mullins, 1894. Winterthur Museum and Library.

Steel Ceilings. Ottawa: McFarland-Douglas, n.d. National Science and Technology Museum Library, Ottawa, Canada.

Steel Ceilings and Side Walls. St. Paul, Minn.: St. Paul Roofing, Cornice and Ornament, 1915. Avery Library, Columbia Univ.

The Story: A Story of People, the Story of Mullins, the Story of Your Job. Salem, Ohio: Mullins Manufacturing, Salem, 1947. Hagley Museum and Library.

Told in the Store: An Interesting Tale of a Buyer's Experience. Lancaster, Pa.: Armstrong Cork, 1915. Library of Congress.

"Two Boys from Osgoode." *Ideal Ideas.* London, Ontario: Ideal Concrete Machinery, 1913. Boyd Brothers Papers, vol. 1, file 2, National Archives of Canada.

Tynecastle Canvas, Vellum, Textures, Leathers, Mosaics, Wood Moldings. Edinburgh: Tynecastle, 1900. Bodleian Library, Oxford.

What People Say: General Testimonials for 'Eastlake' Galvanized Steel Shingles. Toronto: Metallic Roofing Company of Canada, 1894. National Archives of Canada.

Index